MUSIC NAVIGATION WITH SYMBOLS AND LAYERS

MUSIC NAVIGATION WITH SYMBOLS AND LAYERS

Toward Content Browsing with IEEE 1599 XML Encoding

Edited by
Denis L. Baggi
Goffredo M. Haus

IEEE
computer society

WILEY

Published by John Wiley & Sons, Inc., Hoboken, New Jersey.
Published simultaneously in Canada.

For general information on our other products and services please contact our Customer Care Department within the U.S. at 877-762-2974, outside the U.S. at 317-572-3993 or fax 317-572-4002.

Wiley also publishes its books in a variety of electronic formats. Some content that appears in print, however, may not be available in electronic format.

Library of Congress Cataloging-in-Publication Data:

Music navigation with symbols and layers : toward content browsing with IEEE 1599 XML encoding / edited by Denis L. Baggi and Goffredo M. Haus.
     p. cm.
  Includes index.
  ISBN 978-0-470-59716-3 (cloth)
1. Information storage and retrieval systems–Music. 2. XML (Document markup language)
I. Baggi, Denis. II. Haus, Goffredo.
  ML74.3.M87 2012
  780.285'674–dc23

                                       2012027836

Printed in the United States of America.

10 9 8 7 6 5 4 3 2 1

Illustration of IEEE 1599, artwork by Marco Mariotta, Marco Mariotta Designs, Ascona, Switzerland.

CONTENTS

PREFACE

Computer Generated Music is the term used by the IEEE Computer Society to indicate the vast scientific and engineering area that deals with computer applications to music and musicology. At one extreme, one finds *artistic music* created, composed, and/or performed with the help of computers—as are the majority of contemporary music pieces. At the other extreme is *electronic signal processing*, in which the Technical Committee dedicated to this discipline, in existence since 1992, is happy to include all kinds of projects, including extremes.

Fortunately for both the layman and the practitioner, thousands of publications are in existence on the subject, as interest in this field has grown ever since the inception of the computer.[1] Here, we provide a brief review of a few well-known textbooks as a starting point for interested readers, and to allow a positioning of this new work within the existing literature.

Experimental Music [Hiller and Isaacson 1959; see also Chapter 7] has the merit of being the first-known experiment from which a piece of music was obtained from a computer program. One of the authors, Hiller, also contributed an important chapter in [Lincoln 1970], providing an up-to-date report for the time of the publication. Since then, collections of reports on interesting projects have steadily published, such as Roads [1989] and Roads and Srawn [1985], the extension of the special issue of IEEE COMPUTER dedicated to Computer Generated Music [Baggi 1992] with companion audio CD, and, earlier, one of the first collections with a floppy record included in the finished result von Foerster and Beauchamp [1969], as well as Brook [1970] with its mention of symbolic code. As curiosities, we shall mention an early work by Barbaud [1965], with programming code in ALGOL, while Forte [1973] is a model for atonal music that could easily be implemented as a programmed system similar to Macsyma, Mathematica, and other systems for symbolic mathematics.

This book is therefore not a mere addition to the existing collections on the subject, but instead emphasizes the *symbolic representation of music*—as practiced in virtually all musical cultures worldwide—and retains all other aspects of music, especially sound. IEEE 1599 standard is a new technology in which the core of music representation is a symbolic file in Extensible Markup Language (XML) that refers to all musical *layers* representing sound, audio, images (scores), video, metadata (historical details, catalogs, visual art), and the like. It is therefore an encompassing guide that represents, addresses, and incorporates all aspects of music, even those not anticipated at the time of standard approval. It includes all past, present, and future formats and standards for sound, performance, representation, and so on.

---

[1] And for several centuries, if not millennia, if one considers Babylonian algorithms; see the Introduction.

The following is a brief overview of the book.

Chapter 1 gives a simple, brief technical overview to understanding all applications, in particular I to VII, which exist and are complete, as well as VIII and IX, which have been considered, but are not fully realized.

Chapter 2 is a technical chapter that describes in detail how synchronization among different layers is achieved, mostly thanks to the role of the *spine*, the data structure that holds all different layers together.

Chapter 3 describes how, in addition to dealing with all entities of Common Western Notation such as notes, rests, music symbols, and so on, IEEE 1599 also covers complete structures, music excerpts, segments, and the like, thus becoming a useful tool for musical analysis.

Chapter 4 describes in deep detail how collections and music can be described, modeled, sought after, and indexed for musicological applications. Understanding some of the modeling may require elements of mathematical and analytical tools that are not supplied in this text.

Chapter 5 describes in detail how musical events—for example, notes, note symbols, and audio and video renditions—can be referenced in a unique way, thus allowing synchronization among different piece versions, representations, and multimedia renditions that, as the examples of Chapter 1 demonstrate, are unique to IEEE 1599.

Chapter 6 explains the versatility of audio rendering inherent in IEEE 1599 and how other synthesis languages (e.g., Csound) can be made isomorphic to an IEEE 1599 symbolic representation.

Chapter 7 describes future applications for entertainment and education made possible by the availability of such a complete and encompassing technology such as IEEE 1599.

Chapter 8 does not particularly refer to IEEE 1599, but describes past projects that have used the technique of Symbol Manipulation for music, a technique that has culminated in the development of IEEE 1599. Had that technology been available at that time, it could have been used for all these projects. It relates to Chapter 7, which describes future projects that can and will be carried out using IEEE 1599 Technology.

Appendices A, B, and C conclude the book.

To summarize, the purpose of this book is to demonstrate that it is possible to attain systems and applications that take into account *all* aspects of a music piece, making it *navigable* and *interactive* as a whole, without sacrificing past interpretations, formats, representations, and performances.

DENIS L. BAGGI
GOFFREDO M. HAUS

REFERENCES

Baggi, D., ed., and author. 1992. *Readings in Computer Generated Music*. IEEE CS Press.

Barbaud, P. 1965. *Initiation à la composition musicale automatique*. Paris: Dunod.

Brook, B.S., ed. 1970. *Musicology and the Computer*. City University of New York Press.

Forte, A. 1973. *The Structure of Atonal Music*. New Haven, CT: Yale University Press.

Hiller, L.A., and Isaacson, L.M. 1959. *Experimental Music: Composition with an Electronic Computer*. New York: McGraw-Hill.

Lincoln, H.B., ed. 1970. *The Computer and Music*. Ithaca, NY: Cornell University Press.

Roads, C., ed. 1989. *The Music Machine, Selected Readings from the Computer Music Journal.* MIT Press.

Roads, C., and Srawn, J., eds. 1985. *Foundations of Computer Music*. MIT Press.

von Foerster, H., and Beauchamp, J.W. 1969. *Music by Computers*. John Wiley and Sons.

A BRIEF INTRODUCTION TO THE IEEE 1599 STANDARD

Denis L. Baggi and Goffredo M. Haus

Proposed and de facto standards that focus on some aspects of music have been around for several decades—ever since the need arose to apply computer techniques to music and musicology. Some deal with audio aspects; some with the graphical representation or score of music; some with performance; some with specialized standards with choreography; and so on.

At the same time, the idea of representing music with *symbols* is not new. If we consider music notation, it has been used for several centuries in the West, and for computer applications, several decades, as shown by the the Plaine and Easie Code [Brook 1970] and Digital Alternate Realization of Musical Symbols (DARMS) [Erickson 1975].

More recently, attempts have been made to use the new technology brought about by SGML, a subset of which has been defined for music, namely, SMDL or Standard Music Description Language [Newcomb 1991]. Though well-defined, it failed to attract much attention, perhaps because of lack of applications.

Presently, there are some de facto standards using Extensible Markup Language (XML), two of which can be seen as the ancestors of this work. MusicXML is a proprietary standard by company Recordare [Recordare] and is used in dozens of existing applications on the market (including the popular program Finale). This standard has been in existence for several years, and new versions are constantly being released. The Music Encoding Initiative (MEI) [Roland] is a project by the Digital Library of the University of Virginia and it has been used in a few instances of music encoding.

In fact, music has been annotated for at least the past forty centuries in practically all cultures with *symbols* that represent musical events—such as *notes, rests, clefs, performance indications*—and therefore attempts have been made to capitalize on this experience and create music standards based on symbols. Some of these standards include SMDL, MEI, and MusicXML, as mentioned, as well as Hy Time, SMIL, MusiXML, MusiCat and MDL, WEDELMUSIC, MNML, MML, MuTaTeD, MusicML, and ChordML (for a detailed description, see Haus and Longari [2002]).

It would therefore seem that no need exists for a new standard such as IEEE 1599, were it not for the fact that this new recommended practice has some features not found anywhere else. These features include:

- Musical events and other indications are represented with *symbols*—just by itself, this is not new.
- The symbols are expressed in language *XML*, thus inheriting the features of XML such as: *natural extensibility, flexibility*, and *durability*, which may allow the standard to evolve beyond Common Western Music Notation and toward notational

formats not yet established—such as those used by the music avant-garde [Cage 1968].

- The concept of *layers*, that allow integrated representation of several aspects of music, such as its *graphic notation*, *texts* (as in songs and opera), *audio* (from a recording), *performance indications*, and everything that is related to the piece, such as title, composer, interpreter, dates, posters, and discographical and bibliographical data.

- Applications that *synchronize* all layers and events, as with a running indicator on the score or the libretto during an audition, that allow music fruition *independently of the version or the rendition*, and *independently of the audio or video format*, thanks to a special data structure called *spine*.

- As a consequence, all previous encoding of a piece of music can be *recuperated* as desired, since they remain in their original format (e.g., WAV, MP3, MIDI, acoustical recording), and are put under a single *comprehensive meta-language* in which every media file is related to all others with links, thus creating an all-encompassing *music information system* that can be *navigated* in all its aspects.

The idea of *music navigation* is akin to entering the virtual world of a great poem or novel, such as Homer's *Iliad* or Dante's *Divine Comedy*. This extends the enjoyment of music beyond that of *simple listening*, by providing information on who is doing what—as in a jazz piece or an opera—on how the piece is built—both at structural and at the detailed level—and on the constituents of a piece, up to a musicological analysis—which can be supplied by *semantics webs* and *ontologies*.

REFERENCES

Brook, B.S. 1970. "The Plaine and Easie Code." In *Musicology and the Computer*, ed. Barry S. Brook. New York: City University of New York Press, pp. 53–56.

Cage, J. 1968. *Notations*. New York: Something Else Press.

Erickson, R.F. 1975. "The Darms Project: A Status Report." *Computers and the Humanities* 9(6):291–298.

Haus, Goffredo, and Longari, M. 2002. "Towards a Symbolic/Yime-Based Music Language based on XML." *Proceedings of the First International Conference MAX2002*, IEEE, pp. 38–45.

Haus, Goffredo, and Longari, M. 2005. "A Multi-Layered Time-Based Music Description Approach based on XML." *Computer Music Journal*, 29(1):70–85.

Newcomb, S.R. 1991. "Standard Music Description Language complies with hypermedia standard." *IEEE Computer*, pp. 76–79 (July).

Recordare. http://www.recordare.com/xml.html.

Roland, P. "The Music Encoding Initiative (MEI) DTD and the Online Chopin Variorum Edition." http://www.lib.virginia.edu/digital/resndev/mei/mei_ocve.pdf.

CONTRIBUTORS

Denis L. Baggi
Think-Lab
Lugano, Switzerland

Adriano Baratè
LIM, Laboratorio di Informatica Musicale
Università degli Studi di Milano
Dipartimento di Informatica e
Comunicazione
Milano, Italy

Antonello D'Aguanno
Laboratorio di Informatica Musicale
(LIM)
Dipartimento di Informatica e
Comunicazione (DICo)
Università degli Studi di Milano
Milano, Italy

Goffredo M. Haus
Dipartimento di Informatica e
Comunicazione
Università degli Studi di Milano
Milano, Italy

Luca A. Ludovico
LIM, Laboratorio di Informatica Musicale
Università degli Studi di Milano
Dipartimento di Informatica e
Comunicazione
Milano, Italy

Davide A. Mauro
LIM, Laboratorio di Informatica Musicale
Università degli Studi di Milano
Dipartimento di Informatica e
Comunicazione
Milano, Italy

Alberto Pinto
Laboratorio di Informatica Musicale
(LIM)
Dipartimento di Informatica e
Comunicazione (DICo)
Università degli Studi di Milano
Milano, Italy

THE IEEE 1599 STANDARD

Denis L. Baggi and Goffredo M. Haus

Summary: This chapter gives a brief and simplified technical overview useful in the understanding of all IEEE 1599 applications, in particular from I to VII, which exist and are complete, and VIII and IX, which have been studied but not yet fully realized.

1.1 INTRODUCTION

IEEE 1599 is both a standard and a technology to represent and encode music, in all its aspects, making music enjoyment a total experience akin to that lived with literary masterpieces and great movies, well beyond the rendering of a binary file through a micro earphone.

Every music lover has always known that music is much more than audio and noise. The musical experience is similar to the act of entering a new world, enjoying a new experience, understanding a narration, and recognizing descriptions, as in the case of seriously reading a work of literature such as Tolstoy's *War and Peace* or Shakespeare's *Hamlet* and as in a parallel reality. In addition, music offers the possibility of investigating how the whole is built from its technical standpoint, which is the object of *musicology*, the science of music.

For such an experience, music must be represented with something that goes beyond *unreadable, binary standards* for audio, such as WAV and MP3, which are not music standards—they are audio standards. Musical aspects beyond audio must be represented in human-readable form, such as *symbols* and characters. This has always been the case for music scores in classical music, and for music notation in all civilizations for at least

Music Navigation with Symbols and Layers: Toward Content Browsing with IEEE 1599 XML Encoding,
First Edition. Edited by Denis L. Baggi and Goffredo M. Haus.
© 2013 the IEEE Computer Society. Published 2013 by John Wiley & Sons, Inc.

40 centuries (e.g., Babylonian tablets; see the Introduction). This is also the case with other symbols, such as the *harmonic grid* in jazz, and also in other written codes, as in non-Western music.

This is also true for the *new standard for music encoding IEEE 1599*, which uses Extensible Markup Language (XML) clauses [XML]. This work represents the culmination of decades of efforts of specialists in the field of computer applications to music and musicology, of which the "Plaine and Easie Code" [Brook 1970], Digital Alternate Realization of Musical Symbols (DARMS) [Erickson 1975], and SMDL [Newcomb 1991] are worth mentioning, while MusicXML [Recordare] and the Music Encoding Initiative (MEI) [Roland] are the direct ancestors of this technology. However, IEEE 1599 goes beyond such past efforts, as described next.

The characteristics of IEEE 1599 are described in detail in Chapter 2; however, for the purpose of this chapter at least two important ones will be mentioned: *symbols* and *layers*.

IMPORTANT FEATURES OF IEEE 1599

The main distinguishing features of the IEEE 1599 technology are the use of *symbols* to represent music, and the concept of *layers*.

Every element of Common Western Notation (see Chapter 2) can be represented by XML clauses that can be nested as needed, as in the example:

```
<clef type="G" staff_step="2" event_ref="c1"/>
```

This is described in several pages of Document Type Definitions (DTDs) listed in Appendix B and posted at http://standards.ieee.org/downloads/1599/1599-2008/, a site of the IEEE Standards Association. In addition, thanks to the inherent extensibility of XML, it is possible to add clauses for special needs—such as proprietary characters used by a particular music publisher or notation that is not yet standardized [Cage 1969].

In recognition of the different aspects of music, the concept of *layers* has been introduced [Haus and Longari 2005] and is an integral feature of the standard, as shown in Figure 1.1.

The *general layer* provides a general description of the music work and groups information about all related instances, including titles, author, type, number, date, genre, and related items. The *logic layer* provides music description from a symbolic point of view and represents the core of the format. It contains the main time-space construct for localization and synchronization of music events, the description of the score with symbols, and information about a graphical implementation of the symbolic contents, as well as the *spine* with *Logically Organized Symbols* (*LOS*), a sorted list of music events. Again, this is described in more detail in Chapter 2.

All layers are related to each other, and possibly synchronized, as shown in Figure 1.2, which shows that standard IEEE 1599 allows *representation*, *performance*, and *audible* and *visual fruition* of a piece of music *independently* of the original standard or format with which it was previously encoded. It therefore supports existing formats and recognizes that music contents that are already encoded in pre-existing file formats cannot

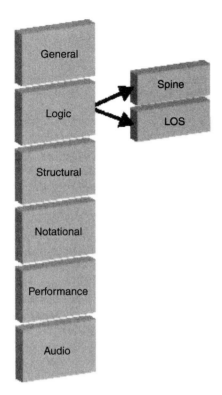

Figure 1.1. The layers in IEEE 1599.

be ignored. Since no overall description has ever existed for all aspects of music in one single format, it provides a meta-language in XML to describe all related music elements as well as to link all corresponding media objects already encoded. Thus, music contents are either newly encoded in the proper layers (the *general*, *logic*, and *structural* layers actually store information) or they remain in their original format, with links from the corresponding layers to files (the Notational, Performance, and Audio layers contain mappings to external files). Hence, media files are handled as they are, and media contents are still available in their original encoding. The comprehensive format described in the standard uses the layers to represent the relationships between music events and their occurrence in media files, thus allowing an overall synchronization. In other words, it is possible to navigate music in all its aspects.

The interaction and synchronization among these layers will become clear through the following examples.

EXAMPLES OF APPLICATIONS OF IEEE 1599 TO INCREASE MUSIC ENJOYMENT

The following are examples of applications of the standard, which can be realized easily thanks to the *symbolic representation of music* and the presence of *synchronized layers*, thus opening up a new way for music fruition.

- **An opera.** A DVD of an opera allows the user to *see the play* on the screen, to *hear the music*, *to see the score* (including *manuscripts*), *to read the libretto*, and *to choose alternative renditions* (see item 5 below).

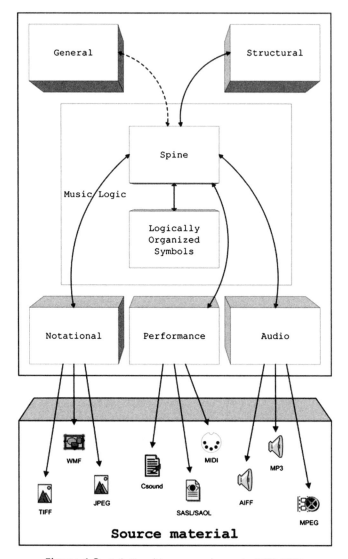

Figure 1.2. Relationship among layers in IEEE 1599.

- **Pieces by a jazz band.** The *harmonic grid* is displayed and the *name of the soloist* pops up at the beginning of each solo—with didactical tools as presented in jazz textbooks [Baggi 2001] (see item 2 below).
- **Music with a "program" or story.** For example, Vivaldi's *Four Seasons* come with poems by the composer that refer to segments of the music (see item 8 below).
- **Music with no apparent meaning.** For instance, free jazz of the 1960s–70s is perceived by many as a random collection of meaningless sounds, while an associated video, generated anew each time, may help the listener understand what is meant (see item 2 below).
- **A fugue.** The *theme* is highlighted as it gets passed among the different voices.
- **A piece of Indian classical music.** The *scale* of the raga is shown and the melodic development is highlighted.

- **A piece of several drums**, for example, as in African drumming, shows how the rhythmic pulse come from the fact that the hits do not fall together.
- **Preservation of the music heritage from the past.** To store documents in any media [Haus].
- **Musicological study.** Ease of queries, for example, all pieces utilizing the lowest note of a grand piano, and questions as to why a certain note is used in a given harmonic context.
- **Books about the making of a masterpiece**, for example, *Kind of Blue*, by Miles Davis and John Coltrane [Kahn].

The following is a list of existing and planned realizations of IEEE 1599:

I.   **"King Porter Stomp,"** by New Orleans pianist and composer Jelly Roll Morton (1889–1941), with versions played by the composer, two different scores, seven versions (of which one is a video from a movie) for solo piano and for orchestra, and 10 related images.

II. **"Crazy Rhythm,"** a jam session with no score and a *harmonic grid*, with Coleman Hawkins and Alix Combelle, tenor sax; Bennie Carter and André Ekyan, alto sax; Stéphane Grappelli, piano; Django Reinhardt, guitar; Eugène D'Hellemmes, bass; and Tommy Benford, drums. Recorded in Paris, April 27, 1937, record Swing #1.

III. *Tosca*, by Giacomo Puccini, 1858–1924, application realized on the original manuscript of 1900, courtesy of Ricordi. With three versions, including one video.

IV. **"Peaches en Regalia,"** by Frank Zappa, an example of control at the symbolic and structural levels.

V.   **"Il mio ben quando verrà,"** from Giovanni Paisiello's *Nina, o sia la pazza per amore*. It allows the user a choice of instrument, voice, versions of the score and of the libretto.

VI. **Brandenburg Concerto No. 3**, by J.S. Bach, allows a user to select a view of any section of the orchestra from several different vantage points running simultaneously.

VII. **Blues**, a didactical tool to learn jazz improvisation on a 12-bar blues structure.

Not yet realized are the following:

VIII. **"La caccia,"** from Antonio Vivaldi's *Four Seasons* ("Autumn"), with links to the score, sonnets, and music.

IX. *Tauhid,* by Pharaoh Sanders, a piece of free jazz with a moving screen meant to represent the feeling of the music.

Notice that items V and VI are also available on the Web as "canned versions" at

http://www.mx.lim.dico.unimi.it/videos/ieee1599_movie_short.wmv
http://www.mx.lim.dico.unimi.it/videos/rtsi_movie.wmv

They are "canned" in the sense that they are not interactive; they are videos of a user using the applications.

Example I: A Score with Different Versions: "King Porter Stomp," by Jelly Roll Morton

This is an application built, like all the others, at the Laboratory for Musical Informatics of the University of Milan [LIM]. The screenshot shown in the figure contains different windows, of which those with the extra caption *real time* operate in synchronism while the music is being played.

The user starts with the *piece selection window*: in this case, there are two choices, "King Porter Stomp 1924" and "King Porter Stomp 1939." They refer to two published scores of that piece, popular in the 1930s, by American composer and pianist Jelly Roll Morton (born Ferdinand Joseph La Motte, 1889–1941).

In the *file selection* window, the user can choose among alternate multimedia files, in this case a recording from 1926 in MP3 format, a MIDI rendition of the 1924 score encoded in MP3, and an excerpt from Louis Malle's movie *Pretty Baby* of 1977, in which a character patterned after Morton is heard composing the piece in the background. The movie is the one shown here in the window player display, which for plain music looks instead like a common music player. Two more choices are versions—one recorded in 1928 and one in 1932—by the jazz orchestra of Fletcher Henderson, who was a bandleader, composer, and arranger who popularized the piece for a band with a section of trumpets, trombones, and reed instruments (clarinets and saxophones). This shows how music pieces that appear very different have the same root and structure.

Once the selection is made, several synchronized activities start and execute in real time. The music starts playing, and in the case of the movie a video segment starts together with its sound. On the *score*, the *running cursor* indicates what is being played (in the figure, the beginning of the seventh bar). The user can move the red cursor with the mouse and initiate playing from another point in the score, while all other real time windows adjust synchronously.

The *XML code* window shows the encoded events, in this case those of the Logical Organized Symbols (LOS) of Figure 1.1 and Figure 1.2, scrolling with the music. In the *command window*, the user can select which XML code is displayed: *spine*, *LOS*, *notation*, and *audio*, again those of Figure 1.1 and Figure 1.2, and in the same window one can choose the *voice* the running cursor will follow; there are three voices in this case.

The *chords* window displays the elements of the music harmony of the piece, again synchronously with the playing, and the window for the *multimedia files* allows selection of other material, such as pictures of Morton or his band, or other curiosities, including a map of Storyville at the turn of the 20th century, a New Orleans district that was torn down in the 1930s.

Example II: A Jazz Piece with No Score: "Crazy Rhythm"

Figure 1.4 shows the screenshot for the jazz piece "Crazy Rhythm." Instead of a score, it displays the *harmonic grid*, pointed to by the running cursor, and the picture and name of each soloist pop up at the appropriate moment. There are four saxophonists taking solos: André Ekyan on alto and Alix Combelle on tenor, both from France, followed by Bennie Carter on alto and Coleman Hawkins on tenor. The rhythm section consists of violinist Stéphane Grappelli on the piano, Django Reinhardt on guitar, Eugène d'Hellemmes on bass, and Tommy Benford on drums. Though entirely improvised, the recording, made in Paris on April 27, 1937, counts among the best of jazz history and

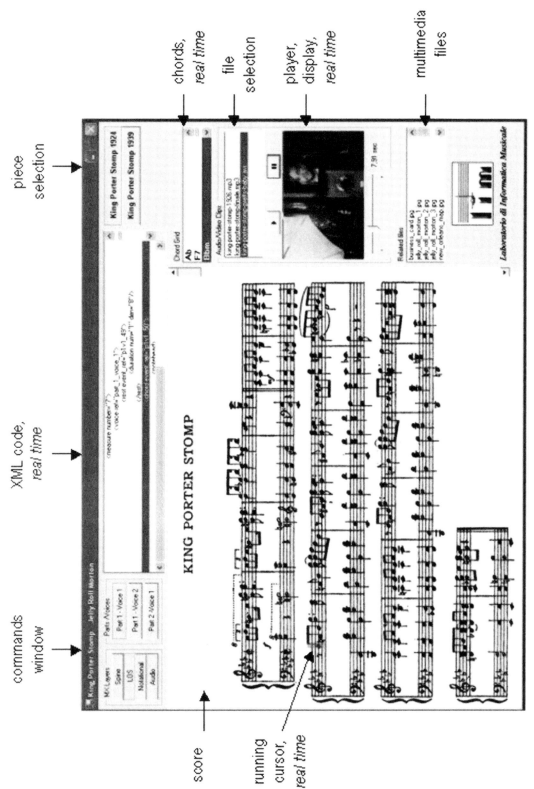

piece selection

commands window

XML code, *real time*

chords, *real time*

file selection

player, display, *real time*

multimedia files

score

running cursor, *real time*

KING PORTER STOMP

Figure 1.3. The screenshot for "King Porter Stomp." See color insert.

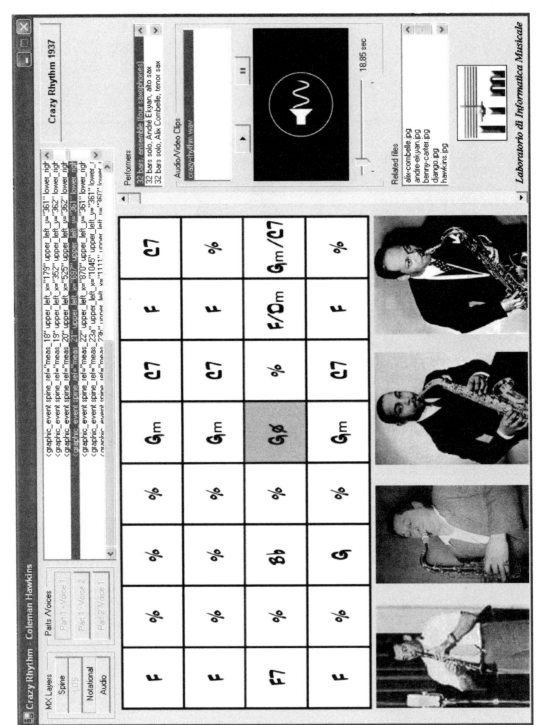

Figure 1.4. The screenshot for "Crazy Rhythm," with a harmonic grid instead of a score. See color insert.

appears as number 1 in the catalog of Swing, the first recording company dedicated entirely to jazz.

The ensemble exposes the theme once, in four voices, for all 32 bars. At each solo, the image and the name of the soloist appears; thus, it is possible to compare styles by clicking on the image of another soloist, and even to compare the sound and style of the alto saxophonist with that of the tenor. The bars and grid are of course synchronized. Each soloist takes 32 bars, except for Hawkins, who, in the middle of the development of sentences that keep building up, takes an unplanned second chorus, after the encouraging shout by Django, "Go on, Go on," which is automatically displayed at the 31st bar. Details like this would be totally lost to a casual listener, and instead can constitute the key for understanding improvised music. The ensemble takes over at the 30th bar of Hawkins's second chorus.

In this application, the standard and its browser can be used to teach a would-be jazz expert to distinguish among soloists and instruments, to detect sound and style differences (in this case between alto and tenor saxophone), and to follow the improvisation at each bar, in order to understand what everybody is playing, from horn to horn to rhythm section and to the ensemble.

Example III: An Opera Using the Composer's Manuscript: *Tosca*, by Giacomo Puccini

This example demonstrates how it is possible with this standard to preserve documents from the past and make them "live." Instead of simply digitizing an old document subject to degradation, this technology allows both the preservation and the realization of an application that allows exploration of music with everything it contains.

The opera is *Tosca*, with music and original manuscript by Giacomo Puccini. The application has been presented at the exhibition called "Tema con variazioni: musica e innovazione tecnologica," held in Rome in December 2005 to January 2006. The manuscript has been made available by publishing house Ricordi, which holds the manuscripts of practically every great Italian composer of the last two centuries.

The usual synchronization of events applies here, as in the other examples. The user can select between the original manuscript and a printed score with the words, or between clarinet and canto. Three tenors can be selected: Giuseppe di Stefano and Enrico Caruso from a 1909 Victor recording, or a video with tenor Jaime Aragall. There are also various images of the time, of Rome, Castel Sant'Angelo, contemporary posters, and the like.

The application shows how easy it is to gain knowledge of a complex piece like an opera, including libretto and different performances that differ considerably. The switch from Di Stefano and Caruso is illuminating, especially because of the difference in voice and style, but also to highlight the recording technique of different epochs, which was entirely acoustic in the case of Caruso—neither electricity nor electronics were available for recording before 1925.

Example IV: "Peaches en Regalia," by Frank Zappa

This example presents an approach to music interaction and creativity at both the *symbolic* and *structural levels*. Even if the creation of music occurs at the symbolic level, the structural level allows interaction with music content at a higher level, provided that a tool

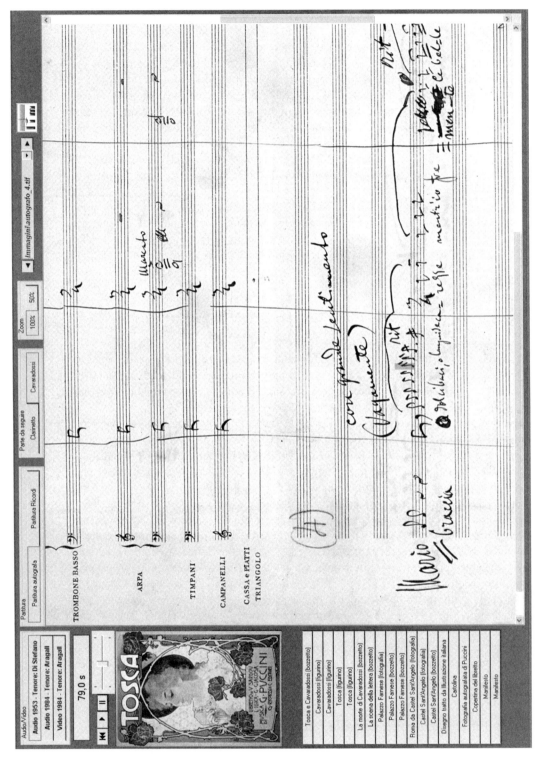

Figure 1.5. An application built on an original manuscript. See color insert.

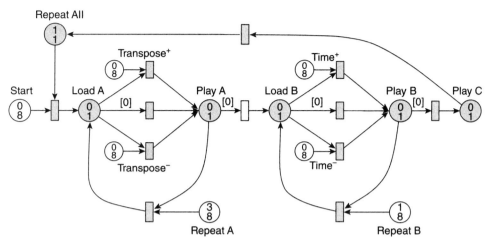

Figure 1.6. Representation of "Peaches en Regalia" in Petri Nets, an application to navigate music structures.

exists to formalize music fragments and their relations in terms of transformation functions. *Petri Nets* is such a tool, thus making real-time music composition possible. Thanks to IEEE1599, this interaction can be performed simultaneously at different levels. The application represents a case study based on "Peaches en Regalia," by Frank Zappa, presented at the International Conference of Esemplastic Zappology, which took place in Rome in June 2006.

Music Petri Nets have been shown since 1982 to be applicable both as a description and as a compositional tool [Degli Antoni and Haus]. The Net shown in Figure 1.6 models the original version of the music piece as recorded by Frank Zappa; thus, if the net is executed without changing the number of tokens in real time, the original version is reproduced. The piece consists of two *fragments*, (a) and (b).

In this model, interaction is limited to *addition/subtraction* of tokens in the places represented by a white background, in order to maintain a similarity to the original result, operations that would have the following results:

- The number of tokens in the **Start** node controls how many times the entire music piece is repeated.

- The number of tokens in **Repeat A** and **Repeat B** places controls how many times fragments (a) and (b) are repeated.

- The presence of one or more tokens in the white input nodes of the two transitions **Transpose +** and **Transpose −** causes the transposition of fragment (a) by a major third higher or lower, respectively. From the execution rules of Petri Nets, it follows that if both nodes have more than zero tokens, a transition is chosen at random.

- The presence of one or more tokens in the white input nodes of the two transitions **Time +** and **Time −** causes time warping of fragment (b) to twice or half the original tempo, respectively. Again, from the execution rules of Petri Nets, it follows that if both of these places have more than zero tokens, a transition is selected at random.

To conclude, the originality of this approach is that music manipulation is performed at a higher level than in the other application mentioned above. Thanks to the IEEE 1599 format, the composer can concentrate on music *structures* and *fragments* that are part of his or her music creation, since music information is automatically handled in a synchronized and heterogeneous way, and lower level integration is automatically performed by the computer.

Example V: "Il mio ben quando verrà," by Giovanni Paisiello

Navigating and Interacting with Notation and Audio (NINA) is an application built to illustrate how to use the standard for symbolic music works, and to show its power [Baggi et al.]. It was designed and implemented for the exhibition "Napoli, nel nobil core della musica," held in May 2007 in Salzburg, Austria, with the purpose of making music tangible and visible by bringing together all five senses beyond hearing. The music piece chosen for this demonstration is the operatic aria "Il mio ben quando verrà," from Giovanni Paisiello's *Nina, o sia la pazza per amore*.

The XML encoding contains the logical information about the piece and the synchronization among the various linked multimedia objects. Overall synchronization is provided among graphic objects representing scores, audio and video clips containing human performances, and the libretto. For the context of the exhibition, a rich but simple user interface has been designed, conceived for laymen, to let them listen to a track with various interpreted scores, and to look at different score versions simultaneously.

The screenshot of Figure 1.7 illustrates the interface of NINA. Music browsing is based on windows that contain different representations of multimedia contents, which operate in synchronism while the music is being played. The user is given some selection windows: in the lower window, there are four choices among scores that can be loaded, namely, full autograph score, manuscript copy, printed score for piano, and libretto. In the left window, the user chooses either an audio track or a video clip to listen to; the movie is represented in a dedicated player. The upper window allows selection of the instrumental part to be followed in real time on the score previously chosen.

The main part of the interface contains key graphical contents, namely, the score of the aria in one of its versions. Upon selection, several synchronized activities start and execute in real time: the music starts playing, the running cursor indicates what is being played on the score (here the beginning of the second bar). The user can change the position of the red cursor with the mouse and initiate playing from another point in the score, which causes other real time windows to adjust synchronously, including the audio/video player cursor that changes its current position accordingly.

In addition, the user is able to follow the evolution of any single voice. Hence, another selection window is provided in the upper part of the interface, in which instruments are listed. Thus, a user can change the instrument to be followed, the audio being played, and the score, by clicking on any point of the current graphical score (the synchronization is driven by spatial coordinates), by dragging the slider of the audio/video player (the synchronization is driven by time coordinates), or by selecting syllables from the libretto (navigation by text), while of course overall synchronization is always immediately obtained. The figure shows only the graphical effects of such operation, which is nevertheless visible in the video mentioned above.

In conclusion, NINA is a browser to represent music with readable symbols that can be accessed and manipulated even by nonmusicians. A significant result is that only one

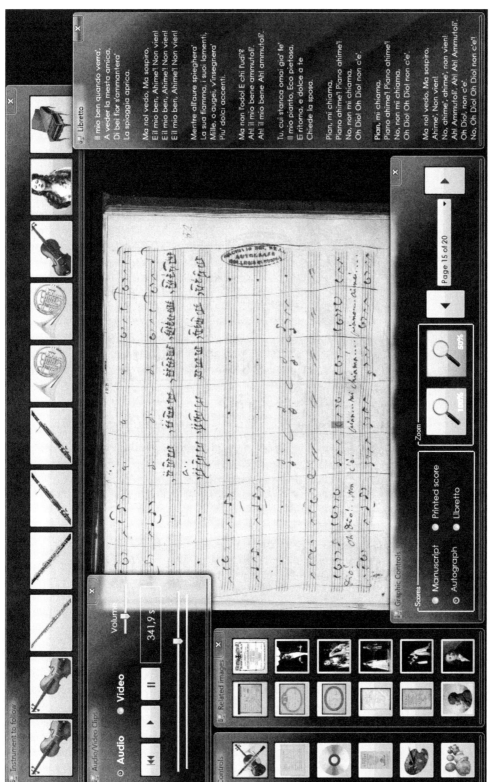

Figure 1.7. Control windows for Navigating and Interacting with Notation and Audio (NINA). See color insert.

single XML file is needed for several renditions of the same piece, all synchronized, to illustrate once more that the format used for audio and graphical contents is irrelevant.

Example VI: Brandenburg Concerto No. 3, by J.S. Bach

The main purpose of this application is to take advantage of the material provided by the Radio della Svizzera Italiana (RSI), the state radio and television station of Italian-speaking Switzerland, located in Lugano-Comano, Switzerland, which sponsors the internationally renowned orchestra I Barocchisti, specializing in 17th- and 18th-century music, directed by conductor Diego Fasolis.

The institute possesses a set of video recordings for concerts in which several fixed video cameras are constantly recording, individually, sections of the orchestra. Hence the idea was to realize an application such that a user could select which orchestra section to follow, a kind of video mixer—even though the audio remains the same. So, a user could choose to see what the harpsichord player is doing while the viola soloist is playing a solo.

Figure 1.8 shows how this controlled. In this case, the user has chosen four possible video channels, shown on the right-hand side, all of which of course move in real time, from the several options displayed at the bottom. By clicking on one, the user can enlarge that video window and follow it, while all others continue to move. Of course, selection of the musical instant is always possible from the complete score that runs in real time, as for all applications.

An application is planned for a piece of music in which not only are the video tracks available separately, but also the audio tracks, thus allowing a user to "mix" a new original version of the piece, beyond what is offered commercially.

Example VII: Blues, a Didactical Tool to Learn Jazz Improvisation

This is didactical tool, a game to learn jazz improvisation, is realized with the IEEE 1599 technology [Baggi and Haus]. The 12-bar blues is one of the simplest structures to improvise upon in jazz and underlies the vast majority of jazz tunes. Its basic structure is shown in the grid of Figure 1.9. For readability, however, the grid has been reduced to its simplest expression and does not exactly represent what advanced musicians use by substituting chords of the grid, even though hints appear on bars 2 and 10 where the parentheses indicate possible disregard of the chord.

The game currently contains three versions of the blues evolved from the basic grid, corresponding to different historical stylistic epochs: 1920s–30s, 1940s–50s, and 1960s–70s, selected from the central buttons. The user plays a solo instrument (e.g., an acoustic one such as a wind instrument or a guitar), a MIDI device connected to the computer as a keyboard, or even a piano keyboard simulated on the computer keyboard. While the rhythm section consisting of piano (or guitar), bass, and drums plays, the chord and the bar are displayed, and the user can enter his or her own solo.

Still under development are the didactical tools for beginners, for example, to favor the use of notes included in the grid chord, so that little by little the user experiments with other notes. Ultimately, the system would grade and comment according to criteria that would be set up by the user, such as basic correctness, stylistic consistency, originality, and similar criteria that have been defined according to jazz musicology (as has been done in the past by Baggi; see NeurSwing, Chapter 8). The same author has given several demos to jazz audiences on his soprano saxophone evolving from New Orleans style to bebop and free jazz.

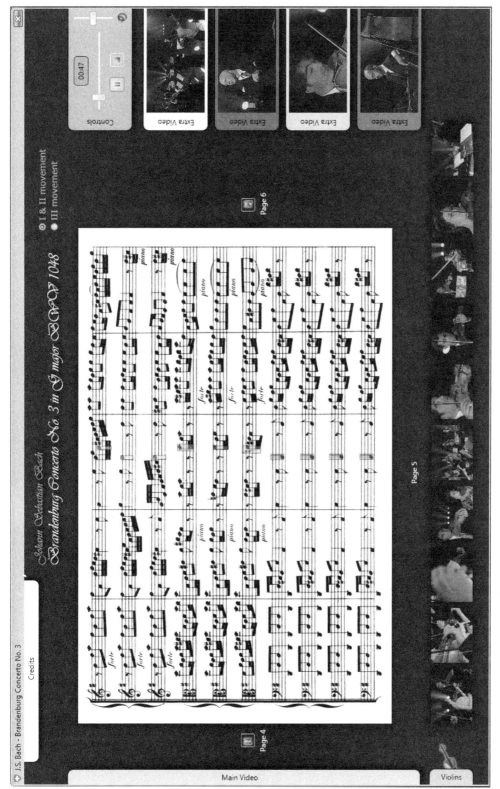

Figure 1.8. An application to control and select different videos. See color insert.

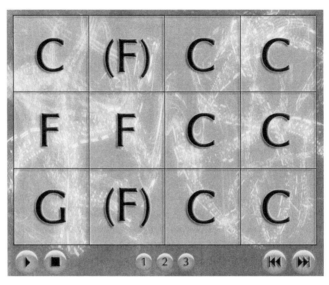

Figure 1.9. A didactical application.

Figure 1.10. The opening screen for the "La caccia" (the hunt), music by Antonio Vivaldi. See color insert.

Example VIII: "La caccia," from Antonio Vivaldi's *Four Seasons* ("Autumn")

Each movement of Vivaldi's *Four Seasons*, composed in 1723, is accompanied by a sonnet that refers to and describes sections of the music. "La caccia" (the hunt) is the third part of "Autumn" (see Figure 1.10), and six verses refer to it as follows:

I cacciator alla nov'alba a caccia
Con corni, schioppi, e cani escono fuore
Fugge la belua, e seguono la traccia;

Già sbigottita, e lassa a gran rumore
De' schioppi e cani, ferita minaccia
Languida di fuggir, ma oppressa muore.

At dawn the hunters
With horns and guns and dogs leave their homes;
The beast flees, they follow its traces.

Already terrified and tired by the great noise
Of the guns and the dogs, and wounded, it tries
Feebly to escape, but exhausted dies.

There are therefore several identifiable themes referring to episodes of the hunt, including:

1. The hunters riding their horses.
2. The hunters blowing their horns.
3. The hunters approach and see the fox.
4. The fox runs away fast (several themes, which change depending on how tired the fox is).
5. The hunters shoot, the dogs bark.
6. The fox is hit and dies.

The idea is to realize an application with the music running in synchronism with text, score, and a series of pictures (in this case, prepared by Swiss artist Jean-Marc Bühler) that illustrate the scene, as shown in Figure 1.11.

The application has the following purpose:

• To make people aware that there is whole story behind the audio of the music, something that even people who like this piece are often unaware of
• To relate and synchronize all connected aspects of the piece: music audio, music score, poetry and narration, pictures.

This is an example of a multimedia representation of a piece of music, which has become possible only with the technology of IEEE 1599.

Example IX: A Musicological Fantasy: *Tauhid*, a Piece of Free Jazz

"Free jazz" is a musical style popular in the 1960s and 1970s that broke with jazz tradition. It rejected tonality, diatonic scale, regular tempo and meter, and the structure in measures; it used sounds extracted outside the range of the instrument, and favored any device that was not part of a learned repertoire. It was, therefore, hard even for seasoned jazz lovers to make sense of such music, which sounded to many like a set of random sounds.

Figure 1.11. Pictures referring to themes 1, 4, 5, and 6 of "La caccia." See color insert.

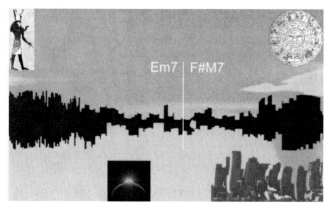

Figure 1.12. The display meant to illustrate and explore a section of the record *Tauhid* by tenor saxophonist Pharoah Sanders (Impulse, 1969).

However, experience shows that most people require to be told the meaning—true or supposed—of a piece of art, so that often just a simple gesture, image, or explanation opens up something akin to a revelation, as in the case of abstract painting. Figure 1.12 represents a proposal for a "creative" display that automatically shows varying images meant to convey the mood of the piece, in this case, the segment "Aum" in the suite containing also "Venus" and "Capricorn Rising" from the record *Tauhid* by saxophonist Pharoah Sanders (Impulse, recorded in 1969; [Kahn 2006]). While the music, represented by the central (blue) stripe, scrolls with musical symbols over an imaginary landscape, pictures appear that represent ancient Egypt (pride of the ancient past heritage claimed by the composer), rising cosmological events, astrological charts, and the fallacy of a modern urban landscape that shakes while it hides social injustice. A generative grammar in XML can be used to that end, and it ensures that the user would approach the system with renewed curiosity to discover new aspects of the music, since the display would look different every time it is accessed.

CONCLUSIONS

The example applications described in this chapter are meant to show that IEEE 1599 technology is wide open: it is not restricted to any particular musical genre, culture (ethnic, geographic, or other), or multimedia convention nor to any pre-established context, and it can therefore be used in as-yet-unforeseen cultural domains (see Chapter 8).

The flexibility of its display makes it usable in any graphic context beyond Common Western Notation, and able to incorporate and integrate any existing standard, audio and other, which guarantees the survival of the standard in different epochs. Beside obvious applications such as a navigable DVD of a piece of music, which can reuse existing material, the technology can be used in didactical tools—for example, to learn music and harmony—to explain particular musical techniques and styles, as part of a digital library that would not only exhibit manuscripts but make them come alive, in databases and queries, and for the recuperation and preservation of cultural heritage. And these are only a few of the applications possible.

ACKNOWLEDGMENTS

The Sponsor for Standard IEEE 1599, from 2001 to 2008, has been the Standards Activities Board of the IEEE CS, and financial support has been obtained from the Commission for Technological Innovation of the Swiss Federal Government, thanks to approval by the global organization Intelligent Manufacturing Systems.

REFERENCES

Baggi, D. 2001. *Capire il jazz: Le strutture dello swing*. Surveys of CIMSI/SUPSI, with CD with 500 musical didactical examples. Manno, Switzerland.

Baggi, D. 2005. "An IEEE Standard for Symbolic Music." *IEEE Computer*, pp. 100–102 (November).

Baggi, D., and Haus, G. 2009. "IEEE 1599: Music Encoding and Interaction." *IEEE Computer*, pp. 84–87 (March).

Baggi, D., Baratè, A., Haus, G., and Ludovico, L.A. 2007. "NINA: Navigating and Interacting with Notation and Audio." *Proceedings of the 2nd International Workshop on Semantic Media Adaptation and Personalization*, December 17–18, 2007. London: IEEE Computer Society.

Brook, B.S. 1970. "The Plaine and Easie Code." In *Musicology and the Computer*, ed. Barry S. Brook. New York: City University of New York Press, pp. 53–56.

Cage, John. 1969. *Notations*. New York: Something Else Press.

Degli Antoni, G., and Haus, G. 1983. "Music and Causality." In *Proceedings of the 1982 International Computer Music Conference*, La Biennale, Venezia. San Francisco, CA: Computer Music Association, pp. 279–296.

Erickson, R.F. 1975. "DARMS, Digital Alternate Realization of Musical Symbols. The Darms Project: A Status Report." *Computers and the Humanities*, 9(6):291–298 (June).

Haus, G. 1988. "Rescuing La Scala's Audio Archives." *IEEE Computer*, 31(3):88–89.

Haus, G., and Longari, M. 2005. "A Multi-Layered Time-Based Music Description Approach Based on XML." *Computer Music Journal*, 29(1):70–85.

Kahn, A. 2000. *Kind of Blue: The Making of the Miles Davis Masterpiece*. New York: Da Capo Press.

Kahn, A. 2006. *The House That Trane Built: The Story of Impulse Records*. New York: W.W. Norton.

LIM. http://www.lim.dico.unimi.it.

MusicXML: http://www.recordare.com/xml.html

Newcomb, S.R. 1991. "Standard Music Description Language Complies with Hypermedia Standard." *IEEE Computer*, pp. 76–79 (July).

Recordare. http://www.recordare.com/xml.html.

Roland, P. "The Music Encoding Initiative (MEI) DTD and the Online Chopin Variorum Edition." http://www.lib.virginia.edu/digital/resndev/mei/mei_ocve.pdf.

XML. http://www.w3.org/standards/xml.

2

ENCODING MUSIC INFORMATION

Luca A. Ludovico

Summary: This technical chapter describes in detail the multi-layer structure of IEEE 1599 and how synchronization among different layers is achieved, mostly thanks to the spine, the data structure that holds all of the different layers together.

2.1 INTRODUCTION

Music is a rich and complex type of communication, which can be represented in a number of forms and conveyed through different media. In the digital age, file formats for music are generally restricted to a particular aspect of music, such as score symbols or audio recordings. Until now, a standard to represent all music aspects has not emerged. It should represent neither a set containing all heterogeneous descriptions of a single music piece nor a group of homogeneous descriptions of the piece itself. Instead, it must be able to synchronize documents thanks to content-based pointers. In this chapter, the problem of representing and organizing heterogeneous contents involved in a comprehensive description of music is analyzed first. These are organized as a multi-layer structure, so that *layers* can be used to realize a top-down approach for describing music, starting at the symbolic level (e.g., score symbols) and reaching notational and audio levels. Thus, each layer can be interpreted as a different level of abstraction in *music information.*

The technology of IEEE 1599 will be presented. It is a format based on Extensible Markup Language (XML) that reflects the multi-layer structure mentioned above. In a

Music Navigation with Symbols and Layers: Toward Content Browsing with IEEE 1599 XML Encoding,
First Edition. Edited by Denis L. Baggi and Goffredo M. Haus.
© 2013 the IEEE Computer Society. Published 2013 by John Wiley & Sons, Inc.

single IEEE 1599 document, all music symbols, printed scores, audio tracks, computer-driven performances, catalogue meta-data, and other content related to one music piece can be encoded, linked, and synchronized.

The main concepts of the standard are discussed, including its multi-layer organization and its key data structure, known as the *spine*. An adequate number of examples are provided to clarify all matters. Other relevant aspects of the format, such as the techniques to synchronize multimedia objects, are provided in other chapters of the book.

2.2 HETEROGENEOUS DESCRIPTIONS OF MUSIC

As shown in Chapter 1, the IEEE 1599 standard essentially provides a comprehensive way to describe music in all its aspects. A unique but comprehensive representation of music is highly desirable, for instance, to satisfy the needs of musicologists as well as those of performers, music students, and untrained people interested in music. A format that catches all the different aspects of a piece of music in a single document is rich in information and suited to a huge audience.

The term "music description" can be used in different contexts, all of which have to be considered. Music is conceived, and often written, as a set of organized symbols. In Common Western Notation, they take the form of *notes* and *rests*, with the addition of other conventional signs to modify the basic notation and to provide articulation and expression information. Even if this way to represent music is almost universally accepted, other cultures and music genres use different ways to notate scores. For instance, to notate Indian *rāga*, a solfège-like system called *sargam* is used, while in many other cultures, such as Chinese and Indonesian, "sheet music" consists primarily of numbers, letters, or native characters representing notes. These systems are often known as *cipher notations*. Western cultures, such as American and European, have also adopted alternative ways to encode score information. One example is the *tablatures* for Medieval and Renaissance music. This technique is still in use, and many contemporary players use tablatures to read, write, and exchange music. A completely different way to represent scores is *graphic notation*, namely, the contemporary use of non-traditional graphic symbols and text to convey information about the performance of a music piece. It has been used in Western culture for 20th century experimental music; graphic notation counts among its practitioners well-known composers such as Luciano Berio, Earle Brown, John Cage, Morton Feldman, Luigi Nono, Krzysztof Penderecki, and Christian Wolff [Cage 1969].

It follows that most representations of scores share the same goal: to provide a common and well-known way to write and preserve music works for future generations. This trend justifies the efforts to find a standardized and commonly accepted way to describe music. Furthermore, a certain richness emerges from specialized discussions on a given topic, such as score notation. Needless to say, a comprehensive format to encode score information, from any culture and from any historical period, must be able to include Common Western Notation, as well as other graphical representations, cipher notations, and so on.

It is thus possible to go back to the question of what the term "music description" includes. Until now, only score information has been considered; however, notation is just one of many ways to describe music. Another aspect is audio related to a performance. An audio file is often the result of a recording chain, where the signal starts as a live sound source, is picked up by a microphone, amplified, filtered, mixed, and finally digitally recorded. But in the computer field, an audio file may also come as a result of digital synthesis, or from some other digitization of an analog signal. While this is not the context to discuss the various ways to obtain an audio file, suffice it to restate the richness and heterogeneity of music, even if one concentrates on a particular aspect of music description.

And this is by no means the end. For example, when people mention a music work, a classical piece, or a pop song, they usually refer to so-called *metadata* such as title, authors, performers, and instrumental ensemble. Everyone knows that it is sufficient to utter a few words, such as a title, to evoke music contents—for instance, "Air on the G String" by J.S. Bach or "Let It Be" by The Beatles. This is also another way to describe music, by using metadata or catalog information, instead of music characteristics. Composers, performers, and music experts would mention still another level of music description, namely, *music structures*, aggregations of music objects emerging as a whole from composition processes or a posteriori analyses. This is dealt with in Chapter 3.

Finally, there exist important documents that are not directly related to music characteristics but that concur with the description of a music piece: on-stage photos of a performance, iconographic material related to staging, posters, and so on. For instance, an opera house is a very rich and complex environment for music-related information [Haus and Ludovico 2006], since the materials and documents stored in its database may include:

- Scores and other symbolic representations of music
- Audio/video recordings
- Photos, sketches, and fashion plates
- Fliers, playbills, posters
- Images of costumes and related accessories
- Images of stage tools, equipment, and maps
- Other text documents, such as librettos and reviews of music works.

This incomplete list is sufficient to show the heterogeneity of data and metadata pertaining to a music piece. The IEEE 1599 format discussed in this book aims at integrating all the descriptions mentioned within a single XML document. In a certain sense, it can be seen as a database of music-related documents and descriptions, with some relevant differences:

- It is limited to a single music piece and does not handle collection of pieces.
- It presents content-based relationships among information sources, and in particular synchronization among media files.

2.3 AVAILABLE FILE FORMATS

Currently, many file formats are available to represent either symbolic or multimedia information. For example, AAC, MP3, and PCM are commonly used to encode audio recordings; Csound, MIDI, and SASL/SAOL are well-known standards for computer-driven performance; GIF, JPEG, and TIFF files can be used to represent music scores; DARMS, NIFF, and MusicXML are examples of formats for score typing and publishing. Needless to say, many other formats could be listed to cover all other aspects of music description. Specific encoding formats to represent music features are well known and used; however, they are characterized by an intrinsic limitation: they can describe music data or metadata for score, audio tracks, computer performances, and so on, in a very specific way, but they are unable to encode all these aspects together. Thus, a new format to describe music had to be designed according to a comprehensive vision; at the same time, commonly accepted standards could not be ignored.

There are at least two good reasons to take into account available standards. First, most existing ad hoc encodings work well for the application fields for which they have been designed. Hence, trying to obtain the same result in XML would be both unnecessary and redundant. Second, huge collections of already encoded documents are available.

Thus, the two-sided approach of IEEE 1599 allows intrinsic music descriptions to be retained within the IEEE 1599 file, while media objects outside the XML document remain in their original format. In other words, IEEE 1599 provides syntax to define music events and music objects in XML, as a commonly accepted standard with the required features. On the other hand, media files can be linked to the IEEE 1599 format, integrated, and synchronized, although their media information remains in its original form. Hence, for media files, an IEEE 1599 document represents a sort of wrapper, as will be seen below.

2.4 KEY FEATURES OF IEEE 1599

The advantages of IEEE 1599 over other formats and of its possible applications have been already mentioned, and they will be discussed in depth in the following chapters of the book. For instance, Chapter 4 deals with the activities of modeling and searching music collections, which can be improved thanks to the features provided by IEEE 1599 format, while Chapter 7 introduces some relevant possible applications of the standard.

To show the potentialities of this format, the present section aims at explaining its main concepts, namely, those characteristics that implement a comprehensive description of music within a single XML document.

During the design phase, the features to be implemented in IEEE 1599 were:

- Richness in multimedia descriptions for the same music piece. Symbolic, logic, structural, graphic, audio, and video content can be encoded within or linked by the same document.
- Possibility of linking a number of digital objects for each type of supported multimedia description. For instance, many performances of the same piece or many score scans from different editions can be related to a single file, when available.
- Synchronization among time-based contents. As explained in Chapter 1, through a dedicated player, audio and video content can be shown while the related score advances, even when switching from a particular performance to another or from a score edition to another. Even though such features clearly belong to a specific software implementation, it is worth noticing that all the information needed to perform score following is encoded within the XML document.
- Full support to user-friendly interaction with music content. This format presents all the characteristics to implement software applications that make interaction with music content intuitive. For example, through an ad hoc IEEE 1599 browser, the user could click any region of the score and jump to that point, and the audio—and the libretto if present—would reposition accordingly. Likewise, audio can be navigated through a slider control, while the score follower responds consequently.

To obtain these results, IEEE 1599 has been designed with a multi-layer architecture, as described in the following section. Layers virtually correspond to different ways and abstraction levels to describe music information, ranging from metadata to structure, from score symbols to audio signals. If music descriptions for the same objects (say, a measure or single note) are located in different layers, a common data structure is used to keep such descriptions together and to synchronize them. This is the role of the *spine*, a concept that will be introduced below.

2.5   MULTI-LAYER STRUCTURE

An IEEE 1599 document contains information about a single piece of music. However, as already mentioned, a comprehensive description of the piece should support a number of different materials, which differ in regard both to their type (e.g., audio and graphic information) and to their number (e.g., different audio recordings or different score versions). Hence, an effective and efficient organization to store heterogeneous information within a unique XML document has to be found. This issue has been addressed in many research works, such as Haus and Longari [2005] and Steyn [2002].

In particular, IEEE 1599 employs six different layers to represent information, as shown in Figure 2.1:

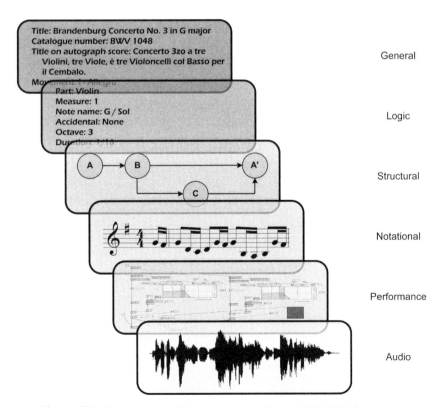

Figure 2.1. The typical multi-layer structure for an IEEE 1599 document.

- *General.* This layer contains metadata about the music piece. Information stored there is not directly related to music events such as notes and rests, and refers rather to the piece as a whole. Content examples include music-related metadata, that is, catalog information about the piece, genre classification, and a number of ancillary documents such as playbills or on-stage photos.
- *Logic.* This is the most important layer of the IEEE 1599 format, as it provides both the description of score symbols and the *spine*, namely, the common data structure mentioned before and discussed in Section 2.7. For now, it is sufficient to view the spine as the glue among all layers. For these reasons, the presence of the logic layer is mandatory.
- *Structural.* In this layer, a number of music objects can be identified, together with their relationships. Thus, different kinds of musicological analyses can be hosted here.
- *Notational.* This layer contains graphical representations, namely, graphical files potentially coming from traditional scores scans and the output of notation software.
- *Performance.* The name of this layer recalls computer-based performances, that is, descriptions and executions of music represented in formats such as MIDI or SASL/ SAOL.
- *Audio.* Within this layer, we find digital and digitized recordings of the current music piece.

Consider the problem of organizing a heterogeneous set of materials within a single document. From this point of view, XML is effective since it provides a strongly structured language to represent information.

The Document Type Definition (DTD) for the root element IEEE 1599 is the following:

```
<!ELEMENT ieee1599 (general, logic, structural?, notational?,
performance?, audio?)>
<!ATTLIST ieee1599
    version CDATA #REQUIRED
    creator CDATA #IMPLIED>
```

Consequently, a generic IEEE 1599 document presents an XML structure similar to the one shown below:

```
<?xml version="1.0" encoding="UTF-8"?>
<!DOCTYPE ieee1599
SYSTEM "http://standards.ieee.org/downloads/1599/1599-2008/
ieee1599.dtd">
<ieee1599>
   <general>...</general>
   <logic>...</logic>
   <structural>...</structural>
   <notational>...</notational>
   <performance>...</performance>
   <audio>...</audio>
</ieee1599>
```

In reality, not all layers must be present for a given music piece to generate a valid IEEE 1599 file. DTD states that only logic and basic general information are mandatory. This aspect provides great flexibility for possible uses of the format. For instance, it is possible to create a file containing a non-traditional graphic score bound to an audio performance, useful, for example, for electronic music, as well as a document where only the logic and structural layers are provided, to be used in musicological analysis. Of course, the higher the number of layers, the richer the description of the piece.

Up to this point, richness has been mentioned with regard to the heterogeneous types of media descriptions. But the philosophy of the IEEE 1599 standard lets each layer contain one as well as many digital instances. Thus, the audio layer could link to several audio tracks, and the structural layer could provide many different analyses for the same piece.

The concept of *multi-layered structure* (i.e., as many different types of descriptions as possible, all mutually related and synchronized) together with the concept of *multi-instance support* (i.e., as many different media objects as possible for each layer) provides rich and flexible means for encoding music in all its aspects.

It follows that the general, logic, and structural layers adopt XML to represent information content, whereas the notational, performance, and audio layers mainly encode pointers to external media files. The overall framework is more complex, as in the latter group of layers some additional information is required to identify the occurrence of music events. Figure 2.2 shows the relationship among layers inside an IEEE 1599 document, as well as the relationship between the document itself and external media files. Intrinsic music descriptions, such as catalog metadata and logical representations of music events, are completely defined inside the XML file (see the upper block in Figure 2.2), whereas external media files are linked from the corresponding IEEE 1599 layers (see the lower part of Figure 2.2).

In conclusion, the description provided by an IEEE 1599 file is both flexible and rich with regard to the numbers and to the type of media involved. In fact, thanks to the multi-layer approach, a single file can present one or more descriptions of the same music piece in each layer. For example, in the case of an operatic aria, the file could contain the catalogue metadata about the piece, its authors and genre, the corresponding portion of the libretto, scans of the original manuscript and of a number of printed scores, several audio files containing different performances, and related iconographic content such as sketches, on-stage photographs, and playbills.

2.6   THE LOGIC LAYER

The *logic* layer is the core of IEEE 1599, since it contains information fundamental for and referenced by all other layers. This layer has been called "logic" because it emphasizes one interpretation of music symbols (i.e., notes, rests, etc.) that traditionally are used in two contexts:

1. As symbols printed on a paper or digital score, including layout, paging, and font information
2. As symbols as they were conceived by the composer, flowing on a unique and virtual staff system with no specific layout, paging, or font information.

The former meaning is strictly related to the graphic aspect of music symbols on specific score versions and editions and is thus treated in the notational layer. However, it is the

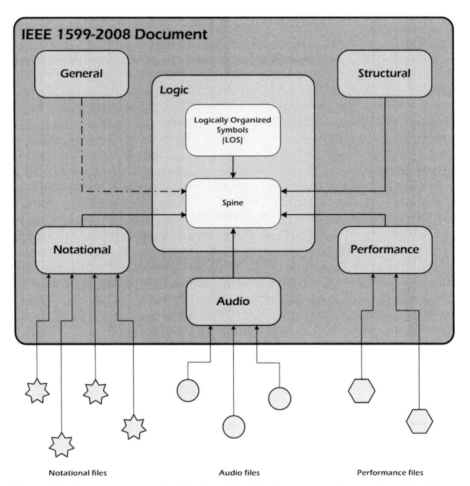

Figure 2.2. Contents encoded inside the IEEE 1599 document and external media objects.

latter interpretation that provides an abstract view of the score, in which music symbols have relation not to graphical objects but to their music essence, their intrinsic meaning. This kind of description is provided by the logic layer, which serves as a semantic reference for all the other layers.

Therefore, one of the key concepts of the format is the separation between *music content*—encoded in the logic layer—and *multimedia representations* contained in other layers. The musical meaning of a note is unique, whereas its aural or visual rendering depends on the specific version we are considering.

Even though syntax and other implementation details will be provided later, the following example shows the central role of this layer in IEEE 1599 documents. Consider a particular music event, say a note: in the notational layer, one or many graphical versions of the note are referenced; in the audio layer one or many tracks containing this sound can be indexed. However, the characteristics of the note from a symbolic point of view can always be retrieved from the logic layer, for example, an octave-3, pitch-C eighth note in measure 1, piano part, right-hand voice.

Hence the logic layer addresses mainly two problems: the unique identification of music events and their description from a symbolic point of view. As a consequence, this layer is composed of the following:

1. A mandatory subelement, known as the *spine*, containing the common data structure referenced by all layers. The spine will be discussed in the next section.
2. An optional subelement, called Logically Organized Symbols (LOS), where symbols are described with regard to their music meaning.
3. An optional subelement, namely *layout*, which contains the specifications for a generic presentation of symbols. Once again, specific graphic versions are dealt with by the notational layer.

The DTD part which defines the logic layer is the following:

```
<!ELEMENT logic (spine, los?, layout?)>
```

Music symbols, data structures, and layout information are completely represented in XML syntax. Examples of the spine are provided in the next section, after the main concepts have been defined.

2.7 THE SPINE

The *spine* is the main data structure in an IEEE 1599 document. Its presence is mandatory for a file to be valid. It is a subelement of the logic layer that aims at listing music events and identifying them univocally by assigning unique labels.

Accordingly, IEEE 1599 DTD defines the `<spine>` subelement as a list of events:

```
<!ELEMENT spine (event)+>
```

The concept of "music event" is left intentionally vague, since the format has to be flexible and suited to a number of different purposes and applications.

A music event can be defined as the occurrence of something that is considered important by the author of the encoding. For instance, in a normal case, all notes and rests within a score can be interpreted as music events: each symbol will be identified univocally and inserted in a sorted list of events. How to build this list is discussed in Section 2.7.3. In a more general case, all score symbols (and not only notes and rests) could be considered music events, ranging from clefs to articulation signs.

There are other, less trivial, interpretations of the concept of music event. For instance, often in jazz music a traditional score is not available for a given piece. It could be obtained by an a posteriori transcription process, but this would generate the score of a particular performance of the piece, and not the original score of the piece itself. Rather, for this music genre the concept of score often collapses to a harmonic grid. In this case, music events could be occurrences of new steps of the harmonic path (regions on the same chord). Similarly, in dodecaphonic music, events of interest could occur when a series begins, and, needless to say, many other interpretations could emerge. In a framework for music analysis, events could refer to the highest and lowest notes within a given instrumental part, or to all C-pitched dotted eighth notes, and so on.

Figure 2.3. The violin incipit from J.S. Bach's Brandenburg Concerto No. 3 in G major, BWV 1048, Allegro.

Thus, against common sense, the list of events of interest does not have to match the whole score. Because if it were, musical works with no notation, pieces where the performance is improvised, or music whose score is unknown could not be encoded in IEEE 1599. On the contrary, thanks to the flexible definition of music event, neither traditional score notation nor a complete encoding of the piece is required to generate a valid IEEE 1599 document.

The spine is a sort of glue needed in a multi-layer framework like IEEE 1599. In this approach, heterogeneous descriptions of the same music piece are not simply grouped together, but further relationships are provided: whenever possible, structural and media information is related to single music events, whatever meaning is adopted for this locution. This common data structure is called "spine" because it serves as a backbone for the music work. This concept was first used in 1975 by D.A. Gomberg [1977], who based a system for electronic music publishing on a similar structure, also called "spine." Figure 2.3 gives a graphical representation of the role of the spine within IEEE 1599 framework.

Since the spine simply lists events without defining them from a musical point of view, the mere presence of an event within the spine has no semantic meaning. It could represent a note as well as a clef, a measure as well as a harmonic region. As a consequence, what is listed in the spine must have a counterpart in some layer, otherwise the event would not be defined and its presence in the list (and in the XML document) would be useless. For example, in a piece made of *n* music events, the spine would list *n* entries without defining them from any point of view.

Consider the following example. Figure 2.3 shows a score incipit, whereas the IEEE 1599 snippet below illustrates the corresponding spine, under the hypothesis that only notes are considered music events (the *timing* and *hpos* attributes of event will be explained later).

```
<ieee1599>
  <logic>
    <spine>
      <event id="p0e0"  timing="0"  hpos="0"/>
      <event id="p0e1"  timing="1"  hpos="1"/>
      <event id="p0e2"  timing="1"  hpos="1"/>
      <event id="p0e3"  timing="2"  hpos="2"/>
      <event id="p0e4"  timing="1"  hpos="1"/>
      <event id="p0e5"  timing="1"  hpos="1"/>
      <event id="p0e6"  timing="2"  hpos="2"/>
      <event id="p0e7"  timing="1"  hpos="1"/>
      <event id="p0e8"  timing="1"  hpos="1"/>
      <event id="p0e9"  timing="2"  hpos="2"/>
      <event id="p0e10" timing="1"  hpos="1"/>
      <event id="p0e11" timing="1"  hpos="1"/>
    </spine>
    <los>...</los>
  </logic>
</ieee1599>
```

Each note event can be contained in many graphical scores and played in a number of audio tracks. Its musical meaning, presence, and behavior cannot be inferred by the spine structure, and these aspects are treated in logic, notational, and audio layers.

2.7.1 Inter-layer and Intra-layer Synchronization

The previous discussion stated that a basic, but valid, IEEE 1599 document could contain only the spine, but this would have little meaning since the spine only lists events without defining them. The definition, according to different semantic meanings, has to be provided in other layers. In general terms, each spine event can be described and linked:

- In 1 to n layers, for example, in the logic, notational, and audio layers. This is the case of a music symbol with a logic definition (a G-pitched eighth note), a graphical representation, and an audio rendering;
- In 1 to n instances within the same layer, for example, in n different audio clips mapped in the audio layer. Another example regarding the notational layer is shown below.
- In 1 to n occurrences within the same instance. For example, each spine event of a song refrain could be mapped n times in the audio layer, at different timings.

Thanks to the spine, IEEE 1599 is not a mere container of heterogeneous semantic and media descriptions related to a single music piece. In fact, those descriptions represent a number of references to a common structure, which puts them in relation on the base of the concept of music event. Hence, two kinds of relationship can emerge within an IEEE 1599 document:

1. Synchronization among instances within a layer (*intra-layer synchronization*);
2. Synchronization among contents disposed in many layers (*inter-layer synchronization*).

These relationships represent a form of synchronization because, as shown in Figure 2.3, if a particular event listed in the spine, for example, labeled *p0e0*, were the first note appearing in the violin part of a piece, then, by referring to the same identifier, its note pitch and rhythmic value could be investigated in *los* subelement of the logic layer. Besides, if a printed score and an audio track are attached, the same identifier appears somewhere in the notational and audio layers, respectively, so that a graphical rendering and an audio definition of the note could also be retrieved. Inter-layer synchronization is given by a number of references from heterogeneous description levels to the same identifier within the spine.

Now, assuming that the piece has three score versions attached, in the notational layer there must be three references to event *p0e0*. A graphical example of this case is provided in Figure 2.4, where the horizontal lines represent real references (from notational instances to the common data structure, the spine), and the vertical lines show the consequent intra-layer synchronization. In other words, the fact that three different areas over three different graphic files are related to the same spine entry automatically creates an implicit synchronization among instances.

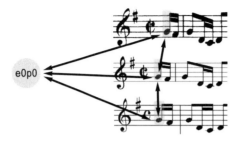

Figure 2.4. Many graphical instances of the same spine event.

2.7.2 Virtual Timing and Position of Events

The spine is not only a way to list and mark music events by assigning unique identifiers, but it also provides information lo locate them in space and time. IEEE 1599 DTD defines *event* subelement as follows:

```
<!ELEMENT event EMPTY>
<!ATTLIST event
    id ID #REQUIRED
    timing CDATA "null"
    hpos CDATA "null">
```

In IEEE 1599, the spine is composed of events, each with a reference both in the time domain, expressed through the *timing* attribute, and in the space domain, encoded by the *hpos* attribute. As a consequence, the spine is also a structure that relates time and spatial information.

However, this kind of information cannot be expressed in absolute terms. Consider once again the example of many tracks related to a given piece. The same music events have—in general—as many different descriptions as the number of audio instances.[1] In this case, the exact time when a music event occurs depends on the performance; thus, such a value is not unique for the piece. Similarly, a given music symbol has different graphical representations (i.e., shape, position, etc.) depending on the score version. As a consequence, in the spine, the values that characterize music events in space and time should be expressed in virtual units.

The adoption of virtual units implements an abstraction from specific instances. If one refers to Figure 2.3, it is evident that an eighth note should take twice the time of a sixteenth one, and virtually also twice the horizontal space. On the contrary, in the aural (audio layer) and visual (notational layer) renderings of the piece, such values can be computed using absolute units, for example, milliseconds or frames for time and pixels or millimeters for space.

The virtual values for timing and hpos must be integers. As explained in the next subsection, they are relative to the previous music event in the spine. Thus, when the spine

---

[1] Note that a music event could be mapped a number of times even within the same audio track (e.g., for refrains), and also that the author of the encoding could decide to omit a given music event from a particular audio mapping (e.g., when a given performance skips the intro).

has to be compiled, it is necessary to find a correspondence between rhythm and virtual units (VUs). Two approaches can be used:

1. Assign to a rhythmic value a number that can be divided by many divisors, in order to represent virtually any other rhythmic subvalue. For instance, a power of 2 (say 1024 VUs) could be assigned to quarter notes, so that an eighth note takes 512 VUs, a sixteenth note takes 256 VUs, and so on. This approach recalls the one of MIDI ticks. Please note that irregular groups, such as triplets, would require rounded values.

2. Find algorithmically the right granularity in order to represent any rhythmic value exactly. For instance, in a piece with quarters, eighth notes, and quintuplets of sixteenth notes, the value assigned to quarters should give integer results when divided both by 2 and by 5: it could be 10 VUs—of course, in this trivial example, no rhythmic value in score would correspond to 1 VU.

2.7.3 How to Build the Spine

As explained above, the spine is the main data structure for an IEEE 1599 document. Figure 2.2 clearly shows that all layers, even the general, present references to the spine in order to define and synchronize music events. Hence, at a high level of abstraction, the spine can be defined as a linearly sorted list of music events.

However, in a Common Western Notation score, symbols are not placed following a linear layout. Even if one considers a virtual staff system with no line breaks (i.e., a group of staves running on a single line from the beginning to the end of the piece), music symbols have both a horizontal position and a vertical one—the former refers to the melodic and rhythmic dimension of music, whereas the latter is related to harmony and instrumental parts. So, even narrowing the field to Common Western Notation, it is necessary to map a two-dimensional structure to an XML hierarchical tree.

Since in general there is no father–child relationship, rather a brother relationship, among music events, the problem consists of flattening a two-dimensional structure into a one-dimensional list. The solution adopted in the IEEE 1599 format consists of referring each spine event to the previous one, using a path that covers music score as follows:

• First, a linear abstraction of the score is employed, hence no line breaks.
• Over this score, a vertical scan is performed, from upper to lower symbols in the staff, and from upper to lower staves.
• When all simultaneous (vertically aligned) events have been considered, the process moves to the next event on the right. Note that such an event does not necessarily belong to the first staff.

In a certain sense, events are linearly sorted by meandering through the score, from top to bottom and from left to right. In respect to space, vertical alignments are expressed by 0 values for the hpos attribute. Similarly, a simultaneous occurrence of notes in time (i.e., a chord) is represented through 0 values for the timing attribute. Of course, as each event in the spine refers to the previous one, in a chord 0s are used for all notes except the first one. Also, *null* values are supported by IEEE 1599 for those cases when a value cannot be determined: for instance, the first symbol of a score follows no other, so its timing and hpos could be conventionally set to 0 or null.

Figure 2.5, Figure 2.6, and Figure 2.7 are some examples to clarify these concepts.

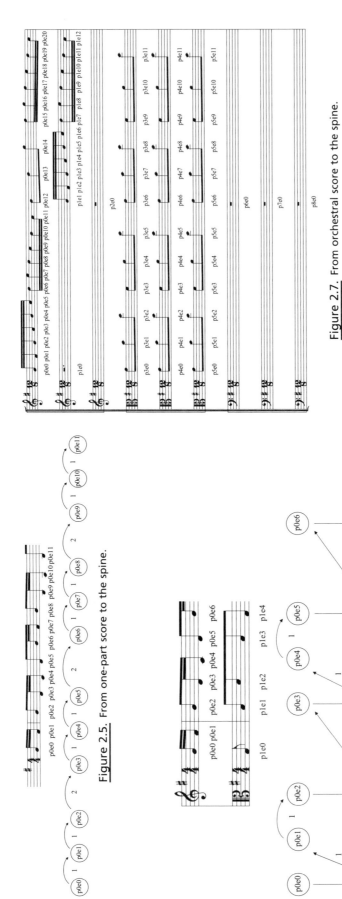

Figure 2.5. From one-part score to the spine.

Figure 2.6. From two-part score to the spine.

Figure 2.7. From orchestral score to the spine.

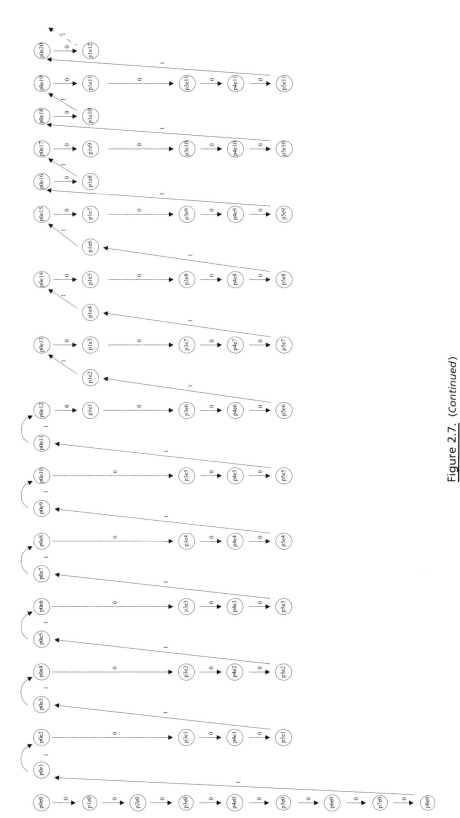

Figure 2.7. (Continued)

REFERENCES

Cage, J. 1969. *Notations*. New York: Something Else Press.

Gomberg, D.A. 1977. "A Computer-Oriented System for Music Printing." *Computers and the Humanities*, 11(2):63–80.

Haus, G., and Longari, M. 2005. "A Multi-Layered, Time-Based Music Description Approach Based on XML." *Computer Music Journal*, 29(1):70–85.

Haus, G., and Ludovico, L.A. 2006. "The Digital Opera House: An Architecture for Multimedia Databases." *Journal of Cultural Heritage*, 7(2):92–97.

Steyn, J. 2002. "Framework for a Music Markup Language." In *Proceedings of the First International IEEE Conference on Musical Application Using XML (MAX2002)*, Milan, IEEE, pp. 22–29.

STRUCTURING MUSIC INFORMATION

Adriano Baratè and Goffredo M. Haus

Summary: This chapter describes how IEEE 1599, in addition to dealing with all entities of Common Western Notation such as notes, rests, and music symbols, can also consider complete structures, music excerpts, segments, and the like, thus becoming a useful tool for musical analysis.

3.1 INTRODUCTION

Music pieces can be described in different ways, depending on the information one wants to convey. For instance, Common Western Notation is nowadays widely considered the most appropriate formalism to represent a score to be performed by occidental musicians.

However, when addressing higher levels of description, little interest is paid to melodic, rhythmic, and harmonic aspects related to single music events (such as notes and rests). Instead, characteristics shared by groups of elementary events have to be considered. Thus, music objects must be described together with their mutual relationships, where the term "music object" refers to all music phenomena or events perceived as a whole.

Music description and processing require formal tools that are suitable for the representation of iteration, concurrency, ordering, hierarchy, causality, timing, synchrony, and non-determinism. Petri Nets are a tool that allows description and processing of musical objects within both analysis/composition and performing environments. To this objective,

Music Navigation with Symbols and Layers: Toward Content Browsing with IEEE 1599 XML Encoding,
First Edition. Edited by Denis L. Baggi and Goffredo M. Haus.
© 2013 the IEEE Computer Society. Published 2013 by John Wiley & Sons, Inc.

a specific extension known as Music Petri Nets has been developed and is presented in this chapter.

3.2 MUSIC OBJECTS AND MUSIC ALGORITHMS

A *music object* is everything with a musical meaning, including a note, a sequence of notes, rests, devices, and control commands. A sequence of notes can be expressed as MIDI commands, MP3 files, textual representation, and so on, and what is important is the intrinsic concept of music object.

While music objects represent music entities of some kind, a *music algorithm* is whatever function can be applied to such objects. Music algorithms include well-known transformations of music fragments, such as transposition, retrogradation, inversion, loudness control, instrument change, and complex mathematical functions.

3.2.1 Music Objects

According to the definition in Haus and Rodrigues [1989], a music object may be anything that could have a musical meaning and could be thought of as an entity, either simple or complex, either abstract or detailed. Such an entity may have some relationship with other music objects.

The concept of music objects is similar to what is defined in Lerdahl and Jackendoff [1983] as *grouping structure*. A group can be defined as any contiguous sequence of pitch events and undetermined beats or rests, and it can be subdivided in smaller groups. In this sense, a music piece, as well as a single note, can constitute a group.

Music objects extend the definition of groups by considering not only contiguous notes and rests but also detached ones, as well as other objects that have a musical meaning, such as MIDI commands or textual representations. The concept of music object can embrace also vertical slices of a music piece, allowing various sorts of harmonic analysis.

According to previous definitions, the analytical process for a music work can be thought of—in general terms—as the identification of music objects together with their relationships inside the piece.

3.2.2 Music Algorithms

From the musicologist's perspective, identifying music objects is only the first step to establish relationships among them, highlighting similarities and differences. For instance, the music form known as *sonata* is characterized by the presence of two contrasting themes (the principal and the secondary theme) that are re-proposed in a literal or slightly varied form during the piece, according to given rules and to the inspiration of the composer. After identifying these music objects, it is possible to show the alternations and recurrences of themes and other transition music objects; in other words, the analysis also focuses on the relationships among music objects.

The analytical process can be conducted at different degrees of abstraction, addressing movements in a complex composition, macro-episodes in a piece, themes in an episode, or even atomic music events in an elementary music object.

To specify the relationships among music objects, *music algorithms* must be specified. In Haus and Sametti [1991] a number of typical modification algorithms are presented, oriented mainly toward processing MIDI sequences. Since in IEEE 1599 the *performance* layer is only one of a number of other representations, new music algorithms can be created depending on other materials.

3.2.3 Music Objects and Music Algorithms in IEEE 1599

Music objects can be expressed in IEEE 1599 using the `segmentation` element; it contains a list of single references to the spine structure:

```
<!ELEMENT segmentation (segment+)>
<!ATTLIST segmentation
  id ID #IMPLIED
  description CDATA #IMPLIED
  method CDATA #IMPLIED>

<!ELEMENT segment(segment_event+, feature_object*)>
<!ATTLIST segment
  id ID #REQUIRED>

<!ELEMENT segment_event EMPTY>
<!ATTLIST segment_event
  event_ref IDREF #REQUIRED>
```

Music algorithms have specific elements such as `relationships` and `feature_object_relationships`, together with their subelements:

```
<!ELEMENT relationships (relationship+)>

<!ELEMENT relationship EMPTY>
<!ATTLIST relationship
  id ID #REQUIRED
  description CDATA #IMPLIED
  segment_a_ref IDREF #REQUIRED
  segment_b_ref IDREF #REQUIRED
  feature_object_a_ref IDREF #IMPLIED
  feature_object_b_ref IDREF #IMPLIED
  feature_object_relationship_ref IDREF #IMPLIED>

<!ELEMENT feature_object_relationships (feature_object_
relationship+)>

<!ELEMENT feature_object_relationship (ver_rule)>
<!ATTLIST feature_object_relationship
  id ID #REQUIRED>

<!ELEMENT ver_rule (#PCDATA)>
```

3.3 PETRI NETS

A Petri Net is an abstract and formal model to represent the dynamic behavior of a system with asynchronous and concurrent activities [Petri 1976; Peterson 1981]. Such a net can

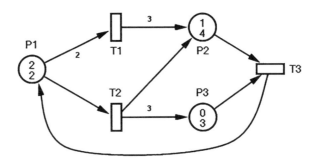

Figure 3.1. An example of a Petri Net.

be represented as a bipartite graph in which nodes are called places and transitions, graphically represented, respectively, with circles and rectangles. Oriented arcs connect only nodes of different kinds, that is, places to transitions and vice versa.

In Figure 3.1, an example of an elementary Petri Net is shown. P1, P2, P3, and P4 are places; T1, T2, and T3 are transitions; and the oriented lines represent arcs. The number sometimes shown on arcs is called the *arc weight*, the meaning of which is explained below.

Petri Nets evolve and self-modify themselves by using *tokens*: at a given time, every place holds a non-negative number of tokens, indicated by the upper numerical value inside the circle. The lower value indicates the capacity of the place, that is, the maximum number of tokens that the place can house.

In a certain way, tokens can be transferred from place to place according to policies known as *firing rules*. The dynamic evolution of a Petri Net is determined by the following rules:

- A *transition* is enabled when all the incoming places of that transition present a number of tokens greater or equal to the weights of the corresponding incoming arcs, and—after the fire of the transition—the marking of all the output places will be less than or equal to their capacities.
- When a transition is enabled, its *firing* subtracts from the incoming places a number of tokens equal to the weights of the incoming arcs, and adds to each outgoing place a number of tokens equal to the weights of the corresponding outgoing arc.

The execution of firing rules is illustrated in Figure 3.2 and Figure 3.3. In this example the only transition **T1** has two incoming places (**P1** and **P2**) and three outgoing places (**P3**, **P4**, and **P5**). Since the markings of the incoming places are greater or equal to the weights of their arcs, and the capacities of the outgoing places are greater or equal to the corresponding arcs' weights, the transition is enabled. When the transition fires, it takes from **P1** two tokens and from **P2** one token, and puts to **P3** and **P4** one token and to **P5** three tokens. The final situation is presented in Figure 3.3. Note that **T1** is no longer enabled, since **P1** and **P2** do not have enough tokens, and the capacity of places **P3** and **P5** do not permit reception of other markings.

3.3.1 Petri Nets Extension: Hierarchy

When working with complex Petri Nets models, it is preferable to create a *hierarchy* to split the whole model in various subnets. In the main net, special kinds of nodes serve as

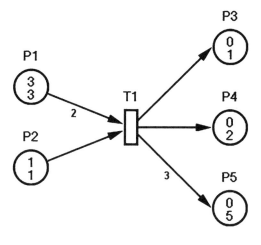

Figure 3.2. Fire rule example: before firing.

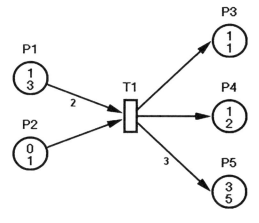

Figure 3.3. Fire rule example: after firing.

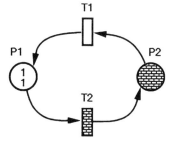

Figure 3.4. An example of refinement: the original Petri Net.

links to the underlying Petri Nets, and will be substituted with the nets when the execution is started.

Figure 3.4 shows an example of hierarchies. Nodes that incorporate subnets are graphically represented in the figure. In this case, transition **T2** contains the subnet shown in Figure 3.5, while the place **P2** contains the subnet of Figure 3.6.

When the net is executed, the subnets are substituted to the corresponding nodes, thus creating the final plain Petri Net. For such reason, in every subnet the input/output nodes

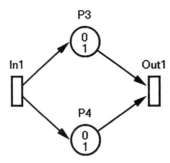

Figure 3.5. The subnet associated to transition T2.

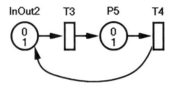

Figure 3.6. The subnet associated to place P2.

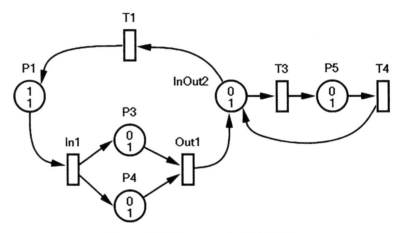

Figure 3.7. The expanded Petri Net.

must be specified, since the incoming/outgoing arcs must be connected to the correct nodes. In the example shown, the subnet in Figure 3.5 has **In1** as input transition and **Out1** as output, and the subnet in Figure 3.6 has only one place, **InOut2**, assigned as input/output node. The unfolded Petri Net is presented in Figure 3.7. In this net, the original arc that connects **P1** with **T2** now connects **P1** with **In1**, the arc from **P2** to **T1** now connects **InOut2** to **T1**, and the arc outgoing from **T2** and incoming to **P2** connects the output transition of the first subnet **Out1** to the input place of the second subnet **InOut2**.

Here is a summary of the operation from a practical point of view:

- A node *n* can contain another entire net called *subnet*.
- The subnet must have an input and an output node of the same type of n. It is possible to have the same node as input/output.

- When n is substituted by the subnet:
  - ○ The incoming arcs of n are connected to the input node of the *subnet*.
  - ○ The outgoing arcs of n are connected to the output node of the *subnet*.
- The same *subnet* can be used several times in the same net: when this happens several different instances of the subnet are used.
- If a net contains nodes that incorporate the same net as a subnet, an infinite loop is generated.

3.3.2 Petri Nets Extension: Probabilistic Arc Weights

Two kinds of non-deterministic situations may arise when considering the firing rule. When two or more transitions are enabled at the same time, one of them may fire, but not all the transitions enabled must fire.

In the net in Figure 3.8, both transitions are enabled, but when, for instance, **T1** fires, in the new state of the net **T2** does not become enabled, since tokens are no longer present in the incoming place **P1**. The same happens if **T2** fires first. This kind of situation, caused by lack of input tokens, is called *alternative*.

Another type of non-determinism is the *conflict* situation, due to capacity of filled places. An example is shown in Figure 3.9. In this net, both transitions are enabled but firing one changes the marking of **P3** to **1**, causing the inhibition of the other transition.

The use of these types of non-determinism situations is investigated afterward in this chapter from a musical point of view.

In these non-deterministic cases, various transitions are enabled, but it is unknown which transition will fire. A mechanism can be introduced to control this kind of situation,

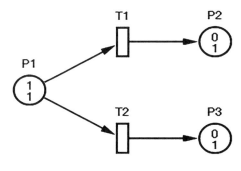

Figure 3.8. A first example of non-determinism: alternative.

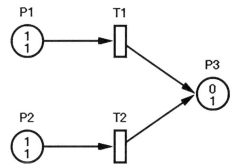

Figure 3.9. A second example of non-determinism: conflict.

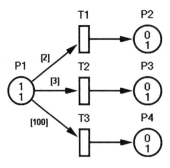

Figure 3.10. An example of probabilistic arc weights.

namely, the *probabilistic arc weight*: if **E** is the set of enabled transitions, each one having a probabilistic weight indicated by a non-negative number, the probability of firing a certain transition **T** is computed by dividing the probabilistic weight of **T** by the sum of all the probabilistic weights of arcs in alternative/conflict.

An example of the probabilistic weight is shown in Figure 3.10. In this net, there are three transitions and an input place with only one token. **T1**, **T2**, and **T3** are enabled, but in alternative. The three incoming arcs of the transitions have different probabilistic weights, represented as numbers inside square brackets, while the outgoing arcs have the same probabilistic weight equal to zero (omitted by convention). In this case, the probabilities to fire are:

$$P(T1) = \frac{2+0}{2+0+3+0+100+0} = \frac{2}{105} = 0.019$$

$$P(T2) = \frac{3+0}{2+0+3+0+100+0} = \frac{3}{105} = 0.029$$

$$P(T3) = \frac{100+0}{2+0+3+0+100+0} = \frac{100}{105} = 0.952$$

It must be noted that when all probabilistic weights are equal to zero in a net, the net behavior is the same as a net without this special extension, while if only an arc has a positive probabilistic weight, the associated transition will be the first to fire.

3.4 MUSIC PETRI NETS

Petri Nets have been applied to the music field since 1982 [Camurri et al. 1986; Pope 1986]. In particular, early papers [e.g., Degli Antoni and Haus 1983] investigated the possibility of describing causality in music processes through the formal approach of Petri Nets. Apparently, different applications of this formalism to music analysis have led to contradictory results. Even though Haus and Rodriguez [1993] have described Ravel's *Bolero* successfully, some limitations of this approach have become evident when attempts were made to model a complex work, such as Stravinsky's *Rite of Spring* [De Matteis and Haus 1996].

In Music Petri Nets *music objects* can be associated to places and *music algorithms* to transitions (see Section 3.2). A particular parameter of *places* controls whether the associated music object has to be played or only transferred in the net. The following rules apply when a Music Petri Net is executed:

- When a place **P** receives *n* tokens from an input transition **T:**
  - If **P** has an associated music object **MO1** and the *playing* parameter is set:
    - *n* simultaneous executions of **MO1** are played (while playing, the tokens cannot be considered in other transition's firings).
    - After the playing is finished, the *n* tokens are free to leave **P.**
    - **MO1** is passed to output transitions.
  - If **P** has an associated music object **MO1** and the *playing* parameter is unset:
    - The *n* tokens are free to leave **P.**
    - **MO1** is passed to output transitions.
  - If the place has no associated music objects.
    - If **T** has a music object **MO2** in output:
      - **MO2** is retrieved from **T.**
      - *n* simultaneous executions of the **MO2** are played (while playing, the tokens cannot be considered in other transition's firings).
      - After the playing finished, the *n* tokens are free to leave **P.**
      - **MO2** is passed to output transitions.
    - If **T** has no music objects in output:
      - The *n* tokens are free to leave **P.**
- When a transition **T** fires and receives $n_1, n_2, \ldots, n_m$ tokens from input *m* places $P_1, P_2, \ldots, P_m$, eventually having associated music objects $MO_1, MO_2, \ldots, MO_m$
  - If **T** has an associated music algorithm **MA**, it is applied to input music objects:
  - The *k* non-empty input music objects, modified by **MA**, are mixed, obtaining a final new music object **MO**
  - **MO** is ready to be passed to all outgoing places

When a Petri Net is in execution, a place that receives a token plays the associated music object, thus retaining the token while the object is in execution. In the following figures we present these rules in their graphical counterparts: all places and transitions without associated objects are called **P#** and **T#**, while places with associated music objects and transitions with associated algorithms are named **MO#** and **Alg**, respectively. Places with the playing parameter unset are named with lowercase.

In Figure 3.11, **T** is ready to fire, and its firing transfers three tokens into **MO1**, resulting in three concurrent playings of the same music fragment.

In Figure 3.12, when **T** fires, the music fragment contained in **mo1** is transferred unchanged to places **P1** and **p2**, and only two instances are played by **P1**, since **p2** has the playing parameter unset.

In Figure 3.13, the transition **Alg** takes the input music object contained in **mo1**, applies the associated music algorithm, and transfers the resulting fragment to **P** that plays it.

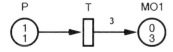

Figure 3.11. Music objects: example 1.

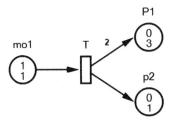

Figure 3.12. Music objects: example 2.

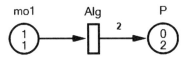

Figure 3.13. Music objects: example 3.

Figure 3.14. Music objects: example 4.

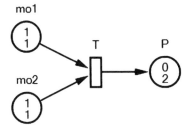

Figure 3.15. Music objects: example 5.

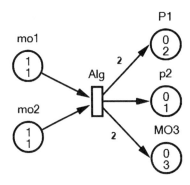

Figure 3.16. Music objects: example 6.

In Figure 3.14, the situation is similar to the previous one, except that the music object associated to the output place **MO2** is played instead of the incoming object.

In Figure 3.15, the two music objects contained in **mo1** and in **mo2** are mixed by **T** and then transferred to **P**, where the final mix is played.

In Figure 3.16, the two music objects contained in **mo1** and in **mo2** are mixed and an algorithm is applied by **Alg**; after that, the modified fragment is played two times by

P1, is passed to **p2** without playing it, and is discarded by **MO3**, which plays instead the associated music object.

3.4.1 Music Petri Nets in IEEE 1599

In IEEE 1599, along with other structural descriptors (see Section 4.3), Music Petri Nets can be linked to music objects using the element `petri_nets` and its subelements. Music objects can be stored in place elements, while the musical algorithms can be stored in the transition elements:

```
<!ELEMENT petri_nets (petri_net+)>

<!ELEMENT petri_net (place | transition)+>
<!ATTLIST petri_net
 id ID #IMPLIED
 author CDATA #IMPLIED
 description CDATA #IMPLIED
 file_name CDATA #REQUIRED>

<!ELEMENT place EMPTY>
<!ATTLIST place
 place_ref CDATA #REQUIRED
 segment_ref IDREF #REQUIRED>

<!ELEMENT transition EMPTY>
<!ATTLIST transition
 transition_ref CDATA #REQUIRED
 feature_object_relationship_ref IDREF #REQUIRED>
```

3.5 MUSIC ANALYSIS USING MUSIC PETRI NETS

This section presents a complete example of applicability of Music Petri Nets to music analysis. For other examples concerning analysis, as well as application of the same formalism to music synthesis, see Baratè et al. [2006, 2007].

While the works mentioned discuss the application of Petri Nets to classical music, the case study presented here is focused on a piece of contemporary music, the minimal field. Philip Glass is a pioneer of this kind of music, and we have chosen as an example "Opening," contained in his *Glassworks* album. This piece is characterized by the repetition of short music fragments with micro-variations of the material, a compositional method encountered in several minimal compositions.

The score of "Opening" is shown in Figure 3.17, Figure 3.18, Figure 3.19, and Figure 3.20. Three musical sections, identified in the figures by numbers on the right, are repeated three times. This leads to the initial net presented in Figure 3.21, where a simple loop is implemented.

Every section of the composition can be described by a corresponding subnet. In Figure 3.22, the model of section 1 is presented: after a loop repeated two times (fragment 1 is thus repeated three times), the fragment is changed and proposed one time only. Section 2 has the same kind of model, while section 3 has two variations and is modeled in Figure 3.23.

Figure 3.17. Philip Glass's "Opening," first part.

Fragment 1 has been modeled by splitting the formalization procedure into three, constructing single nets for the melody (right hand) and the upper and the lower parts of the harmony (left hand). The Petri Net that models the right hand is shown in Figure 3.24. In this net, only the place named **1.1 D** has an associated music object containing the first measure; when the outgoing transition fires the associated algorithm applies a retrogradation and substitutes the A flat notes with Cs.

Similar algorithms are associated to the other transitions. The entire net contains a loop to execute the whole section four times; the first three times the algorithm **G = Ab** is applied to the fragment contained in place **1.3 D**, while the in last execution of the loop the fragment is proposed unchanged one more time and place **1.4 D** is not reached.

Figure 3.18. Philip Glass's "Opening," second part.

Figure 3.25 shows the Petri Net related to the upper part of the left hand: the entire section is repeated four times, and in every loop the two main places **1.1 S / 1.2 S** and **1.3 S / 1.4 S** are proposed two times each, applying an algorithm to diatonically transpose two degrees (i.e., a third) down along the E flat major scale. In the net that formalizes the lower part of the left hand (Figure 3.26) the structure is similar, except the third and fourth measures are different and have thus different places (**1.3 S** and **1.4 S**, in the final loop with variations). The Petri Nets that describe sections 2 and 3 are similar to the presented ones.

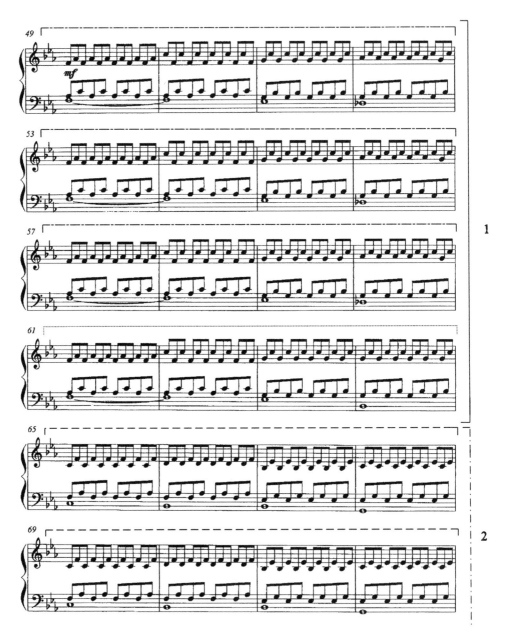

Figure 3.19. Philip Glass's "Opening," third part.

3.6 REAL-TIME INTERACTION WITH MUSIC PETRI NETS

This section presents a perspective on how Petri Nets can be used in a real-time environment, by changing net parameters on the fly, that is, when a model is being executed and the music is playing. All allowed modifications to Petri Nets affect the model itself and the firing rule from a theoretical point of view.

Figure 3.20. Philip Glass's "Opening," fourth and last part.

The following concepts are related to standard Petri Nets, since music implications are considered in the next section:

- Modification of place marking (PM): when adding or subtracting a number of tokens in a place, the place capacity is automatically incremented to contain the new number of tokens.

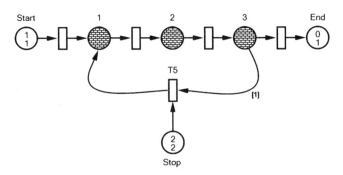

Figure 3.21. The macro-net of "Opening."

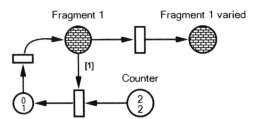

Figure 3.22. Petri Net of "Opening," section 1.

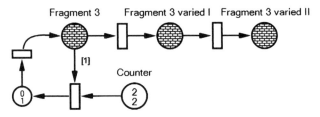

Figure 3.23. Petri Net of "Opening," section 3.

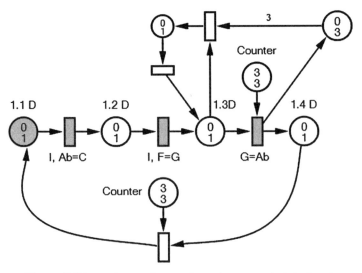

Figure 3.24. Petri Net of "Opening," fragment 1, right hand.

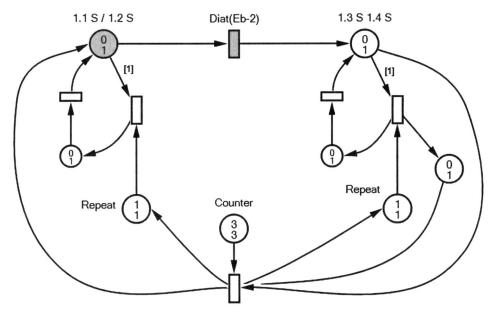

Figure 3.25. Petri Net of "Opening," fragment 1, left hand 1.

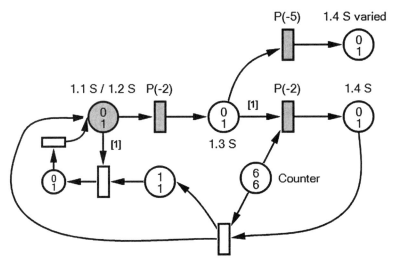

Figure 3.26. Petri Net of "Opening," fragment 1, left hand 2.

- Modification of place capacity (PC): the marking is automatically decremented if the specified capacity is less than the number of tokens contained in the place.
- Modification of arc tokens weight (ATW).
- Modification of arc probabilistic weight (APW).
- Modification of the set of places (PP): the new place has by default marking equal to zero, capacity equal to one, and timing equal to zero.
- Modification of the set of transitions (TT).

- Modification of the set of arcs (AA): the new arc has by default a token weight equal to one and a probabilistic weight equal to zero.

When a modification occurs, the transition firing rule must be instantly applied, since the new parameters could have created new firing conditions.

Since a real-time Petri Net can be constructed from scratch, a Petri Net can be empty or can have unconnected nodes.

When speaking of Music Petri Nets, the presented real-time modifications generate changes in the produced music. Particular implications in the first two modification types introduced early are discussed here from a music perspective, together with new changes related to music objects and music algorithms.

Types of modifications with new considerations:

- Modification of place marking (PM): if the place does not contain an associated music object, nothing happens in terms of music production. If a music object is present and n tokens are added, n new instances of that object are played, while if m tokens are subtracted, m current playing music objects are stopped.
- Modification of place capacity (PC): if the capacity is decremented, the considerations about place marking modifications must be applied.
- Modification of associated music objects (MO): if the place has marking n greater than zero, the playing of the previous music object, if present, is stopped, and n new instances of the new music object are executed.
- Modification of associated music algorithms (MA).

In general terms, the only instantaneous effect of these modifications is the playing of n new music objects, while most of the changes modify the net structure but their effects are produced when the net continues its execution.

Since music objects are encoded in IEEE 1599, a net execution creates a comprehensive IEEE 1599 document that mixes all these music objects, thus creating a final result where the logic part reflects the mixing process, and the linked media maintain their synchronization.

As an example of real-time interaction, a Petri Net that models the original version of the music piece "Peaches en Regalia," as recorded by Frank Zappa, is presented in Figure 3.27. In this Petri Nets model, interaction is limited to addition/subtraction of tokens in the places represented with a white background, in order to maintain a similarity to the original result. Addition and subtraction of tokens has the following results:

- The number of tokens in the Start place controls how many times the entire music piece is repeated.
- The number of tokens in repeat A and repeat B places controls how many times fragments (a) and (b) are repeated.
- The presence of one or more tokens in the white input places of the two transitions Transpose + and Transpose − causes the transposition of fragment (a) by a major third higher or lower, respectively. From Petri Nets execution rules, if both these places have more than zero tokens, a transition is chosen at random.
- The presence of one or more tokens in the white input places of the two transitions Time + and Time − causes time shrinking of fragment (b) to double or half the original time, respectively. From Petri Nets execution rules, if both these places have more than zero tokens, a transition is selected at random.

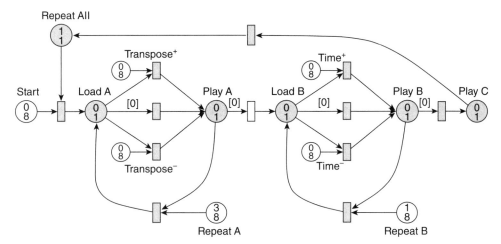

Figure 3.27. The Petri Nets model of "Peaches en Regalia."

Even though this model is very simple, the application demonstrates how an original music structure can be formalized, and how a performer can create different versions of the piece every time the net is executed.

3.7   CONCLUSIONS

The possibility to encode in IEEE 1599 music objects, music algorithms, and Music Petri Nets opens new possibilities to analysis and composition of music pieces. From a musicological perspective, an existing piece can be described by Petri Net models that can be linked together with other information in a single IEEE 1599 file. With specific applications, the analyst is therefore able to have a global perspective at various levels of abstraction, described in different IEEE 1599 layers.

Another interesting aspect concerns music creation. By using the IEEE 1599 format, a composer could concentrate the structure of the music piece he or she wants to obtain, without addressing lower-level material involved in the mixing process, such as the file formats of the linked objects. Thanks to IEEE 1599 and to Music Petri Nets, the final result automatically generates synchronization of various kinds of music representation, permitting a new type of musical experience.

REFERENCES

Baratè, A., Haus, G., and Ludovico, L.A. 2006. "Music Analysis and Modeling through Petri Nets." Paper presented at the Computer Music Modeling and Retrieval, Third International Symposium, CMMR 2005, Pisa, Italy, September 26–28, 2005. In *Revised Papers*, ed. Richard Kronland-Martinet, Thierry Voinier, and Solvi Ystad, LNCS, 3902. Berlin: Springer, pp. 201–218.

Baratè, A., Haus, G., and Ludovico, L.A. 2007. "Petri Nets Applicability to Music Analysis and Composition." In *Proceedings of the International Computer Music Conference '07* (ICMC 2007), Holmen Island, Copenhagen, Denmark, pp. 97–199.

Camurri, A., Haus, G., and Zaccaria, R. 1986. "Describing and Performing Musical Processes by Means of Petri Nets." *Interface*, 15:1–23.

De Matteis, A., and Haus, G. 1996. "Formalisation of Generative Structures within Stravinsky's 'Rite of Spring.'" *Journal of New Music Research*, 25(1):47–76.

Degli Antoni, G., and Haus, G. 1983. "Music and Causality." In *Proceedings of the 1982 International Computer Music Conference*, La Biennale, Venezia. San Francisco, CA: Computer Music Association, pp. 279–296.

Haus, G., and Rodriguez, A. 1989. "Music Description and Processing by Petri Nets." In *1988 Advances on Petri Nets, Lecture Notes in Computer Science*, no. 340. Berlin: Springer-Verlag, pp. 175–199.

Haus, G., and Rodriguez, A. 1993. "Formal Music Representation; a Case Study: the Model of Ravel' Bolero by Petri Nets." In *Music Processing*, Madison, Computer Music and Digital Audio Series, A-R edn., pp. 165–232.

Haus, G., and Sametti, A. 1991. "Scoresynth: A System for the Synthesis of Music Scores Based on Petri Nets and a Music Algebra." *Computer*, 24(7):56–60.

Lerdahl, F., and Jackendoff, R. 1983. *A Generative Theory of Tonal Music*. Cambridge: MIT Press.

Peterson, J.L. 1981. *Petri Net Theory and the Modeling of Systems*. Englewood Cliffs, NJ: Prentice Hall.

Petri, C.A. 1976. "General Net Theory." In *Proceedings of the Joint IBM & Newcastle upon Tyne Seminar on Computer Systems Design*, Newcastle upon Tyne: University of Newcastle upon Tyne.

Pope, S.T. 1986. "Music Notation and the Representation of Musical Structure and Knowledge." *Perspectives of New Music*, 24(2):156–189.

4

MODELING AND SEARCHING MUSIC COLLECTIONS

Alberto Pinto

Summary: This chapter describes in detail how collections and music can be described, modeled, searched for, and indexed for musicological applications. Understanding some of the modeling may require elements of mathematical and analytical tools, which are not supplied in this text.

4.1 INTRODUCTION

Modeling and searching music collections is an inherently complex task that usually involves multidisciplinary expertise obtained from library science, information science, musicology, music theory, music perception, audio engineering, mathematics, and computer science.

Different points of view from different disciplines produce different descriptions and retrieval models of music pieces, from statistical analysis on symbolic performances (MIDI), signal analysis on audio (WAV, MP3) and musicological analysis on scores. And all of them need the integration of a description framework, in order to interact effectively.

This need is particularly felt in a number of Internet-related areas such as music exchange, digital libraries and education, digital rights management, and XML formats for music description and retrieval within IEEE 1599, as described in Chapter 1.

IEEE 1599 is the first standard that allows the representation of multiple music models within the same format and provides an effective tool to handle this integration through an ad hoc music information retrieval (MIR) environment in the structural layer.

Music Navigation with Symbols and Layers: Toward Content Browsing with IEEE 1599 XML Encoding, First Edition. Edited by Denis L. Baggi and Goffredo M. Haus.
© 2013 the IEEE Computer Society. Published 2013 by John Wiley & Sons, Inc.

In this chapter, a general overview of formats related to music description and of music search engines is given, followed by the basic components and structures of a music representation.

Section 4.3 recalls the main structures of the abstract layer of IEEE 1599, the structural layer, to show how music structures can be encoded in the same format, together with different analyses of the same piece. Section 4.4 provides the theoretical framework to understand the implementation of MIR models within IEEE 1599. Section 4.5 describes in detail the concepts of MIR models, objects, morphisms, and features, and Section 4.6 provides a concrete implementation of the framework through a case study.

4.2 DESCRIBING MUSIC CONTENT

As stated in Chapter 2, music has an intrinsically layered structure [Kranenburg 2007], from raw audio to purely structural information. For each layer of music information, there is at least one accepted standard. For example, PCM and compressed formats such as MP3 and AAC are de facto standards for digital audio [Bosi and Goldberg 2003], while Musical Instrument Digital Interface (MIDI) is the most widely accepted standard for music performance, since it is actually a "low-level" language for digital devices that allows real time information exchange. From the notational side, Notation Interchange File Format (NIFF) has been the first standard format for music notation, but has been surpassed by other formats, many of them based on XML such as MusicXML by Recordare. Among notational standards, it is worth to cite SCORE, still one of the best notational formats, and several proprietary formats such as Finale and Sibelius. Formats such JPEG and TIFF may represent the result of an Optical Music Recognition (OMR) process. The number of such standards is growing, since more and more libraries are "going digital" and make their material such as manuscripts and drawings available in such formats [Haus 1984; Diana et al. 2001].

In this context, XML is an effective way to describe music information, since none of these formats can be suitably applied to other layers of music [Roads 1996]. There are presently a number of good dialects to encode music by means of XML, such as MusicXML, MusiXML, MusiCat, MEI, and MDL (see Longari 2004 for a thorough discussion). In particular, MusicXML [Hewlett and Selfridge-Field 2000] is a comprehensive way to represent symbolic information and has been integrated in a number of commercial programs. Another leading application for music notation is Coda Music Finale. One of the key advantages of MusicXML over other XML-based formats is its popularity in the field of music software. However, none of the listed encoding formats deals with semantic descriptions of metadata.

Moving Picture Experts Group (MPEG)-7 allows integration of Ontology Web Language (OWL) ontologies in a framework developed for the support of ontology-based semantic indexing and retrieval of audiovisual content [Hunter 2001; Haus et al. 2004; Arndt et al. 2007]. This initiative follows the Semantic Level of MPEG-7 Multimedia Description Schemas (MDS) and the TV-Anytime standard specifications for metadata descriptions [Good 2001; Garcia and Celma 2005].

Unlike the IEEE 1599 semantic layer, the semantic level of MPEG-7 allows description of music information from the real world, giving the emphasis on events, objects, concepts, places, time in narrative worlds, and abstraction. Therefore, the MPEG-7 ontology is aimed at the description of music performance and not score information, as in IEEE 1599. A complete discussion of these topics is given in Tsinaraki et al. [2004].

Semantic analysis in MPEG-7 has the purpose of standardizing a core set of quantitative measures of audio-visual features in order to provide content-derived metadata that a music search engine can handle. Its audio descriptors are subdivided in low- and high-level descriptors:

I. Low-level descriptors
   a. Timbral Temporal
      i. LogAttackTime
      ii. Temporal Centroid
   b. Timbral Spectral (specific to harmony perception)
      i. Harmonic Spectral Centroid
      ii. Spectral Spread
   c. Spectral Basis

II. Additional low-level (added in 2003)
   a. Audio signal quality description
      i. Background noise, channel cross-correlation, relative delay, balance, DC offset, bandwidth, transmission technology
      ii. Errors in recordings (clicks, clipping, drop outs), musical tempo (bpm)

III. High-level descriptors
   a. Audio signature
   b. Musical instrument timbre
   c. Melody description.

Even if a semantic analysis is sufficient for many purposes, such as general sound recognition or indexing, instrument timbre search, motif search, audio identification, and fingerprinting, it presents a main drawback because of its low flexibility. For instance, it is not possible to encode custom-made descriptors obtained from custom-made MIR models for the raw material and in conjunction with different analyses of the piece. In the next sections, a richer and more flexible description of the MIR layer for multiple MIR models is introduced.

4.2.1 Music Search Engines

Figure 4.1 shows a rather general architecture of a music search engine, local or web-based. It consists of two main components: the *Musical Storage Environment* and the *Musical Query Environment*. The former is basically similar to the latter and provides methods to perform query-by-content on music scores, starting from a score or an audio fragment as input. These two main blocks perform similar steps in order to create a semantic description of music content [Maddage et al. 2006], graphically illustrated in Figure 4.1:

- Segmentation: scores or audio files are segmented into temporal slices
- Feature extraction: the input is converted into a sequence of feature vectors
- Analysis/decision making: higher level features are identified, and, depending on the MIR model applied, connections among different parts of the music piece are established.

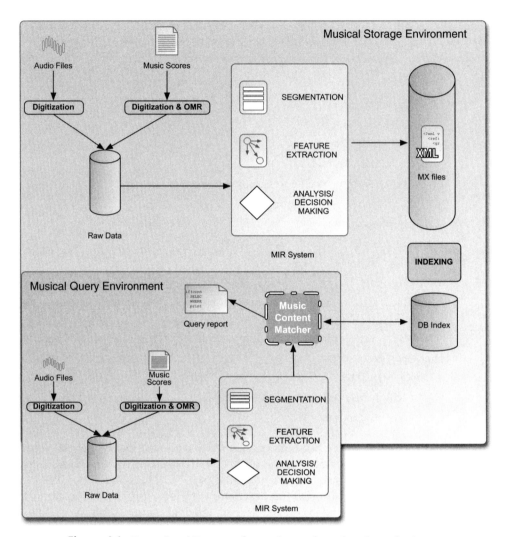

Figure 4.1. General architecture of a music search engine. See color insert.

The matching phase is performed by the *Music Content Matcher*, which applies matching algorithms based on different similarity functions. The next sections describe how the extracted features can be suitably encoded within IEEE 1599 as semantic metadata into its structural layer.

4.3   MUSIC DESCRIPTION IN IEEE 1599

The key characteristics that the IEEE 1599 standard is able to support are summarized as the following:

- Multimedia descriptions related to the same music piece: the format has to support graphical information, as well as audio and video content, with already defined and accepted common standards

- Ability to link and play a number of media objects of the same type, for instance, many performances of the same piece or many score scans coming from different editions, since this is a basic requirement in multimedia fruition
- Complete synchronization among time-based contents, meaning that audio and video content are kept synchronized as the score advances, even when the user switches from a particular performance to another or from a particular score edition to another (see Chapter 5 for a complete description of these features)
- Interaction, that is, the abiliity for users to click at any point of the score and jump to a point in the audio, as well as the ability to navigate the audio track by moving the related slider control and highlighting the related portion of score
- High-level structural descriptors that allow embedding of different music analyses, for musicological purposes
- Embedding of music/audio content descriptors that allow efficient queries on multimedia files.

XML provides an effective way to represent multimedia information at different levels of abstraction, and XML metadata provide useful tools for the retrieval processes [Baeza-Yates and Ribeiro-Neto 1999]. As stated in Chapter 2, IEEE 1599 represents music information according to a multi-layered structure and to the concept of a space–time construct. In fact, music information can be structured by a layer subdivision model, as shown in Figure 4.2 and Figure 4.3.

Each layer is specific to a different degree of abstraction in music information: general, structural, music logic, notational, performance, and audio. The main advantage of IEEE 1599 is the richness of its descriptive features, which are based on other commonly accepted

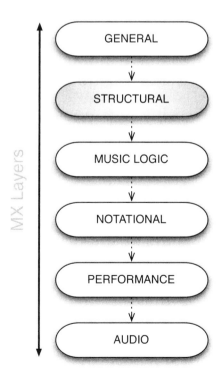

Figure 4.2. Music information layers.

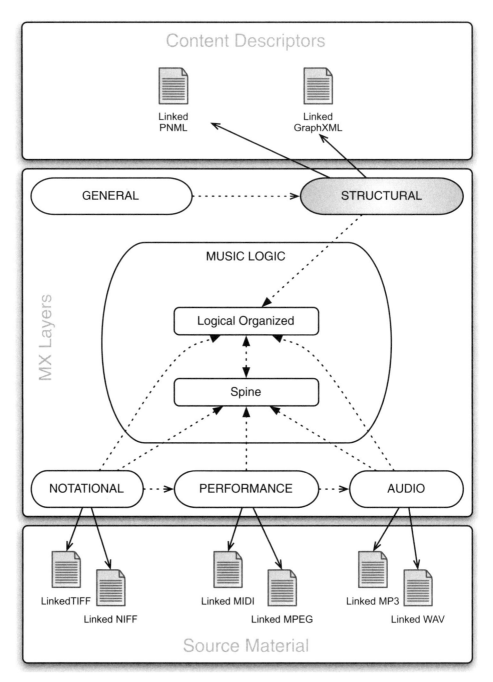

Figure 4.3. IEEE 1599 layers and their relationships.

encodings aimed at more specific descriptions. The multi-layered music information structure is kept together by the concept of the spine, which relates time and spatial information. Through such a mapping, it is possible to fix a point in a layer instance, for example, notational (see Figure 4.5), and investigate the corresponding point in another one, for example, performance or audio (see Figure 4.4).

Musicians could benefit from the presence of these features, because they would be able to handle each representation of a music piece as a unique entity, for example, by simultaneously watching the score and listening to the music of a particular audio recording, or even by watching the related video, if present. Music analysts would have complete control over notational information, for example, by easily comparing the notational content with the aural features of a recording. Music vendors could access a database in which each piece of music would be stored along with different instances of its rendition, their own different properties related to a single product. Music producers would benefit as well because they could set up a music database in which all related material could be handled in a structured way. For example, a Web service could be created to

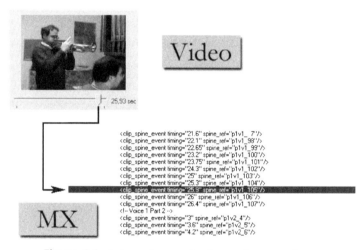

Figure 4.4. *Spine* reference for the performance layer.

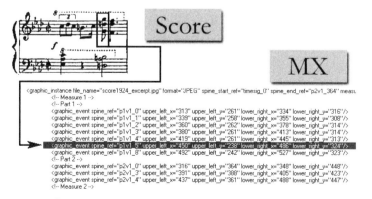

Figure 4.5. Spine reference for the notational layer.

which users connect and select a piece of music, accessing a MIDI rendition of it for practicing, along with a visualization of the score.

The integration of all music aspects would greatly improve the management of multimedia documents in digital libraries, especially from the point of view of human–machine interaction.

IEEE 1599 organizes information in a hierarchic structure so that each layer is represented as a secondary branch of the source element. The conceptual hierarchy is represented in Figure 4.2. The central element of Figure 4.3 is the logic layer. All other layers relate to this core element in a star-like structure, and only the general layer does not link explicitly to the logic layer. Relationships among layers are implemented by means of XML references. Audio source material is directly linked to the spine and thus indirectly to the Logic Organized Symbols (LOS). Notational and performance source material can also be directly linked to elements in the LOS, because they represent analogous information.

As stated in previous chapters, the audio layer describes properties of the source material, which contains musical audio information; this is the lowest level of the format. Formats representing audio information can be subdivided in two categories: *compressed* and *uncompressed*. Uncompressed audio are, for example, Pulse Code Modulation in Microsoft WAV file format (PCM/WAV), Audio Interchange File Format (AIFF), and μ-Law. Compressed audio can be further subdivided into *lossy* (e.g., MPEG and Dolby AC3) and *lossless* types (e.g., ADPCM, SHN).

To automatically relate the audio to the time part of the spine structure, it is necessary to extract the features related to the actual temporization of musical events. This information is independent from the format in which the audio information is stored, because compressed formats are uncompressed before elaboration.

All the layers mentioned above deal mainly with audio/video content, format compatibility, and synchronization issues. Actual content descriptors are embedded in the structural layer, which contains the explicit description of music objects and their relationships. The information within this layer contains neither explicit descriptions of time sorting nor any absolute timing of music events. The event localization in time and in space is realized by spine references. The structural layer is subdivided into four main sections:

    I. Chord grid
    II. Petri nets
    III. Analysis
    IV. MIR

where each one corresponds to a different kind of analysis, for instance, the Petri Net–based analysis described in Chapter 3. All these objects may be the output of an automatic segmentation process [Haus et al. 2004], the result of a human analysis, or a mix of the two.

4.3.1 Chord Grid Objects

Element *chord grid* is a container for chord name elements. These objects deal with a simple harmonic description of the score and can be applied to most of Western music when the chord sequence is explicit and there is no need for a deeper musical analysis. The description of attributes allows a text description of the analysis process. The element chord_name points to the representation of single chords, while the attribute root_id allows for the identification of the root of the chord among spine events:

```
<!ELEMENT chord_grid (chord_name+)>
<!ATTLIST chord_grid description CDATA#REQUIRED>

<!ELEMENT chord_name (#PCDATA)>
<!ATTLIST chord_name root_id IDREF #REQUIRED>
```

4.3.2 Petri Net Objects

The element petri_nets is a container for a number of petri_net instances. As described in Chapter 3, Petri Nets represent a powerful descriptor of music at different levels of abstraction. They can be used as a language to describe the temporal flow of music objects [Hunter 2001] together with their mutual interactions. Music objects are stored in *nodes*, and the transformation rules (musical operators) are stored in the *transitions* of the net.

```
<!ELEMENT petri_nets (petri_net+)>

<!ELEMENT petri_net (place | transition)+>
<!ATTLIST petri_net
 id ID #IMPLIED
 author CDATA #IMPLIED
 description CDATA #IMPLIED
 file_name CDATA #REQUIRED>

<!ELEMENT place EMPTY>
<!ATTLIST place
 place_ref CDATA #REQUIRED
 segment_ref IDREF #REQUIRED>

<!ELEMENT transition EMPTY>
<!ATTLIST transition
transition_ref CDATA #REQUIRED
feature_object_relationship_ref IDREF
 #REQUIRED>
```

4.3.3 Analysis Objects

Analysis [Tagliolato 2006] can be made by *segmentation*, that is, a set of relations between segments and a set of relations between feature objects to represent relations among segments. The structural element can contain zero or more analyses as subelements. In this way, it is possible to represent different analytical viewpoints. Each analysis contains an *id*, which provides a unique identifier within an IEEE 1599 file and may identify one or more authors of the analysis and a description or an optional textual description of the analysis.

The basic structure common to almost all analytical schools is the segmentation of a piece, which can be looked as a collection of segments. A segment consists of a set of events in the piece of music and is identified, together with each event, by a unique ID in the IEEE 1599 document. Feature objects are assigned to segments. A relation among segments is identified by a unique identifier in the IEEE 1599 document, and it is defined by references to the two segments involved.

```
<!ELEMENT analysis
 (segmentation,
  relationships?,
  feature_object_relationships?)>

<!ATTLIST analysis
 id ID #IMPLIED
 author CDATA #IMPLIED
 description CDATA #IMPLIED>
```

The analysis element has been developed in order to model different structures discovered by music analysts and can allow a number of different applications such as analytical and educational tools.

4.3.4   MIR Objects

To handle music information retrieval in IEEE 1599, a MIR environment has been implemented within the structural layer. This allows a complete description of MIR models together with their particular structure, internal relationships, and feature objects, as shown in the next sections.

4.4   THE THEORETICAL FRAMEWORK

To allow queries by content, MIR researchers have recently developed formal models and tools for music analysis [Tagliolato 2006] and retrieval [Chai and Vercoe 2003; Pinto et al. 2007; Pinto and Tagliolato 2008]. The next sections focus on the concept of the MIR model and its use in the IEEE 1599 format.

4.4.1   The Model Perspective

Music is a very complex topic; thus, it is not possible to have a unique method to investigate, for example, music similarity, which is also one of the goals of MIR systems [Hewlett and Selfridge-Field 2000, 2005; Kranenburg 2007]. The concept of a MIR model is slightly different from that of analysis, since the aim of an analysis is to give a detailed description of a musical piece from a musicological point of view, while a MIR model is something more technical, abstract, and partial.

It is technical, because usually it makes use of mathematical and computational concepts to describe music content [Mazzola and Müller 2002]. It is abstract, since it usually works with equivalence classes in order to take into consideration standard musical transformations such as transpositions, inversions, and retrogradations [Hewlett and Selfridge-Field 2005]. Moreover, a model can deal with more than just the audio layer of a music piece (see Chapter 5), and this implies that it can also model musical features that are not encoded in these scores, such as timbre [Cook 2002; Muzzulini 2006]. It is partial since, for example, a specific model can consider the rhythm of a composition, its pitch class sets, its harmonic structure, and so on, thus producing a partial viewpoint of the piece [Maddage et al. 2006].

For these reasons, it is important for an XML standard oriented to music description to support multiple model descriptors, so that each individual model can exploit and provide links to multiple analysis.

It thus follows that the MIR layer is meant more for computer scientists, while the analysis layer is for musicologists. However, the development of new MIR models can lead to new analysis techniques that can produce new analytical methods. This layer interplay, which from an end-user perspective coincides more or less with the role of computational musicologists as depicted in Kranenburg [2007], represents the key toward the development of new systems for knowledge discovery in musical documents.

4.4.2 Categories

Music information retrieval models within the structural layer of IEEE 1599 have been represented thanks to a categorical approach [Haus 1997]. A *category* is a powerful mathematical tool that allows extraction of similarities between mathematical concepts that seem very different. Category theory provides a very general language within which one can study mathematical objects via their transformations rather than from their internal structure. For example, it is possible to describe a set simply by stating that it is in bisection with another set. In the context of set theory, the term "transformation" is equivalent to "function."

The aim is to represent very different music information retrieval models. To this purpose, a particular MIR model can be seen as a category whose objects and morphisms are instances of very different concepts, depending on the model under consideration.

The basic ideas and definitions of category theory are listed below, to illustrate the definition of the music content descriptors for score and audio.

A Category C consists of the following three mathematical entities [Eilenberg and Mac Lane 1945; Harkleroad 2006]:

I.   A class $Ob(C)$ of objects
II. A class $Hom(C)$ of morphisms. Each morphism f has a unique source object A and a unique target object B. We write $f:A{\to}B$, and we say "f is a morphism from A to B." We write $Hom(A,B)$ to denote the hom class of all morphisms from A to B.
III. A binary operation • called composition of morphisms, such that for any three objects A, B, and C we have: $Hom(A,B) • Hom(B,C) \to Hom(A,C)$. The composition of $f:A{\to}B$ and $g:B{\to}C$ is written as $g•f$ or gf, governed by two axioms:
   a. Associativity: If $f:A{\to}B$, $g:B{\to}C$, and $h:C{\to}D$, then $h•(g•f) = (h•g)•f$, and
   b. Identity: For every object X, there exists a morphism $1_X:X{\to}X$ called the identity morphism for X, such that for every morphism $f:A{\to}B$, we have $1_B •f = f = f•1_A$

From these axioms, it can be proved that there is exactly one identity morphism for every object. Some authors deviate from this definition by identifying each object with its identity morphism.

A *set* is an example of a category. In this very simple category, the objects are all the possible sets and the morphisms are all the possible functions between sets. Another example of category is the *graph*, which is the category whose objects are all graphs and whose morphisms are functions between graphs that preserve the *adjacency relation.*

4.5 MUSIC MODELING AND RETRIEVAL IN IEEE 1599

In IEEE 1599, the representation of music information retrieval models is obtained with the formalism of category theory. A model is composed of objects, subobjects (for simplicity reasons, a subobject is just like a subset of a set), and morphisms, corresponding respectively to the entities and subentities that the model assigns to music segments and the relationships between segments.

4.5.1   MIR Model

```
<!ELEMENT mir (mir_model+)>
```

The element *mir* is a container for a number of *mir_model* instances. They correspond to different formal models used in music information retrieval. As stated before, current information retrieval research has proved that many different analyses and models can be applied to the same piece of music (see, e.g., Orio 2006; Tagliolato 2006), so that a single model takes into consideration just one aspect of the music piece.

For example, there is a clear distinction between models coming from pure audio and those coming from pure score. The former will focus more on signal processing features such as chroma-based audio features, spectral or cepstral coefficients, relative to the selected *spine* window (see Chapter 5). The latter will be focused on more abstract and symbolic representation of the selected spine window, or segment, such as *pitch-class representation*, *n-grams*, and *graphs*.

```
<!ELEMENT mir_model (mir_object+, mir_morphism*)>
<!ATTLIST mir_model
 id ID #REQUIRED
 description CDATA "null"
 file_name CDATA #IMPLIED>
```

Figure 4.6 shows an example of a MIR object. Element *mir_model* contains a number of *mir_object* and may contain a number of *mir_morphism*s. It allows reference to an external file in GraphXML format in which the model can be stored. The attribute *file_name* represents the name of the GraphXML file.

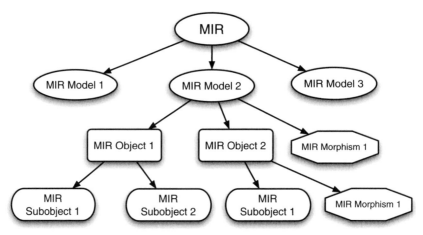

Figure 4.6. An example of a MIR object.

4.5.2 MIR Object

A *mir_object* is the abstract instance of a concrete segment in the analysis layer (see Figure 4.7), which is the representation of a concrete temporal spine window, even if not connected, so that it can refer to audio/video, score, and even notation.

Each *mir_object* corresponds to a specific point of view, given by the MIR model it belongs to, in the group of segments to which it refers.

```
<!ELEMENT mir_object
    mir_subobject+, mir_feature*)>

<!ATTLIST mir_object
    id ID #REQUIRED
    description CDATA null
    displacement_ref (#PCDATA) #IMPLIED>
```

The element *mir_object* contains a number of *mir_subobject*s and may contain a number of *mir_feature* objects. The *displacement_ref* is the reference to its position in *file_name*.

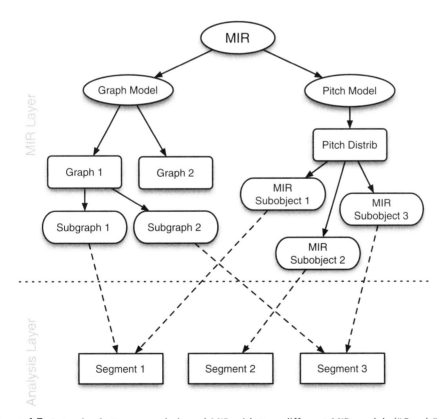

Figure 4.7. Interplay between analysis and MIR with two different MIR models ("Graph" and "Pitch"): each MIR model refers to different segment subsets in the analysis.

4.5.3 MIR Subobject

A *mir_subobject* is an intermediate representation between the abstractness of the *mir_object* and the concreteness of the analysis. This representation is needed to embed in the format an image of the concrete instance present in the analysis layer through the specific modeling process, and it can be used by retrieval algorithms for a refinement of the retrieval process. In Section 4.6, an example will be given to make this concept clear.

```
<!ELEMENT mir_subobject (mir_feature*)>

<!ATTLIST mir_subobject
 id ID #REQUIRED
 description (#PCDATA) "null"
 displacement_ref(#PCDATA) #IMPLIED
 segment_ref (#PCDATA) "null">
```

A *mir_subobject* may also contain a reference to the corresponding segment belonging to an analysis, such as the trivial one (attribute *segment_ref*) and a reference to its position in *file_name* (attribute *displacement_ref*).

4.5.4 MIR Morphisms

MIR morphisms represent the connections among objects and subobjects. For instance, two subobjects might be connected by a *transposition morphism* and two objects by an *inclusion morphism*.

Therefore, *mir_morphism* accounts for the relationships among the different parts of the music piece, which might be also expressed by morphisms in the analysis layer, but which can also represent new relationships from the specific model representation under consideration. For example, in a graph representation, graph A can be a subgraph of graph B, thus revealing an interesting hidden relationship between the corresponding segments in the analysis layer, possibly not revealed by any other analysis.

```
<!ELEMENT mir_morphism (mir_feature*)>

<!ATTLIST mir_morphism
 id ID #REQUIRED
 description CDATA "null"
 domain_ref IDREF #REQUIRED
 codomain_ref IDREF #REQUIRED
 displacement_ref CDATA #IMPLIED>
```

The element *mir_morphism* contains references to its domain and codomain (*domain_ref* and *codomain_ref* attributes) and a reference (attribute *displacement_ref*) to its position in *file_name*.

4.5.5 MIR Features

There are also a number of *mir_feature* objects linked to each *mir_object* that represents the indexes of the object. Those elements are of crucial importance, because they form the database indexes of the music piece. In the retrieval process, indexes are the main elements on which the retrieval process is based; of course, effective indexing is essential for effective retrieval. Multiple indexes are necessary because of the inherent complexity of music semantics.

```
<!ELEMENT mir_feature>

<!ATTLIST mir_feature
 id ID #REQUIRED
 description CDATA "null"
 displacement_ref CDATA #IMPLIED>
```

The element *mir_feature* describes a particular feature used within the model and may create a reference to the GraphXML file (attribute *displacement_ref*).

4.5.6   GraphXML Encoding

Following the categorial representation, MIR objects, subobjects and features, and morphisms are encoded by a graph into a GraphXML file. The following code shows the simplest way to encode a graph with three nodes and eight edges, shown in Figure 4.8.

```
<!DOCTYPE GraphXML SYSTEM "file:GraphXML.dtd">
<GraphXML>
   <graph>
     <node name="A"/>
     <node name="B"/>
     <node name="C"/>
     <edge source="A" target="B"/>
     <edge source="B" target="B"/>
     <edge source="B" target="C"/>
     <edge source="C" target="C"/>
     <edge source="C" target="A"/>
     <edge source="A" target="C"/>
     <edge source="C" target="B"/>
     <edge source="B" target="A"/>
   </graph>
</GraphXML>
```

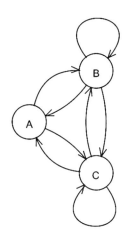

Figure 4.8. Example of a graph descriptor.

The first line specifies that this is an XML application based on the GraphXML document-type definition (DTD) contained in the GraphXML file, while the second and the last lines enclose the real content of the file. The actual content begins with line 3, which defines a full graph. Graph definitions are marked with the *graph* tag, so that a file can contain several definitions for graphs. The body of the graph description is straightforward: two nodes and a connecting edge are defined. Attributes can also be defined for each of the elements as key-value pairs. The GraphXML DTD defines the set of allowable attributes for each element, and it is partly thanks to these attributes that additional information about nodes, edges, or graphs can be used in the application.

In the next section, an example of implementation of a MIR model through a model based on graph theory is shown. This model presents many connections in its structure with the more general approach as categories, since each graph can be looked at as a category [Mac Lane 1998].

4.6   CASE STUDY: GRAPH-CATEGORIAL MODELING

The graph is useful for modeling melodic sequences and indexing music collections in symbolic format. In this model, a graph like the one of Figure 4.8 is associated to each music segment, as described in Pinto and Haus [2007]. An algebraic structure is associated to each graph, namely, an $n \times n$ matrix, with $n = 12$, like the number of vertices in the graph (see also Pinto et al. 2007).

A feature vector is associated to each matrix, and therefore to each music segment; its values are the eigenvalues of the Laplacian matrix, and they have the property that they are invariant through musical transformations. Therefore, an arbitrary melody can be modeled by a 12-dimensional feature vector, which represents the melody.

Figure 4.9 shows the incipit of the "Badinerie" by J. S. Bach from his Orchestral Suite No. 2 in B Minor for flute and strings (BWV 1067), perhaps the best-known example of this type of dance. The example shows the potentials of the new features of the format, for both model description and information retrieval, while the next sections show the XML code relative to the graph model.

4.6.1   Content Description

Badinerie's incipit, shown in Figure 4.9, represents the main recurring motif of the piece, which is presented first in its main tonality, B-minor, and later in the dominant key, F sharp (Figure 4.10).

Figure 4.11 shows the overall description of this motif in the analysis and MIR layers. In the analysis layer there are the two actual instances of the main motif, segments 1 and 2, together with their spine references. In the MIR layer there are the graph model *mir_model* object, which defines the retrieval environment to which the descriptors belong (in the example the environment is the graph model) and an instance of *mir_objects*, the graph 1 object, which is the abstract graph representation of both concrete instances SubGraph 1 and SubGraph 2.

4.6.2   Content Retrieval

Each MIR model provides a particular description (or point of view) of all the segments belonging to the analysis layer. In this example, a 12-dimensional feature vector Graph Spectrum is linked to the abstract graph representation and represents the concrete index

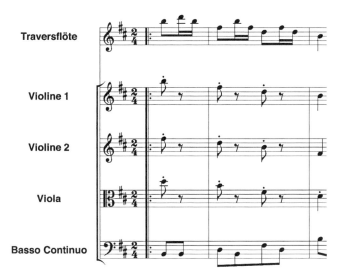

Figure 4.9. Thematic example: "Badinerie," BWV 1067, by J.S. Bach.

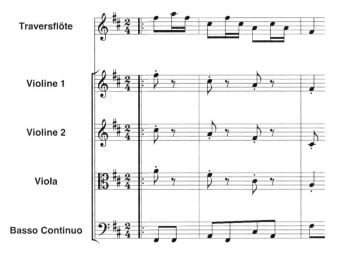

Figure 4.10. Incipit of the second refrain of "Badinerie," BWV 1067, by J.S. Bach: main theme in F sharp minor.

for segments 1 and 2. Thus, any retrieval system can exploit those indexes relative to the graph model. To refine the retrieval process, it is possible to exploit the abstract graph representation of the *mir_object*s and also the raw graph representation of the concrete instances *mir_subobject*s.

4.6.3 MIR Model

The field *mir_model* univocally identifies the particular type of model under consideration; in this case the model is the graph model of music themes. An external XML file (graph. xml) contains all model descriptors.

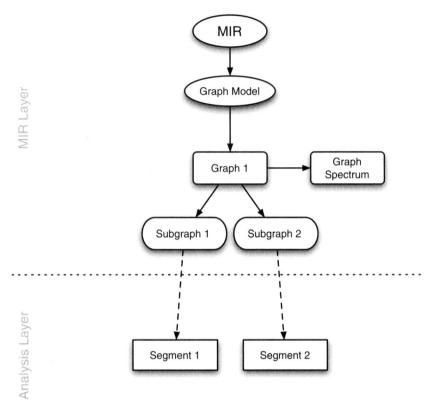

Figure 4.11. Example of a graph model of the themes represented in Figure 4.9 (subgraph 1) and Figure 4.10 (subgraph 2). The two objects are connected by a transposition morphism (see the XML code). The connections with the analysis layer (segments 1 and 2) are also represented.

```
<mir>
  <mir_model id="graph model"
    description="Graph model of music themes"
    file_name="/graph.xml">
```

4.6.4 MIR Object and Subobject

In this case, the *mir_object*s are the graphs representing the melodies. The example is J.S. Bach's "Badinerie," which presents two repetitions of the main theme in different tonalities, as shown in the analysis layer of Figure 4.11. Both expositions share the same representative graph (A); thus, the *mir_object* is the same for the two instances of the refrain together with the *mir_features*, which are graph invariants and are encoded in the same object.

```
<mir_object id="theme-A" description="Traversflote: main theme">
  <mir_subobject id="theme-A1"
    description="First exposition in b minor"
    displacement_ref="node-1"
    segment_ref="segment-1"/>
```

```
<mir_subobject id="theme-A2"
  description="Second exposition in f sharp minor"
  displacement_ref="node-2"
  segment_ref="segment-5"/>
<mir_feature id="inv-first-theme"
  description="Graph spectrum of A"
  displacement_ref="spec-node"/>
</mir_object>
```

4.6.5 MIR Morphism

In this example, in the two expositions of the main theme, one is the transposition of the other. In the following code, this kind of transformation is encoded in the morphism connecting the two subobjects.

```
<mir_morphism id="transformation-1"
  description="transposition"
  domain_ref="segment-1"
  codomain_ref="segment-5"
  displacement_ref="arrow-1"/>
  </mir_model>
</mir>
```

REFERENCES

Arndt, R., Troncy, R., Staab, S., Lynda Hardman, L., and Vacura, M. 2007. "COMM: Designing a Well-Founded Multimedia Ontology for the Web." Paper presented at the 6th International Semantic Web Conference (ISWC).

Baeza-Yates, R., and Ribeiro-Neto, B. 1999. *Modern Information Retrieval*. Addison-Wesley-Longman.

Bosi, M., and Goldberg, R.E. 2003. *Introduction to Digital Audio Coding and Standards*. Springer.

Chai, W., and Vercoe, B. 2003. "Music Thumbnailing via Structural Analysis." In *Multimedia '03: Proceedings of the Eleventh ACM International Conference on Multimedia*. New York: ACM Press, pp. 223–226.

Cook, P.R. 2002. *Real Sound Synthesis for Interactive Applications*. AK Peters.

Diana, L., Ferrari, E., and Hans, G. 2001. "Saving the Multimedia Musical Heritage of Teatro alla Scala for Querying in a Web-Oriented Environment." In *Proceedings of the First International Conference on Web Delivering of Music*, pp. 52–59.

Eilenberg, S. and Mac Lane, S. 1945. "General Theory of Natural Equivalences." *Transactions of the American Mathematical Society*, 58(2):231–294.

Garcia, R., and Celma, O. 2005. "Semantic Integration and Retrieval of Multimedia Metadata." In *5th International Workshop on Knowledge Markup and Semantic Annotation*, pp. 69–80.

Good, M. 2001. "MusicXML for Notation and Analysis." In *The Virtual Score: Representation, Retrieval, Restoration*. MIT Press, pp. 113–124.

Harkleroad, L. 2006. *The Math behind the Music*. Cambridge University Press.

Haus, G. 1984. *Elementi di informatica musicale*. Jackson, Milano.

Haus, G. 1997. "Describing and Processing Multimedia Objects by Petri Nets." Paper presented at the IEEE International Conference on Systems, Man, and Cybernetics, Computational Cybernetics and Simulation.

Haus, G., Longari, M., and Pollastri, E. 2004. "A Score-Driven Approach to Music Information Retrieval." *Journal of the American Society for Information Science and Technology*, 55(12): 1045–1052.

Hewlett, W.B., and Selfridge-Field, E. 2000. "Melodic Similarity: Concepts, Procedures, and Applications." *Computing in Musicology*, vol. 11. Cambridge: MIT Press, pp. 113–124.

Hewlett, W.B., and Selfridge-Field, E. 2005. "Music Query." *Computing in Musicology*, vol. 13. Cambridge: MIT Press.

Hunter, J. 2001. "Adding Multimedia to the Semantic Web: Building an MPEG-7 Ontology." In *First International Semantic Web Working Symposium (ISWC)*, pp. 261–281.

Kranenburg, P. van. 2007. "Towards Integration of MIR and Folk Song Research." In *Proceedings of the ISMIR 2007 Conference*, Vienna, 2007.

Longari, M. 2004. "*Formal and Software Tools for a Commonly Acceptable Musical Application Using the XML Language.*" PhD thesis, Università degli Studi di Milano, Milano.

Mac Lane, S. 1998. *Categories for the Working Mathematician*. Springer.

Maddage, N.C., Li, H., and Kankanhalli, M.S. 2006. "Music Structure Based Vector Space Retrieval." In *SIGIR 2006: Proceedings of the 29th Annual International ACM SIGIR Conference on Research and Development in Information Retrieval*, Seattle, WA, August 6–11, 2006, pp. 67–74.

Mazzola, G.G., and Müller, S. 2002. *The Topos of Music: Geometric Logic of Concepts, Theory, and Performance*. Birkhäuser.

Muzzulini, D. 2006. *Genealogie der Klangfarbe*. P. Lang.

Orio, Nicola. 2006. "Music Retrieval: A Tutorial and Review." *Foundations and Trends in Information Retrieval*, 1(1):1–90.

Pinto, A., and Haus, G. 2007. "A Novel XML Music Information Retrieval Method Using Graph Invariants." *ACM Transactions on Information Systems*, 25(4):19.

Pinto, A., van Leuken, R., and Demirci, F., and Wiering, F., and Veltkamp, R.C. 2007. "Indexing Music Collections through Graph Spectra." In *Proceedings of the ISMIR 2007 Conference*, Vienna, 2007.

Pinto, A., and Tagliolato, P. 2008. "A Generalized Graph-Spectral Approach to Melodic Modeling and Retrieval." In *ACM Multimedia Information Retrieval Conference*, pp. 89–96.

Roads, C. 1996. *The Computer Music Tutorial*. Cambridge: MIT Press.

Tagliolato, P. 2006. "Music Structure Representation: A Formal Model." In *Proceedings of Sound and Music Computing Conference*, Marseille, France.

Tsinaraki, C., Polydoros, P., and Christodoulakis, S. 2004. "*Integration of OWL Ontologies in MPEG-7 and TV-Anytime Compliant Semantic Indexing.*" Paper presented at the Hellenic Data Management Symposium.

5

FEATURE EXTRACTION AND SYNCHRONIZATION AMONG LAYERS

Antonello D'Aguanno, Goffredo M. Haus, and Davide A. Mauro

Summary: This chapter describes in detail how musical events—for example, notes, note symbols, and audio and video renditions—can be referenced in a unique way, thus allowing synchronization among different versions, representations, and multimedia renditions of a piece in a way that, as the examples of Chapter 1 demonstrate, is unique to IEEE 1599.

5.1 INTRODUCTION

Contemporary archives of digital music consist of huge collections of heterogeneous documents. For a music piece, an archive may contain scores of different versions, such as for voice and piano, or for orchestra, as well as several interpretations, namely, the same piece played by different performers and recorded in various formats (CD, MP3, FLAC, and so on). This heterogeneity of information increases the difficulty of retrieval [Downie 2003] and generates problems that remain unsolved.

Synchronization is an important problem that requires a solution through to the implementation of algorithms that automatically link different audio streams of the same piece to symbolic data formats representing the different scores.

As stated in Arifi et al. [2003]: "Such synchronization algorithms have applications in many different scenarios: following some score-based music retrieval, linking structures can be used to accurately access some suitable CD audio to listen to the desired part of the interpretation." This possibility is a useful tool for music students who can listen to music and, at the same time, see the corresponding notes.

Music Navigation with Symbols and Layers: Toward Content Browsing with IEEE 1599 XML Encoding,
First Edition. Edited by Denis L. Baggi and Goffredo M. Haus.
© 2013 the IEEE Computer Society. Published 2013 by John Wiley & Sons, Inc.

Moreover, synchronization creates a strongly interconnected and integrated environment to enjoy music. MXDemo [Baraté et al. 2005] illustrates the full potentialities of an integrated approach to music description.

This goal can be achieved thanks to:

- A comprehensive format to encode music in all its aspects
- A software environment designed for an integrated representation. The software application will provide a graphic interface to read, watch, and listen to music while keeping the different levels synchronized.
- An automatic system to synchronize music scores and the related audio signals.

The first requirement is satisfied by the adoption of the IEEE 1599 format, while the second is covered in other chapters of this book.

The goal of this chapter is to introduce and review algorithms and mechanisms that will at the same time benefit from the encoding and enrich the information contained in the document.

5.2 ENCODING SYNCHRONIZATION INFORMATION

To synchronize all IEEE 1599 layers, a mechanism based on the concept of the *spine* has been realized. The spine allows interconnection of layers in the space and time domains thanks to a relative measure in the spine and an absolute measure in other layers. For a general overview of the format and its structure, see Chapter 2.

Inside the spine, each music event is univocally defined by an identifier (the *id* attribute) and carries information about timing and position. Timing (the *timing* attribute) is expressed in a relative way: the measurement unit is user-defined in the function of the time domain and its value is the distance from the preceding event. For instance, a quarter note may correspond to 1024 timing units, no matter what its absolute timing, even though the absolute timing of a music event depends on the performance and is therefore described in the *audio* layer. The *hpos* attribute, standing for horizontal position, has a similar meaning referred to space domain. The following is a simplified example of the spine:

```
<spine>
  <event id="e1" timing="0" hpos="0"/>
  <event id="e2" timing="1024" hpos="5"/>
  <event id="e3" timing="512" hpos="10"/>
  ...
</spine>
```

In the previous example, three music events are listed within the spine structure. The second event occurs 1024 time units after the first one, whereas the third occurs 512 time units after the second one. Notice that: (1) such values are theoretical, that is, the first score event should last half as long as the second one (but different audio performances could ignore this indication), and (2) those values have no absolute meaning, as neither physical time units nor rhythmical music values are directly involved in their spine definition.

However, the approach is completely different in the audio layer, where every media linked to IEEE 1599 is mapped to spine events through the *track* tag. This element is a container for a number of *track_event* elements, which contain the spine identifier (the *event_ref* attribute) and absolute references (*start_time* and *end_time* attributes) that specify the absolute occurrence of the event in the media file. Thanks to this mechanism, each single music event in the spine can be physically indexed and recognized within one or many digital objects.

Unlike spine timing, the audio layer contains absolute time references, allowing the use of different measurement units in the function of various media. For the *timing_type* attribute, the default unit is the second, but it is possible to use bytes, samples, or frames as well. This solution provides more sophisticated time granularity as required by the different media structures (PCM, MP3, AAC, etc.) supported by IEEE 1599.

The following is a simplified example of the audio layer contents:

```
<audio>
  <track file_name="audio/example.mp3" encoding_format="audio_
mpeg"
    file_format="audio_mpeg">
    <track_indexing timing_type="seconds">
      <track_event event_ref="e1" start_time="0.00" />
      <track_event event_ref="e2" start_time="1.15" />
      <track_event event_ref="e3" start_time="1.67" />
      ...
    </track_indexing>
  </track>
</audio>
```

In general terms, synchronization in the time domain can be obtained thanks to three different methodologies, namely:

- Hand-made approach: Synchronization and spine are completely created by human work. To this end, experience is necessary, both as a musician and as a trained listener.
- Semi-automatic approach: Main beats are manually set, whereas intermediate notes are looked for by an ad hoc algorithms based on interpolation techniques.
- Automatic approach: Every music event is recognized automatically by means of audio-score synchronization algorithms.

The last approach is the most interesting, since it does not require human supervision and allows processing of a large amount of pieces in over short period of time. The state of the art on automatic audio-score synchronization algorithms suggests different approaches; however, most algorithms are performed in two steps: (1) audio and score analysis, and (2) identification of the links between the two layers [Dixon and Widmer 2005].

Several different systems have been proposed to implement audio analysis with well-known tools from audio signal processing and represent the state of the art. For example, in Soulez et al. [2003], a short-time Fourier transform is performed, while in Arifi et al. [2003] an *onset detection* followed by *pitch detection* is employed. In Muller et al. [2004], the audio signal is decomposed into spectral bands related to fundamental and harmonic pitches: for each band, the position of significant energy increases is computed, and such positions are candidates for note onsets. However, the most accepted solution in the literature is a *template-matching technique*, used to select the correct links between audio and score [Dannenberg and Hu 2003; Turetsky and Ellis 2003b]. Such algorithms use a MIDI score to obtain a template of the real execution, then the result is compared with the actual audio, often by employing a dynamic time warping (DTW) programming technique[1] [Rabiner and Juang 1993]. Despite efforts to obtain automatic synchronization and the various algorithms proposed to address this problem, there is no commonly accepted solution for the general problem. However, for our purpose, the representation of synchronization data is more important than the way they are obtained.

What follows is an evolution of the code previously introduced. It is an IEEE 1599 example of the audio layer containing two tracks, where the default time units are the second and the sample-aligned frame, respectively:

```
<audio>
  <track file_name="audio/example.mp3"
    encoding_format="audio_mpeg" file_format="audio_mpeg">
    <track_indexing timing_type="seconds">
      <track_event event_ref="e1" start_time="0.11" />
      <track_event event_ref="e2" start_time="1.15" />
      <track_event event_ref="e3" start_time="1.67" />
      ...
    </track_indexing>
  </track>
  <track file_name="video/example.mpg"
    encoding_format="video_mpeg" file_format="video_mpeg">
    <track_indexing timing_type="frames">
      <track_event event_ref="e1" start_time="10" />
      <track_event event_ref="e2" start_time="45" />
      <track_event event_ref="e3" start_time="63" />
      ...
    </track_indexing>
  </track>
</audio>
```

The code shows, through the same structures, that it is also possible to synchronize videos containing musical contents (e.g., the soundtrack of a movie or the video clip of a song in MPEG format). Once again, the synchronization is based on absolute timing values.

Note that each music event is logically mapped on the spine, and it is accordingly referenced from other layers and, if needed, from other instances in the same layer. In this approach, identifiers are used to jump from one kind of representation to another, and to allow synchronized movements along layers in both the time and space domains.

Figure 5.1 illustrates this method applied to audio and video included in a single IEEE 1599 file. As intuitively shown by the vertical lines, the spine mechanism allows not only investigation of all the encoded representations of the same spine events but also logical jumps from one layer to another, by finding correspondences inside heterogeneous contents.

It is also possible to synchronize video clips containing music that can be related to the *logic/logical organized symbols (LOS)* layer (e.g., the soundtrack of a movie or the video clip of a song). Once again, the synchronization is based on absolute timing values.

---

[1] Dynamic time warping is a technique for aligning time series used in speech recognition since the 1970s.

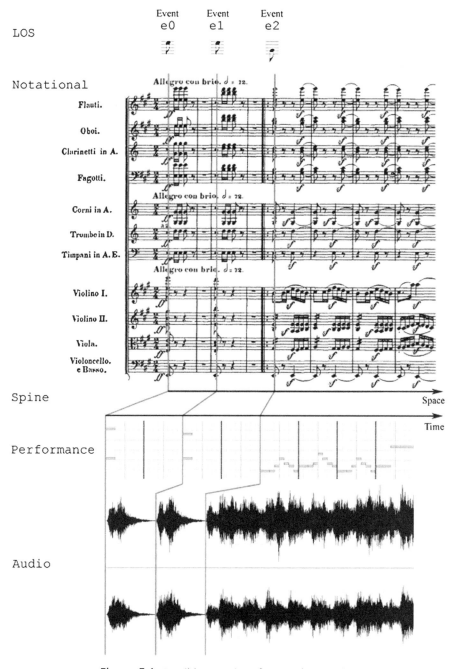

Figure 5.1. Possible mappings from and to a spine.

The *performance* layer provides the same functionality and synchronization mechanisms applied to computer-driven performances. Thus, MIDI, Csound, and MPEG files can also be linked to IEEE 1599.

Synchronization for the *notational* layer is somehow similar. Once again, it is based on the logic/spine layer, where each event is marked in order to be referenced. However,

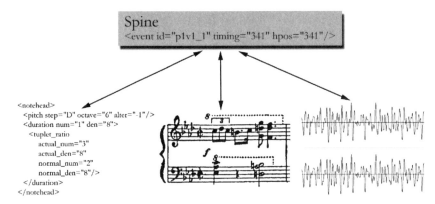

Figure 5.2. Relationships within an IEEE 1599 file.

at the notational level, IEEE 1599 format manages space relationships and not time references. A number of regions in score image(s) are defined with two pairs of coordinates with the purpose of associating spine markers to the corresponding bounding boxes.

Therefore, each music event is logically mapped in the spine and referenced accordingly in the other layers. The spine and all the other layers (except the *general* layer) are linked to each other by event identifiers, acting like pointers. Identifiers are used to jump from one representation to another and allow synchronized movements along layers in both the time and space domains).

Figure 5.2 illustrates some possible relationships within an IEEE 1599 file. Double arrows indicate two-way navigation. In other terms, the spine mechanism allows not only investigation of all encoded representations of the same spine event but also movement from a "peripheral" layer to another one through the spine.

5.2.1 Extraction of Synchronization Data

Multimedia practitioners have had access to many programs that allow use, storage, and sharing of lists of time anchors. Such lists can be used in several ways, such as splitting a movie into chapters thanks to DVD-authoring software or and labeling audio files to obtain synchronization between audio and related symbols.

Currently, there exist no commonly accepted file formats to save both the symbolic information and the audio-related synchronization to use in future computations. However, the present chapter will show that IEEE 1599 can be used to solve this problem. With this technology, synchronization anchors can be inserted in three different layers: the notational, performance, and audio layers. In particular, the audio layer contains a list of time stamps related to the audio/video files (see Section 5.2.2). Thanks to the features of XML, this information can be easily accessed and parsed to design and to implement software tools for export to other recognized standards. Hence, an application can read this list and translate its contents in plain text, to be imported by an authoring program.

Two practical examples illustrate this topic (see Figure 5.3). Most audio editing tools can import files of formatted text to specify markers in a file, as does Sony Sound Forge, which uses a list of entries in one of the formats it supports: time (hr.mn.sc,xxx), time and frames (hr:mn:sc.fr), measures and beats (ms:bt,qbt), and so on. In general, after being imported, the process markers can be saved in audio formats. Another example is the

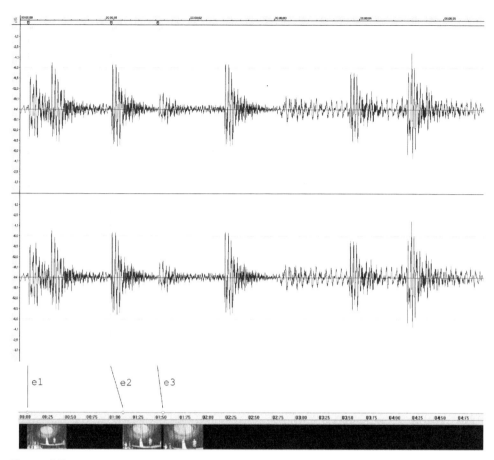

Figure 5.3. Screenshots representing the identification of the same music events in two different digital objects according to the IEEE 1599 sample code described in the text. The events are graphically shown as markers in a popular audio editing tool and as key frames in a DVD authoring software.

automatic creation of chapters in an authoring environment for a DVD, which are described in some detail in the next section.

The software used in IEEE 1599 reads the entire audio layer and separates the time-related information from its event name and other XML syntax. For example, the event `<track_event event_ref="e1" start_time="1.67"/>` can originate a text line such as 1.67 or 00:00:01.670 depending on the required format. By performing this operation on a whole track, a sequence of formatted time data is obtained. Furthermore, this list can be translated again to adhere to the time format of other programs.

In addition, time information could have different granularity: in an MP3 file it is related to frame dimension, while in a CD-DA to samples. A further example is a DVD that uses the MPEG2 compression standard, for which it is possible to set the starting time of a chapter in a less accurate way, because it has to be attached to an intra-frame (a compressed version of a single uncompressed frame; it does not depend on data in the preceding or following frames and is the only frame kind that a reproduction can start). This is less accurate than one based on milliseconds, because typically an I-frame occurs only every 15 frames, and the National Television System Committee (NTSC) uses 30 frames/second.

To conclude, it is up to the user to decide which clip is related to the examined synchronization.

5.2.2 Case Study

The approach described in the previous sections has inspired the creation of a multimedia entertainment product, realized at the Laboratorio di Informatica Musicale (LIM) of the Università degli Studi di Milano for an exhibition about cultural heritage. The symbolic contents of the aria "Il mio ben quando verrà," from G. Paisiello's *Nina ossia la pazza per amore*, were encoded in the IEEE 1599 format, together with four versions of its score in three different performances and lyrics. All these media have been synchronized semi-automatically.

The final goal was a DVD-like video where the user could skip to different performances of the same piece, switch among different versions of the score, and jump to a particular verse of the libretto in a synchronized environment. For the audio, even though the DVD video format allows various tracks for multi-language support, the standard is conceived to support video synchronization among a number of parallel sequences. Thus synchronization points had to be defined to allow jumping from one video clip to another, which required that the original video material had to be split into a number of chapters. Since synchronization data are already contained in the XML file, they are used to drive the process. The operations to be performed can be summarized as follows:

- Read all synchronization events related to a particular execution.
- Translate this information into an ad hoc plain-text list, and export it to a DVD authoring system.
- For each video, automatically split the movie into chapters.

The authoring system used in this project was Mediachance DVD-Lab Pro. Figure 5.4 illustrates the design phase.

As stated above, the granularity of DVD chapters is not good with respect to time, because of the mechanism of I-frames. Besides, since non-standard controls to navigate DVD content are not comparable in flexibility to those provided by a computer interface [Baraté and Ludovico 2008], relevant events have been selected. From the audio layer, the software extracts only those time stamps related to the first word of each verse. Time-related fixed-point values were translated in the format hh:mm:ss:ccc, as required by DVD-Lab Pro. Eventually, by repeating this process for each audio/video track, a complete synchronization was obtained.

From the user standpoint, this DVD product allows jumps from chapter to chapter—for example, from a libretto line to another—in a conventional way, like scenes in a standard movie. In addition, a number of extra on-screen buttons provide controls to switch the audio/video currently playing practically in real time.

5.3 OVERVIEW OF SYNCHRONIZATION ALGORITHMS

Many algorithms that deal with synchronization have been proposed in the literature. The majority of them can be subdivided into two groups: a first one where audio and score are analyzed to extract the low-level features [Tzanetakis and Cook 2000; de la Cuadra et al. 2001; Goto 2001; Haus et al. 2004; Sethares et al. 2005], and a second one where links between the low-level features extracted from the audio and the related score are realized.

This goal can be reached by implementing *DTW algorithms* [Ratcliff 1999; Arifi et al. 2003, 2004; Dannenberg and Hu 2003; Turetsky and Ellis 2003b; Muller et al. 2004; Dixon and Widmer 2005], hidden *Markov models* [Soulez et al. 2003], discriminative *learning algorithms* [Keshet et al. 2007], and *heuristic models* [D'Aguanno and Vercellesi 2007].

The algorithms proposed in the literature use several different methods to implement audio analysis, with well-known tools from audio signal processing. For example, in Soulez et al. [2003] a short-time Fourier transform (STFT) is used, while Arifi et al. [2003] propose an onset detection followed by pitch detection. In Muller et al. [2004], the feature extraction procedure performs these operations by decomposing the audio signal into spectral bands corresponding to fundamental pitches and harmonics, followed by the computation of the positions of significant energy increases within each band; such positions are candidates for note onsets.

To select the correct links between audio and score, a template-matching technique [Dannenberg and Hu 2003; Soulez et al. 2003; Turetsky and Ellis 2003b] can be used. Such algorithms use a MIDI score to obtain a template of the real execution, which is compared to the real audio using DTW.

The correct synchronization is then obtained from the difference between the duration of the real execution and the one of MIDI. The algorithm described here uses a DTW approach similar to the one proposed in Muller et al. [2004], but the two time series needed to apply DTW techniques are not audio, but some particular low level information extracted from the audio and the IEEE 1599 score. In this algorithm, an STFT is used to obtain the low-level audio feature, similar to the one proposed in Soulez et al. [2003]. The algorithm proposed here uses an approach related to onset detection [Arifi et al. 2003]; however, no pitch analysis is performed.

Turetsky and Ellis [2003a] first convert score data, originally given in MIDI format, into an audio data stream using a synthesizer. Then, both audio data streams are analyzed by means of an STFT, which in turn yields a sequence of feature vectors. Based on the measure of the local distance, which allows pairwise comparison of these vectors, the best alignment is derived by means of DTW.

The approach of Soulez et al. [2003] is similar to that of Turetsky and Ellis [2003a], but with one fundamental difference: in the latter, the score data are first converted into audio format, which is much more complex. In the actual synchronization step, the explicit knowledge of note parameters is not used, while instead Soulez et al. explicitly use note parameters such as onset times and pitches, in order to generate a sequence of attack and sustain as well as silence models, used in the synchronization process.

This yields an algorithm more robust with respect to local time deviations and small spectral variations. However, since STFT is used for the analysis of the audio data stream, both approaches have the following drawbacks: first, the STFT computes spectral coefficients, which are linearly spread over the spectrum, resulting in an inaccurate low-frequency resolution. Therefore, one has to rely on the harmonics in the case of low notes. This creates problems in polyphonic music, where harmonics and fundamental frequencies of different notes often overlap and coincide. Second, in order to obtain a sufficient time resolution one has to work with a relatively large number of feature vectors at the audio side; for example, even with a low time resolution of 46 ms as suggested by Turetsky and Ellis [2003a], more than 20 feature vectors per second are required.

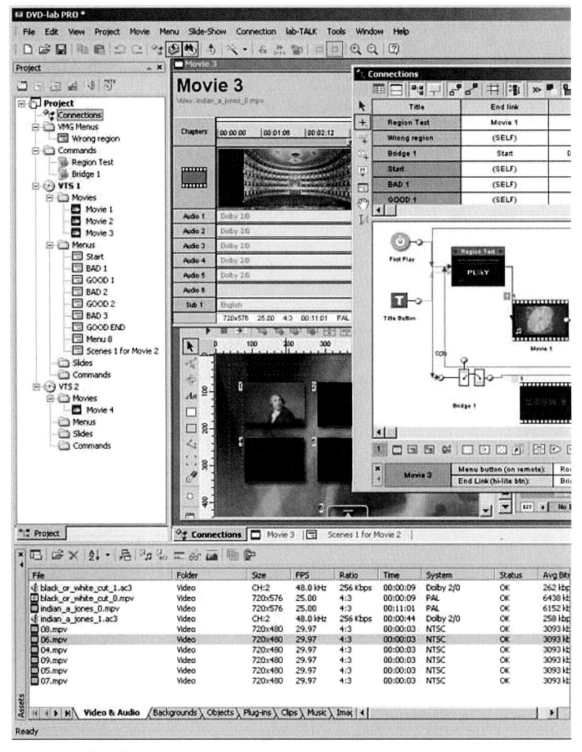

Figure 5.4. The design phase of the DVD product using Mediachance DVD-Lab Pro.

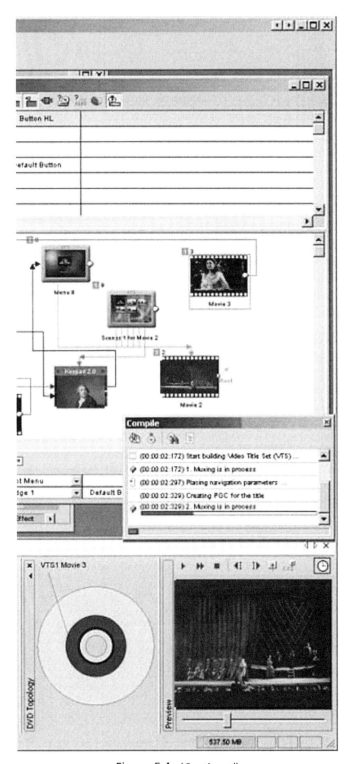

Figure 5.4. (*Continued*)

This leads to a high requirement of memory, as well as long run times for the DTW computation.

Applications of the aforementioned algorithms can be found in Chapter 7.

5.4 VARSI: AN AUTOMATIC SCORE-TO-AUDIO SYNCHRONIZATION ALGORITHM BASED ON THE IEEE 1599 FORMAT

In this section, an example of a synchronization algorithm suited to IEEE 1599 is discussed.

The aim of automatic score-to-audio synchronization is to match every note written in a score to the corresponding temporal position of the audio execution. This can be achieved by deriving from the score and from the pulse code modulation (PCM) signal a set of descriptive parameters to be matched. The *VarSi algorithm* shapes descriptive parameters, making them as similar as possible, so that they are easily comparable.

Some automatic algorithms for score-to-audio synchronization start by analyzing the audio signal, to extract a sort of *execution score*. The synchronization events are then generated by comparing execution and symbolic scores [D'Aguanno and Vercellesi 2007]. However, this procedure has shown some limits, especially in polyphonic music [Klapuri and Davy 2006].

The algorithm adopted here uses a different approach. From the score, a list of *score events* is first obtained. Then the audio signal is analyzed and the *audio events* are generated, containing both the energy and a vector of energy variations over time. These two values are used during the decisional phase to relate score and audio events.

The decisional phase uses a *divide and conquer* approach and implements a DTW [Rabiner and Juang 1993] algorithm. In this phase, a list of certain synchronization events as *anchors* is used, which are computed by matching the vertical rest with the energy computed during the audio analysis. A DTW algorithm is then used to find the best match between audio and score events, working inside the subregions created by the anchors.

The measure of how an audio and a score event are related is called *alignment degree*. Usually, note attacks correspond to a sudden increase of energy, and this variation is more likely to appear at fundamental frequency and harmonics [Tzanetakis and Cook 2000]. In this way, the alignment degree is computed by using the vector of energy variation over time. Finally, the best path is found as the sum of these alignment degrees when it is maximal. This represents the final synchronization, which will be encoded in IEEE 1599. The following definitions will help explain this work.

- **Score symbol**: Note, rest or ornament (acciaccatura, trill, and arpeggio)
- **Fuzzy note**: Note whose attack is not well defined in time, as in an ornament
- **Score attack**: The attack of a symbol in the score, measure, and subdivision
- **Chord event**: The set of notes with the same score attack
- **Vertical rest event**: A rest having at least a quarter duration for each part in the staff system
- **Score event**: Either a chord event or a vertical rest
- **Estimated attack**: The possible attack of a note in the audio signal computed using the temporal information in the score
- **Audio event**: Every audio analysis frame, characterized by both energy and energy variation among frequencies over time

- **Synchronization event**: The synchronization between a score event (score attack) and an audio event (seconds), encoded in the spine of the file in IEEE 1599.

Hence, the overall VarSi algorithm can be summarized as follows:

1. *Score analysis*: The IEEE 1599 score, or MIDI, is read and the relevant score events are extracted.
2. *Audio analysis*: The PCM audio signal is analyzed, and a number of audio events are extracted in order to describe it.
3. *Decisional phase*: Score and audio events are related by a DTW algorithm generating the score-to-audio synchronization, conveniently encoded into the spine.

Each of these steps is described in detail in the following sections.

5.4.1 Score Analysis

The first step in the VarSi algorithm is score analysis. In this phase, the LOS and the spine sublayer of the IEEE 1599 file, or the MIDI file, are parsed to extract a set of score events (Figure 5.5).

Two types of score events are considered:

- Vertical rest events
- Chord events.

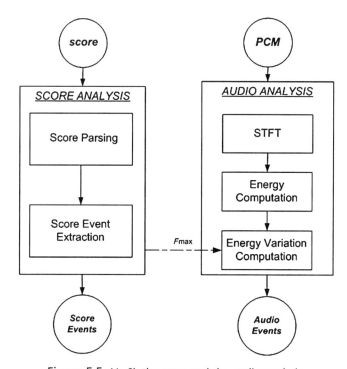

Figure 5.5. VarSi: the score and the audio analysis.

Vertical rest events are characterized only by their score attacks

$$vre_i = \{me_i, su_i\} \tag{5.1}$$

where $me_i \in [1, ME]$ is the measure number, ME is the number of measures in the score, $su_i \in [1, SU]$ is the displacement within a measure expressed in number of temporal units, and SU is the total number of temporal units in a measure.

The vertical rest event set is defined as

$$V\,RE = \{vre_1, \ldots, vre_{MV\,RE}\} \tag{5.2}$$

where $MV\,RE$ is the total number of vertical rests in the score.

Notes with the same score attack are grouped into the same *chord event*. The chord event set is defined as

$$CE = \{ce_1, \ldots, ce_{MCE}\} \tag{5.3}$$

where MCE is the total number of chord events in the score. The ith chord event is

$$ce_i = \{me_i, su_i; no^1_i, \ldots, no^{J_i}_i\} \tag{5.4}$$

where

$$no^j_i = \{f^j_i, z^j_i\}, j \in [1, J_i] \tag{5.5}$$

is the jth note in the ith chord event, J_i is the number of notes in the ith chord event, f^j_i is the frequency of the jth note in the ith chord event, and z^j_i is its fuzzy note indication.

In the case of fuzzy notes, the score attacks are managed as follows:

- In trills or arpeggios, they correspond to the attack of the first note.
- In acciaccaturas, they correspond to the attack of the real notes they are linked to.

The transposition of instruments is managed by encoding the notes at the real fundamental frequency. Even if the algorithm can manage any number of changes in time signature, in this formalization, for simplicity, all the measures are assumed to have the same number of temporal units.

At the end of the score analysis, the score event set is defined as follows:

$$SE = CE \cup VRE. \tag{5.6}$$

5.4.2 Audio Analysis

The second step of the VarSi algorithm consists of audio analysis. In this phase, a set of audio events $AE = \{ae_1, \ldots, ae_{MAE}\}$ is extracted, where MAE is the total number of the audio events.

To obtain these audio events, a frame-based signal analysis is performed. The frame energy (E) and the energy distribution (S) among frequencies are computed in the frequency domain, using an STFT with a Hamming window and a 50% overlap.

Remember that at lower notes, the STFT spectral resolution has been fixed at 10.7665 Hz. In this way, the frame size (N) depends on the sampling frequency (fs), as follows:

$$N = fs/10.7665 \tag{5.7}$$

At the end of the *energy computation block*, a set of frames has been obtained, of which each one is characterized by its energy E_l and a set of values $S^m{}_l$, each of which describes the contribution of the frequency m, where l represents the frame number.

Since note attack is usually characterized by a remarkable and sudden energy variation on the fundamental and the harmonic frequencies [Klapuri and Davy 2006], each frame is characterized by the variation of energy at its spectral frequency component. This characterization generates the *audio events* (*energy variation computation* block).

Let $V^m{}_l$ be the energy variation at frequency m in audio event l. It is equal to

$$V_l^m = \begin{cases} S_l^m - S_{l-1}^m & \text{if } S_l^m > S_{l-1}^m \\ 0 & \text{elsewhere} \end{cases} \tag{5.8}$$

In this way, audio event ae_1 can be defined as $ae_1 = \{E_l; V_l^1, \ldots, V_l^M\}$; each audio event corresponds to a time audio portion and is characterized both by its energy value E_l and by the energy variations among the different frames $V^m{}_l$. To reduce the computational cost, M is the maximum harmonic frequency corresponding to the highest note in the analyzed score (the F_{max} in Figure 5.5).

Furthermore, the maximum number of harmonic frequencies to be considered can be selected by the user in a range from 0 to 8.

The VarSi algorithm can also provide audio analysis using a notch filter bank, as described in Heijink et al. [2000] and D'Aguanno and Vercellesi [2007]. However, this method is less precise and, above all, requires much more time. By using the STFT, the signal is processed only one time, unlike by the method with the notch filter bank, for which the signal is processed M times.

5.4.3 Decisional Phase

The last step of the VarSi algorithm is the *decisional phase* (Figure 5.6). At this stage, the best alignment between score and audio events can be found and the synchronization events created are conveniently encoded into the spine structure.

As mentioned in the previous section, audio events contain two different pieces of information: *energy* and *energy variations*. These are used to relate audio and score events as follows:

- The *energy variations* are used to find the attacks of chord events, usually corresponding to a substantial energy increase at the fundamental frequency and at the harmonics of the notes of the chord event.
- The *energy* is used to find out the estimated attack of vertical rest events, corresponding to the local minima over the whole signal.

First, the vertical rest events are synchronized and used as anchors (*anchor extraction*). Let su be a subdivision (an eighth in the score); its duration, expressed in number of audio events, is

$$SL = MAE/SL \cdot SU \tag{5.9}$$

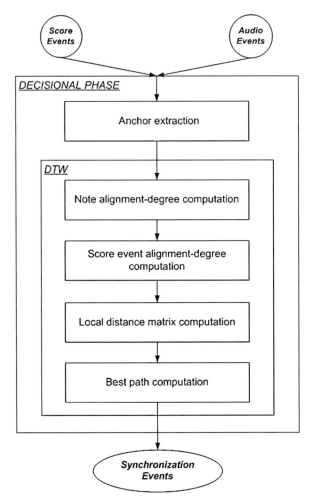

Figure 5.6. VarSi: the decisional phase.

The estimated attack EA_i of a vertical rest event vre_i is then given by

$$EA_i = SL \cdot (me_i - 1) \cdot SU + SL \cdot su_i \qquad (5.10)$$

If we consider a neighborhood, namely, the *analysis window AWi* = {ae_c, . . . , ae_d} $\subseteq AE$ of that estimated attack, the vertical rest event vre_i will be synchronized with the audio event ae_l if $E_l = \min_{h \in [c,d]} E_h$ where $c = \max \{1, \lceil EA_i - R \cdot SL \rceil\}$, $d = \min \{MAE,$ $\lceil EA_i + R \cdot SL \rceil\}$, and R is the radius of the analysis window.

The analysis window is used to look for the vertical rest around the estimated attack—not on the whole audio signal, which yields to a reduction of the computational costs: the longer the signal, the wider the radius.

At the end of this phase, the following subsets are obtained:

- ($MV \, RE + 1$) disjoint subsets $CE_k \subseteq CE$
- ($MV \, RE + 1$) disjoint subsets $AE_k \subseteq AE$.

The chord event synchronization relates the subset CE_k with AE_k, $\forall k \in [1, MV\ RE + 1]$. In the rest of the chapter, to simplify the formalization, we assume that $MV\ RE = 0$, so $CE_1 \equiv CE$ and $AE_1 \equiv AE$. A DTW algorithm is used to find the best alignment between score and audio events. To calculate the local distance matrix ldm, the alignment degree $AD_{i,l}$ between each chord event ce_i and each audio event ae_l has to be found, and it is computed as shown in Figure 5.6.

Note alignment-degree computation: For each note $no^j_i \in ce_i$ the algorithm calculates the alignment degree $G^j_{i,l}$ with respect to the audio events $ae_l \in AW_i$ as follows:

$$G^j_{i,l} = V^{j,fundamental}_{i,l} + \sum_{m \in \Phi^j_i} \frac{V^{j,m}_{i,l}}{2} \tag{5.11}$$

where Φ^j_i is the set of harmonics belonging to the note no^j_i, contained in the chord ce_i. As can be seen, only half of the energy variation of the harmonics is considered.

In Φ^j_i the harmonics are not taken into account, since they are the fundamental frequencies of other notes in the chord event. To obtain the energy variation $V^{j,m}_{i,l}$ at note frequency f^j_i, a linear interpolation is performed between the adjacent energy variations.

Score event alignment-degree computation: The algorithm computes the alignment degree $AD_{i,l}$ between each chord event ce_i and each audio event $ae_l \in AW_i$. There are two possible cases:

1. The chord event contains only one note ($J_i = 1$).
2. The chord event contains two or more notes ($J_i > 1$).

The first case implies that $\forall ae_l \in AW_i \to AD_{i,l} = G^l_{i,l}$. In the second case, the set called $L^j_{i,l}$ is defined as $L^j_{i,l} = [\max(c, l - I^j_i) : \min(d, l + I^j_i)]$, where

$$I^j_i = \begin{cases} \left\lfloor \dfrac{SL}{2} \right\rfloor & \text{if } z^j_i = 1 \\ 1 & \text{otherwise} \end{cases} \tag{5.12}$$

The alignment degree is computed as follows:

$$AD_{i,l} = \begin{cases} \displaystyle\sum_{j=1}^{J_i} \max_{l \in L^j_{i,l}} G^j_{i,l} & \text{if } l \in [c:d] \\ 0 & \text{otherwise} \end{cases} \tag{5.13}$$

The maxima in a range of audio events are added together, since the notes in a chord event could not be executed simultaneously.

Local distance matrix computation: In this phase, the algorithm generates matrix ldm, with the chord events in the rows and the audio events in the columns. To reduce the cost of the DTW computation, only a subset of those audio events is considered: those that have a high degree of *spectral variation* SV_l. This parameter, introduced by Goto and Muraoka [1999], quantifies the novelty degree in the spectrum of audio event ae_l compared with previous ones. It is given by the sum of all the energy variations of the audio event ae_l:

$$SV_l = \sum_{m=1}^{M} V^m_l \tag{5.14}$$

To select alignment indexes, the AE set in ME is subdivided in clusters, and in each cluster the audio events are ordered with respect to SV_l. Then, first $\lceil 3/2 \cdot SU \rceil$ audio events are selected that have the maximum spectral variations and a distance (in audio events) of at least $d = \lceil SL/3 \rceil$. In this way, the following set is obtained: $AE_1 \subseteq AE$.

Recall that the algorithm creates the matrix ldm, which has chord events $ce_i \in CE$ in the rows and audio events $ae_p \in AE_1$ in the columns.

Taking into account chord event ce_i, its alignment degree $AD_{i,l} > 0$ is stored in $ldm(i, u)$, where u is the column number related to audio event $ae_p \in AE_1$ nearest to ae_l.

Best path computation: The best path computation for matrix ldm is performed in two steps: first, the adm—matrix of partial paths—is computed, where $adm(i, u)$ is the quality degree of the best path to *cell* (i, u), and where

$$adm(i,u) = \max[adm(i-1, u-1) + ldm(i, u), adm(i-1, u), adm(i, u-1)] \quad (5.15)$$

The second step is summarized by the following algorithm, which finds the best path related to the adm matrix:

```
i = MCE (the last row number)
u = |AE₁|
    while i > 0 and u > 0
    {
      if adm(i,u) = adm(i,u-1)
        u = u - 1
      else if adm(i,u) = adm(i-1,u)
        i = i - 1
      else
        se(i) = u
        i = i - 1
        u = u - 1
    }
return se
```

where $se = \{se_1, \ldots, se_{MCE}\}$ is the set of synchronization events that relates each chord event with an audio event. This set will be utilized to encode the synchronization in the IEEE 1599 audio layer and in the spine structure.

REFERENCES

Arifi, V., Clausen, M., Kurth, F., and Muller, M. 2003. "Automatic Synchronization of Music Data in Score-, MIDI- and PCM-format." Paper presented at the 4th International Conference on Music Information Retrieval, ISMIR 2003.

Arifi, V., Clausen, M., Kurth, F., and Muller, M. 2004. "Automatic Synchronization of Musical Data: A Mathematical Approach." In *Computing in Musicology*, ed. W. Hewlett and E. Selfridge-Fields. MIT Press.

Baraté, A., and Ludovico, L.A. 2008. "Advanced Interfaces for Music Enjoyment." In *Proceedings of the International Working Conference Advanced Visual Interfaces (AVI 2008)*, Napoli, Italy. ACM Press.

Baraté, A., Haus, G., Ludovico, L.A., and Vercellesi, G. 2005. "MXDemo: A Case Study about Audio, Video, and Score Synchronization." In *Proceedings of IEEE Conference on Automatic Production of Cross Media Content for Multi-Channel Distribution (AXMEDIS)*, pp. 45–52.

D'Aguanno, A., and Vercellesi, G. 2007. "Automatic Synchronisation between Audio and Score Musical Description Layers." In *Semantic Multimedia*, vol. 4816 of LNCS. Berlin: Springer-Verlag, pp. 200–210.

Dannenberg, R.B., and Hu, N. 2003. "Polyphonic Audio Matching for Score Following and Intelligent Audio Editors." In *Proceedings of the 2003 International Computer Music Conference*.

de la Cuadra, P., Master, A., and Sapp, C. 2001. "Efficient Pitch Detection Techniques for Interactive Music." In *Proceedings of the 2001 International Computer Music Conference*.

Dixon, S., and Widmer, G. 2005. "Match: A Music Alignment Tool Chest." In *6th International Conference on Music Information Retrieval, ISMIR 2005*.

Downie, J.S. 2003. "Music Information Retrieval." In *Annual Review of Information Science and Technology*, vol. 37, chapter 7, pp. 295–340. Medford, NJ: Blaise Cronin.

Goto, M. 2001. "An Audio-Based Real-Time Beat Tracking System for Music With or Without Drum-Sounds." *Journal of New Music Research*, 30(2):159–171.

Goto, M., and Muraoka, Y. 1999. "Real-Time Beat Tracking for Drumless Audio Signals: Chord Change Detection for Musical Decisions." *Speech Communication*, 27(3):311–335.

Haus, G., Longari, M., and Pollastri, E. 2004. "A Score-Driven Approach to Music Information Retrieval." *Journal of the American Society for Information Science and Technology*, 55(12): 1045–1052.

Heijink, H., Windsor, L., and Desain, P. 2000. "Data Processing in Music Performance Research: Using Structural Information to Improve Score Performance Matching." *Behavior Research Methods, Instruments, and Computers*, 32(4):546–554.

Keshet, J., Shalev-Shwartz, S., Singer, Y., and Chazan, D. 2007. "A Large Margin Algorithm for Speech-to-Phoneme and Music-to-Score Alignment." *IEEE Transactions on Audio, Speech and Language Processing*, 15(8):2373–2382.

Klapuri, A., and Davy, M. 2006. *Signal Processing Methods for Music Transcription*. Springer.

Mediachance Web site. http://www.mediachance.com/dvdlab/dvdlabpro.html.

Muller, M., Kurth, F., and Roder, T. 2004. "Towards an Efficient Algorithm for Automatic Score-to-Audio Synchronization." In *5th International Conference on Music Information Retrieval, ISMIR 2004*.

Rabiner, L.R., and Juang, B.H. 1993. *Fundamentals of Speech Recognition*. Englewood Cliffs, NJ: Prentice-Hall.

Ratcliff, J.D. 1999. *Timecode: A User's Guide*. Focal Press.

Sethares, J.C., Sethares, W.A., and Morris, R.D. 2005. "Beat Tracking of Musical Performances Using Low-Level Audio Features." *IEEE Transactions on Speech and Audio Processing*, 13(2):275–285.

Sony, Sound Forge. http://www.sonycreativesoftware.com/products/soundforgefamily.asp.

Soulez, F., Rodet, X., and Schwarz, D. 2003. "Improving Polyphonic and Poly-Instrumental Music to Score Alignment." In *4th International Conference on Music Information Retrieval, ISMIR 2003*, pp. 143–148.

Turetsky, R.J., and Ellis, D.P. 2003a. "Force-Aligning MIDI Syntheses for Polyphonic Music Transcription Generation." In *Proceedings of International Conference on Music Information Retrieval (ISMIR)*.

Turetsky, R.J., and Ellis, D. 2003b. "Ground-Truth Transcriptions of Real Music from Force-Aligned MIDI Syntheses." In *4th International Conference on Music Information Retrieval, ISMIR 2003*.

Tzanetakis, G., and Cook, F. 2000. "Sound Analysis Using MPEG Compressed Audio." In *Proceedings of the IEEE International Conference on Acoustics, Speech, and Signal Processing ICASSP'00*, 2.

6

IEEE 1599 AND SOUND SYNTHESIS

Luca A. Ludovico

Summary: *This chapter explains the versatility of audio rendering inherent in IEEE 1599 and how other synthesis languages (e.g., Csound) can be made isomorphic to the IEEE 1599 symbolic representation.*

6.1 INTRODUCTION

This chapter deals with the relationships between sound synthesis and other music descriptions of the same piece. IEEE 1599 is a format oriented to the description and synchronization of heterogeneous representations of the same music material, including computer-driven performances. From the analysis of sound synthesis applied to materials encoded with IEEE 1599, some relevant applications stand out.

First, it is possible to automatically produce a computer-driven performance of symbolic content, thus generating files in a given performance language (e.g., Csound, MIDI, and SASL/SAOL) as well as the related audio files. Thanks to the features of IEEE 1599, this process may exhibit novel features, for instance, the possibility to synchronize different representations of the same piece. In other words, the same algorithm that generates performance information from the symbolic can equally well produce IEEE 1599 code that keeps all music events synchronized, if they are represented in the logic, performance, and audio layers. The next section of this chapter discusses how performance and audio information in IEEE 1599 can be derived from music symbols.

Another application deals with music originally conceived for sound synthesis, whose score usually cannot be described through Common Western Notation. However, the

Music Navigation with Symbols and Layers: Toward Content Browsing with IEEE 1599 XML Encoding,
First Edition. Edited by Denis L. Baggi and Goffredo M. Haus.

format of IEEE 1599 is flexible enough to accommodate other score representations, such as graphic representations and diagrams, and to synchronize them with the information in the performance or audio layer. In this case, the process requires the identification, in an existing performance or audio file, of all relevant music events and their matching to a score document. Therefore, both a graphical and a symbolic representation of a score can be obtained from synthesized audio with ad hoc algorithms.

These topics require dealing with the following two aspects:

1. The features of IEEE 1599 as a representation format
2. The algorithms needed to implement such processes.

As is to be expected, the first aspect will be privileged. In fact, on one hand, IEEE 1599 has been formalized with stable characteristics, while on the other hand algorithms can change, be updated, and be optimized, depending on the needs and goals of user. Some examples will be presented to clarify the matter.

6.2   FROM MUSIC SYMBOLS TO SOUND SYNTHESIS

The main topic of IEEE 1599 and sound synthesis is the extraction of performance and audio information from symbolic information. When a music piece is encoded in a suitable symbolic format, algorithms can be designed to generate computer performances and audio automatically. In IEEE 1599, music events are identified and described in terms of symbols. These aspects are treated within the logic layer: the identification of music events is carried out through the spine sublayer, whereas their description in terms of traditional notation is implemented within the Logically Organized Symbols (LOS) sublayer. Various types of score description are supported, for example, tablatures and neumes, though the LOS sublayer focuses on Common Western Notation. Hence, this section deals with the translation of Common Western Notation symbols into synthesized sounds. A comprehensive survey about music codes can be seen in Selfridge-Field [1997].

As discussed in other chapters, IEEE 1599 encapsulates symbolic, performance, and audio information in a unique document. It is therefore possible to link the original symbolic information to the performance and audio content thanks to ad hoc algorithms.

Heterogeneous formats are supported even for the same media type. In other words, performance and audio information can be encoded in different formats, such as AIFF, WAV, and MP3 for audio, and Csound, MIDI, and SASL/SAOL for performance. However, the result may change significantly depending on the characteristics of the target format and on the algorithms used in the encoding. An example is the translation of a glissando, or a glide from one pitch to another. For instance, with MIDI it can be reproduced by a channel message that creates a sliding effect by smoothly changing pitch from one note to the next one over a scale, while in Csound it is possible to choose between linear and cubic interpolation directly at the start- and end-pitch of the glissando.

IEEE 1599 is a strongly structured format, like any language based on XML; this allows the viewing of scores in the LOS sublayer as a hierarchical tree, where the score itself is the root with children as parts, measures, voices, and finally chords and/or rests. Since symbolic information is organized hierarchically, it is possible not only to synthesize the whole piece but also to extract a specific section from it, for example, a block of measures, an instrumental part, or even a single note with special features.

The process to go from score to computer-driven performances and finally to audio renderings can be useful for a number of reasons. First, it is possible to generate different performances of a score, to verify encoding errors, and to validate the score itself. In addition, it is possible to perform experimentation on timbres and comparison among different aesthetic results by using both synthesized instruments that imitate real ones and user-defined artificial instruments. Finally, the automatic generation of performance information, possibly enriched by interpretative models or real-time interaction, can also have didactic and entertainment implications. The result is potentially rich in multimedia content, since the translation process can be performed a number of times using different parameters.

The following case will clarify this discussion. IEEE 1559, Csound, and uncompressed PCM format can all be used for symbolic, performance, and audio information, respectively. But in addition, IEEE 1599 also supports other performance (e.g., MIDI) and audio encodings (e.g., MP3). It is not necessary in this section to provide a detailed picture about the possibilities of the format with regard to synthesis, hence an in-depth description of ad hoc algorithms and encodings will not be given.

The process to obtain performance and audio information automatically can be viewed as consisting of the following:

1. A description of the original music content in a suitable symbolic format. This role is played by the IEEE 1599 logic layer, since the spine contains the list of events to be synthesized and the LOS provides their description as music symbols.

2. A translation of the symbolic score into a chosen performance language.

3. An audio rendering coming from the computer-based performance.

6.2.1 Translating Symbols into a Performance Language

The original IEEE 1599 document is conceived to contain all the information required by the second step, namely, a symbolic description of the music events (typically in Common Western Notation form). This is not a trivial point, since, even though an IEEE 1599 file with only the spine information would be valid, it would be unfit for synthesis. Except for this extreme case, both the second and the third step can be performed automatically thanks to ad hoc algorithms.

In this section, *Csound* will be adopted as the computer-driven performance language. Csound, realized by Barry Vercoe at MIT, is a digital synthesizer that permits the simulation of every kind of sound. Music scores encoded in Csound can be played with any timbre to simulate both real instruments and user-defined ones [Boulanger 2000]. The best simulation of existing physical instruments is typically done through physical model synthesis. Of course, Csound also supports other synthesis models: additive, subtractive, non-linear distortion, granular, and formant synthesis.

A key feature of Csound, relevant for the goals of this chapter, is a logical and physical distinction between orchestra and score. Hence, Csound takes two formatted text files in input: the orchestra (file .ORC), which describes the nature of the instruments, and the score (file .SCO), which describes notes and other sound parameters along a timeline. Csound processes the instructions in these files and renders an audio file or a real-time audio stream as output. This is very similar to the approach of another supported performance language, SASL/SAOL [Scheirer and Vercoe 1999].

The symbolic content of the logic layer can be translated into Csound code, potentially both the score and the orchestra. The former is essentially a translation of Common Western Notation into Csound, whereas the latter is related to the interpretation of ensemble information present in an IEEE 1599 document. In addition, there are different approaches for the choice of timbres. For instance, one way is to reproduce with computer-based synthesis the real-world instruments notated in the score; thus, the part of a flute could be assigned to a virtual instrument using a physical model of a flute. But another approach is possible, and has sometimes been used in the history of artistic sound synthesis with computers, namely, to make synthesized timbres explicitly different and provide a new musical experience to the audience. One of the first examples of this method was the album *Switched-On Bach* by Wendy Carlos (released in 1968), a selection of pieces by Johann Sebastian Bach performed on a Moog synthesizer.

This study deals with the generation of score (.SCO) files from the logic layer of IEEE 1599. In Csound syntax, every line of a score file represents a single sound event. In particular, for each sound to be produced, the characteristics that can be specified are the instruments used and its starting time, duration, amplitude, and frequency. Other parameters are also possible, but this set is sufficient for the current goal of this chapter.

With respect to measurement units, time can be expressed in seconds; amplitude as an absolute value; and pitch according to octave-point-pitch-class notation.[1] Once again, other approaches are possible, but these settings make implementation easier.

The first example is the translation of a single note (see Figure 6.1) from the logic layer to a Csound score file. The Csound translation is the following:

```
<chord event_ref="v1_e1">
  <duration num="1" den="1"/>
  <notehead>
    <pitch step="C" octave="5"/>
  </notehead>
</chord>


i1 0 4 10000 8.00
```

The line above should be read as follows: play instrument i1 at time 0 s for 4 s, with an amplitude set to 10000 and originating a natural C in the eighth octave.

This trivial example illustrates a number of problems: first, time is expressed in seconds, whereas the logic layer provides only a rhythmic description in musical terms (a whole note). However, conversion can be done thanks to the tempo and metronome information included in an IEEE 1599 document. For example, an eighth note with 120 quarter-notes BPM (beats per minute) lasts 0.25 s; similarly, an eight note in an *allegro* movement—when a more precise metronome information is not available—lasts approximately 0.21 to 0.25 s.

Figure 6.1. A middle-C whole note in Common Western Notation.

---

[1] In Csound, data concerning pitch and frequency can exist in any of the following forms: cycles per second, MIDI note number, octave point pitch-class, and octave point decimal. For example, the 440 Hz note A can be represented alternatively by 440, 69, 8.09, or 8.75.

Figure 6.2. A C-major chord in Common Western Notation.

Amplitude is also expressed through an absolute value. Csound amplitudes are a simple mathematical representation of the signal that does not take into account the acoustical or perceptual nature of the sound. This format supports $2^{16} = 65536$ raw amplitude values in the range −32768 to 32767. This translates into an amplitude range of over 90 dB, roughly corresponding to 6 dB per bit of resolution. In this case, a default value for key velocity can be chosen, and alternatively, the logic layer can be parsed searching for dynamics indications. In both cases, one problem is *clipping*: in Csound, when two or more sounds are playing simultaneously, their amplitudes are added, and when the result is greater than 32767 the synthesized signal is truncated.

Another example is the case of a C-major chord, as shown in Figure 6.2. The same music events, encoded in Csound, have the following form:

```
<chord event_ref="v1_e1">
  <duration num="1" den="2"/>
  <notehead>
    <pitch step="C" octave="5"/>
  </notehead>
  <notehead>
    <pitch step="E" ctave="5"/>
  </notehead>
  <notehead>
    <pitch step="G" octave="5"/>
  </notehead>
  <notehead>
    <pitch step="C" octave="6"/>
  </notehead>
</chord>
```

```
i1  0  2  2500  8.00
i1  0  2  2500  8.04
i1  0  2  2500  8.07
i1  0  2  2500  9.00
```

In IEEE 1599, each chord is an XML element that contains a number of subelements referring to the notes of the chord. In Csound, instead, every line represents a single sound event. Hence, there are four different sounds whose starting time and duration are the same and played by the same instrument. More articulated cases, such as chords of different rhythmic values, can be managed by encoding sound events with the same starting time and different durations.

For the translation of rests, note that only sounds are coded in a performance-oriented language, so rests are implicitly represented through the absence of sound. Consequently, the Csound code corresponding to Figure 6.3 reads as follows:

```
i1  0  1  10000  8.08
i1  2  2  10000  8.08
```

Figure 6.3. A score excerpt including a rest.

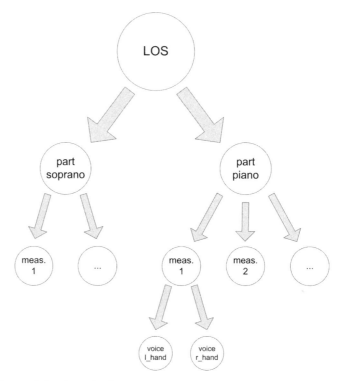

Figure 6.4. Hierarchy for parts, measures, and voices in the logic layer.

Rest encoding is a paradigmatic example of the different approaches between symbolic and performance languages: the former describes every music symbol of the score (also ancillary notations such as articulation and expression signs, if needed), whereas the latter encodes only the information strictly related to sound synthesis.

A complete example of score translation should deal with a number of simultaneous instrumental parts and voices. The spine sorts music events by using relative positions in time and space (see Chapter 2 for further details), so that events from different parts/voices are interpolated within the same list. On the contrary, the logic layer describes the score first part by part, then measure by measure, and finally voice by voice within an instrumental part. This hierarchy is shown in Figure 6.4, and the corresponding XML code is the following:

```
<?xml version="1.0" encoding="UTF-8"?>
<!DOCTYPE ieee1599 SYSTEM "http://standards.ieee.org/
downloads/1599/1599-2008/ieee1599.dtd">
<ieee1599 version="1.0" creator="Luca A. Ludovico">
  <general>...</general>
```

```
<logic>
  <spine>...</spine>
  <los>
    <part id="piano">
      <voice_list>
        <voice_item id="r_hand" staff_ref="staff_3"/>
        <voice_item id="l_hand" staff_ref="staff_3"/>
      </voice_list>
      <measure number="1">
        <voice voice_item_ref="r_hand">
          <rest event_ref="v2_e0" staff_ref="staff_2">
            <duration num="1" den="2"/>
          </rest>
          <chord event_ref="v2_e1">
            <duration num="1" den="2"/>
            <notehead staff_ref="staff_2">
              <pitch step="C" octave="6"/>
            </notehead>
            <notehead staff_ref="staff_2">
              <pitch step="C" octave="5"/>
            </notehead>
          </chord>
        </voice>
        <voice voice_item_ref="l_hand">
          <chord event_ref="v3_e0">
            <duration num="1" den="1"/>
            <notehead staff_ref="staff_3">
              <pitch step="C" octave="4"/>
            </notehead>
            <notehead staff_ref="staff_3">
              <pitch step="C" octave="3"/>
            </notehead>
          </chord>
        </voice>
      </measure>
      <measure number="2">...</measure>
    </part>
    <part>...</part>
  </los>
</logic>
</ieee1599>
```

To translate this example in Csound, where sound events have an absolute time position and duration, an algorithm has to reset the counter of the starting time whenever a new part/voice begins.

A translation algorithm that is easy to implement can follow the same hierarchy used by IEEE 1599's logic layer: parts, measures, and voices are managed in this exact order. Under this hypothesis, the production of Csound code for music symbols that belong to a voice in a measure can be straightforward. Rests are not encoded, even if they are computed to place sound events correctly over the timeline. Single notes (degenerate chords in IEEE 1599) are converted into single sound events, and simultaneous notes belonging to a chord (see Figure 6.3) are translated by setting the same starting time and duration for all the symbols. When there are different simultaneous parts and voices, the translation

Figure 6.5. A piano score with multiple voices.

is performed measure by measure, and the starting time of the measure can be saved in a variable. As soon as the translation of the single voice ends, the counter is reset to the initial value previously saved.

As an example, Figure 6.5 illustrates an excerpt from a piano score. While the first measure contains only two voices, corresponding to the right hand and left hand, in the third measure three rhythmically independent voices can be recognized. The proposed algorithm scans the score part by part (here only the piano part is present), measure by measure, and finally voice by voice. Consequently, the events in the third measure are encoded in Csound with the following steps: first, the global starting time of the measure is saved, then the events belonging to the upper voice are encoded with the proper starting time, and then when the new voice in measure 3 has to be parsed, the global starting time is referred to in order to synchronize the very first event of that voice.

Basic rhythm information can be retrieved and translated as shown in the previous examples. The information in the logic layer allows the computation of starting time and duration. However, detailed management of complex information, namely, rhythm variations due to articulation symbols, ties, and irregular groups, would require a more refined approach. For example, a *staccato* sign implies that notes are cut off during playback; on the contrary, a *tie* adds the durations of the tied notes.

While the cases mentioned are trivial to manage, irregular groups such as tuplets are more challenging. IEEE 1599 specifies the actual duration for each element in an irregular group.

For instance, it is possible to represent an excerpt where three quarter notes take the place of two, as shown in the following example. The attributes of *tuplet_ratio* element reflect the sentence: "Enter three quarter notes in the space of two quarter notes." Note that the symbol under the tuplet is not a quarter but an eighth note:

```
<chord event_ref="p1v1_0">
   <duration num="1" den="8">
     <tuplet_ratio enter_num="3" enter_den="8" in_num="2" in_
den="8"/>
   </duration>
   <notehead>
     <pitch step="D" octave="7"/>
   </notehead>
</chord>
```

Tuplets can be translated by considering both the aggregate duration of all the music objects of the group (in this case, two quarter notes resulting in a half note) and the duration of the single note under the tuplet (one eighth note) related to the internal subdivision

Figure 6.6. The encoding of a note inside a tuplet.

of the tuplet itself (three eighth notes) (see Figure 6.6). The following is the resulting Csound code:

```
i1 0    0.5  10000 9.00
i1 0.5  0.5  10000 9.04
i1 1    0.33 10000 9.02
i1 1.33 0.33 10000 9.04
i1 1.66 0.34 10000 9.05
```

6.2.2 Interpretative Models

The previous section described some techniques to translate the original symbolic information into a performance language. However, execution by a human performer is achieved not only by reading the score but also by interpreting the piece in a unique manner according to the performer's taste and experience. An approach that also takes into account human interpretation is generally very complex. In Widmer and Goebl [2004], a detailed description of the state-of-the-art of interpretative models is presented.

Among the basic parameters usually notated in a score, dynamics is of the utmost importance. The signs typically represent hints for the interpretation and provide indications that can be either absolute and well localized (e.g., *piano*, *mezzo forte*, *forte*, *sforzando*) or relative and distributed over a set of notes (e.g., *crescendo*, *diminuendo*). Moreover, the performer can interpret dynamic symbols in a different manner depending on the historical context, musical genre, personal preferences, and so on. As a consequence, even absolute indications usually do not correspond to standardized values.

Other basic parameters and signs where an interpretative model is required—such as grace notes, articulations, and in general every symbol without a fixed rendering in music—must be treated according to musical practice. The metronome itself, even when a numeric value is expressed by the author, usually requires changes during a human performance.

Sound synthesis can be used for many purposes beyond mere reproduction, for example, to produce a mechanical performance of a music piece, in which case interpretative models are not required. But when the goal is to simulate a human performance, the problems mentioned have to be solved in order to create a "credible" audio interpretation of the symbols. A possible solution is to allow human intervention in the final performance, and this can occur a priori, in real time, or a posteriori. The first approach consists of choosing a set of parameters to be used during the synthesis process (e.g., "translate a *mezzo forte* dynamic to an absolute amplitude of 10000"). The second approach allows a user to modify parameters during the performance (e.g., "raise the volume slider of the mixer when a *crescendo* occurs"). Finally, the third approach can be compared to a post-production phase, when some parameters are modified by human intervention to obtain some effects (e.g., "slow down the performance of the last notes to provide conclusion with a *rallentando* effect").

Another approach to achieve a completely automatic translation is to implement ad hoc algorithms to solve interpretation ambiguity during sound generation. For instance, the absolute dynamic indications can be translated by assigning default values within an allowed range, and hairpins can be implemented through appropriate interpolations. The automatic interpretation of time indications and agogics is a more complex task, as shown by the great number of ways to indicate initial tempo marking. Its definition may consist of basic markings (e.g., *allegro*, *andante*, *adagio*), common qualifiers (e.g., *assai*, *con moto*, *con brio*), mood markings (e.g., *vivace*, *maestoso*, *sostenuto*), and even terms for change in the basic tempo (e.g., *ritenuto*, *stretto*, *rubato*). Moreover, the use of other languages (e.g., *Langsam* is German musical command to play slowly) and non-standard indications (as in many of Erik Satie's works) are quite common. All this information can be encoded in IEEE 1599, but its semantic content cannot in general be inferred automatically.

A number of issues about interpretative models have been mentioned. An algorithm to automatically perform the translation process from the symbolic to the performance level produces a better result if it takes such models into account. IEEE 1599 features that are oriented to interpretative modelingm or that somehow refer to this activity, are described below.

The general layer contains catalog information, including genre classification. The constraints to define genres were left intentionally vague. First, a piece could belong to different music genres, as supported by IEEE 1599 encoding. For each genre, the user can specify a free-text description, thus including a number of acceptable dimensions for classification: historical period (e.g., "20th century"), critical classification (e.g., "Baroque"), type of composition (e.g., "counterpoint"), geographical area (e.g., "Balkan music"), ensemble (e.g., "quartet"), and so on. Finally, each genre is weighted through a numerical value related to other classifications listed within the same document. For instance, a piece can be considered 0.7 classical and 0.3 romantic, such as Beethoven's late compositions—even though a reference scale is not provided; the sum of the values for different genre elements do not have to reach a predefined value such as 1.0. Genre information can be used to influence performance: for example, a jazz piece can present a swing effect, and in a Baroque piece, prelude-dotted notation can be sharper than the corresponding rhythmical values.

The logic layer is the container of symbolic information, and therefore it plays a key role also for interpretative models, of which many aspects have already been discussed. It is worth recalling that the logic layer focuses also on aspects such as tempo (both the basic metronome and its possible variations), dynamics, articulation signs, embellishments, and text indications.

The structural layer helps recognition of structures in music, for example, the occurrences of the same theme or the subdivision of a song into verse and chorus sections. Interpretative models could take this into account and apply similar processes to correlated parts. For example, all the occurrences of a fugue's subject should have the same dynamic contour and articulations to make the subject easily recognizable within complex counterpoint patterns.

Finally, both the performance and the audio layer can host other instances for which interpretative models have been already applied, even though they present no information to influence the current synthesis.

6.2.3 Audio Rendering and Synchronization

Thanks to the features of IEEE 1599, the process from symbolic to performance information can originate a new one, namely, the transformation of symbols into sound. As in the Csound-based case study, this software tool allows the reproduction and saving of the results of sound synthesis in digital format. Similarly, MIDI format can be read and parsed to obtain an audio file. In other words, looking at the whole picture it is possible to enrich the original file with only symbolic information, obtaining a process that originates one or more computer-based performances, and one or more audio renderings.

In IEEE 1599, not only are heterogeneous descriptions not restricted to a unique container, but they are also mutually synchronized. In general terms, it is still difficult to obtain automatic synchronization between performance files and audio tracks, even if the complete score is known; nevertheless, the process is far easier if the score is given. In this case, the problem of finding which music events occur in a media file is replaced by finding where the music events—listed and described in the logic layer—occur. And fortunately for sound synthesis driven by the logic layer, synchronization is easy to obtain, since timing information is produced by an algorithm based on symbolic content. For example, in a Csound score, the starting time and duration of each sound event must be specified, but remain associated with the individual event, while an algorithm that stores these values and associates them to the corresponding audio events and timing achieves a synchronization that is correct by definition.

In the IEEE 1599 multilayer structure, the steps described above are present in the logic, performance, and audio layers, respectively. All these descriptions are connected to the spine, and in this way every music event is linked to its logical, performance, and audio rendering. With respect to the performance layer, it is sufficient to relate the identifier of the spine events to the corresponding line in the Csound score file. An example is provided by the following code:

```
<performance>
  <csound_instance>
    <csound_score file_name="C:\adagio.csd">
     <csound_spine_event line_number="3" event_ref="p1v1_1" />
     <csound_spine_event line_number="4" event_ref="p1v1_2" />
     ...
    </csound_score>
  </csound_instance>
</performance>
```

After obtaining a Csound score and associating instruments to parts and voices through a Csound orchestra, a waveform can eventually be generated. In the Csound score, the starting time and the duration of each sound event is known, so this information can be used also to obtain synchronization between the music symbols in the logic layer and their rendering in the audio layer. This subject has been treated in detail in Chapter 5. For every track event—namely, a music event mapped in an audio track—IEEE 1599 encodes both the current reference to the corresponding spine identifier and the time it occurs in the media file, expressed in absolute term, as shown in the following lines of code:

```
<audio>
  <track file_name="C:\adagio.wav" ... >
    <track_indexing timing_type="seconds">
      <track_event timing="0" event_ref="p1v1_1" />
      <track_event timing="0.1875" event_ref="p1v1_2" />
      ...
    </track_indexing>
  </track>
</audio>
```

In conclusion, IEEE 1599 is a format potentially rich in information needed for sound synthesis. And sound synthesis itself is a way to obtain both a *qualitative* and a *quantitative* improvement in the original music information contained in an IEEE 1599 document. The qualitative enrichment is achieved by adding heterogeneous types of multimedia information—such as performance and audio data—to the original score data, whereas the quantitative improvement comes from a number of new media objects linkable to the document.

6.3 FROM SOUND SYNTHESIS TO MUSIC SYMBOLS

IEEE 1599 provides a way to encode music pieces when no score is available, for example, when there is only an audio rendering. This case is common for improvised and synthesized music that is not expressively produced from a notated score. Fortunately, encoding into IEEE 1599 materials without symbolic information can be discussed in general terms.

There are various reasons for the absence of traditional score, such as a Common Western Notation score:

1. The piece was not composed on the base of any kind of score; rather, it follows a general idea or manipulates audio materials directly. This is the case of some examples of *musique concrète* [Schaeffer and Chion 1967].
2. A written score exists, but it is not a traditional one; instead, it is a graphical sketch or another ad hoc representation of the work [Mathews and Rosler 1968]. This is the case for many contemporary pieces of electronic music.
3. The score notated in Common Western Notation may exist, but the piece itself is the fruit of improvisation, so the resulting score is only one of many possible extemporary instances. This is typical of some jazz music.
4. Only a harmonic grid exists, as the basis for improvisation, as in the case of most jazz pieces; or—even worse—only a general structure such as the 12-bar blues or the 32-bar AABA rhythm changes exists, with no accepted melody or harmony.
5. The original score exists but is unknown at the time of the IEEE 1599 encoding.

Each of these cases implies the presence of audio or multimedia material without knowledge of the corresponding logic symbols. Nevertheless, pieces that fall into these categories can be encoded into IEEE 1599 format, since an IEEE 1599 document can contain symbolic information, although it is not required. In other words, a file is valid also when the logic layer presents no LOS sublayer.

Nevertheless, the spine sublayer is strictly required. Following the definition in Chapter 2, the spine is made up of a list of unique identifiers for music events. As a consequence, the problem consists of recognizing music events inside multimedia material to let the spine structure be compiled, and other descriptions of music events included and synchronized.

With regard to synthesized music, when it is produced through a known performance language (e.g., Csound or MIDI) and the corresponding file is available (e.g., the .SCO or .MID file), a number of parameters can be extrapolated and automatically translated into IEEE 1599. In other cases, when only audio is available, an algorithmic approach based on signal analysis must be attempted. The scientific literature abounds with experiments in the fields of de-mixing, music feature extraction and recognition, and so on. A detailed survey is presented in Klapuri and Virtanen [2008], and more specific aspects are addressed in Schobben et al. [1999], Smaragdis and Brown [2003], Abdallah and Plumbley [2004], Cont et al. [2007], and Virtanen [2007]; however, the goal of this section is not to describe algorithms but to provide an IEEE 1599–oriented vision of the problem.

Even if the computer-performance score is available, not all synthesized music can be translated into Common Western Notation in a straightforward way. Trivial examples are granular synthesis or noise generation in Csound. However, this critical issue can be solved by recalling two key considerations:

1. As stated, the definition of "music event" in IEEE 1599 was left intentionally vague. As a consequence, the occurrence of white noise in an electronic music piece can be viewed as a music event, as needed, or even ignored if the author of the encoding does not consider it relevant.
2. The mandatory part to be compiled is the spine and not the LOS. In other words, music events have only to be identified, but a translation into Common Western Notation notes is not required.

The dilemma of choosing between an automatic and a manual approach for the recognition of music events recalls what has been stated for synchronization: an algorithm is much faster, but in general it is less reliable. Fortunately, some problems have been solved, for example, the automatic demixing of a *n*-part score using *n*+1 audio recordings from different angles, as well as the automatic computer recognition of the notes played by a single, monophonic instrument. Other problems are still difficult to solve without human intervention and will probably remain so; this is the case of the correspondence between an audio and a non-traditional score that graphically represents the performance (see Figure 6.7). Another research field that remains open is the transcription of an orchestral work starting from a stereo recording.

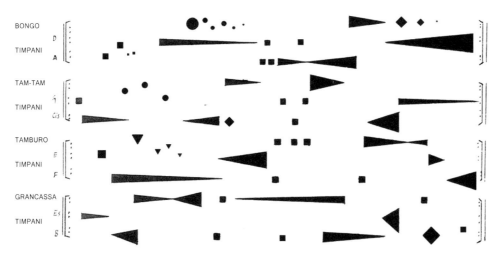

Figure 6.7. A graphical representation of a score for percussions.

6.4   AN EXAMPLE OF ENCODING

The following case study focuses on an electronic music piece not based on a traditional score. The goal is to show the approach of IEEE 1599 to music encoding for pieces for which Common Western Notation symbols are not available.

   The music example is an excerpt from "Points contre Champs," a movement of the work *De Natura Sonorum*, composed by Bernard Parmegiani in 1975 [Mion et al. 1982]. The key idea of the composer is depicting a struggle between antagonist entities, represented by continuous versus punctual sounds. Since the score is not available, the case study adopts a graphical representation derived from the sonogram of the piece (see Figure 6.8). This adaptation, using software called Acousmographe, was produced in 2002 by Benjamin Levaux for the Portraits Polychromes section of the INA Groupe de Recherches Musicales (GRM) [Gayou 2007] Web site. In conclusion, the materials for this piece include a graphical, non-traditional score and an audio rendering. From these objects, a logical representation of the music work has to be inferred.

   The first step consists of identifying music objects, assigning them a unique name, and computing their relative time and space offset. The result of these activities is used to compile the spine in all its parts. On the basis of the audio and graphical information provided, 17 events have been identified in the score excerpt. Needless to say, this value is arbitrary: it would be arbitrary for any composition, even for traditional scores, according to the principles presented in Chapter 2. In this example, based on synthesized music, the identification of music events is even more difficult. Here, the author of the encoding chooses to identify single discrete sounds or small aggregations of punctual sounds, thus omitting continuous ones. With reference to Figure 6.8, the former events are represented by either a sawtooth or straight vertical lines, circles, and solid rectangles, whereas long horizontal marks provide a graphical representation of the latter. For the sake of clarity, in Figure 6.9 the events manually identified within the score are boxed inside light-gray rounded rectangles.

   In Figure 6.10, the audio version of the piece has been aligned to the score by using the scaled graphical representation of its stereo waveform. This is an expedient to show the correspondences among signs and sounds on paper. Nevertheless, it is worth noticing that a graphical representation of sound (i.e., a graphical file containing the image of a waveform) could be considered another non-traditional, alternative version of the score, and it could be treated like any other instance within the notational layer.

   A potential problem is the identification of parts and voices, especially in synthesized music where often the characteristics of instrument timbres cannot help in either an

Figure 6.8. Acousmographie for "Points contre Champs," by Bernard Parmegiani.

Figure 6.9. Sound events highlighted on the graphical score.

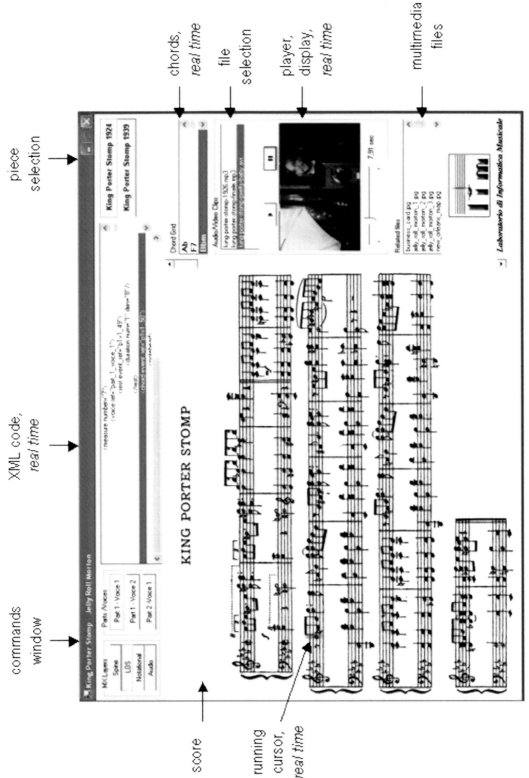

Figure 1.3. The screenshot for "King Porter Stomp."

Music Navigation with Symbols and Layers: Toward Content Browsing with IEEE 1599 XML Encoding,
First Edition. Edited by Denis L. Baggi and Goffredo M. Haus.
© 2013 the IEEE Computer Society. Published 2013 by John Wiley & Sons, Inc.

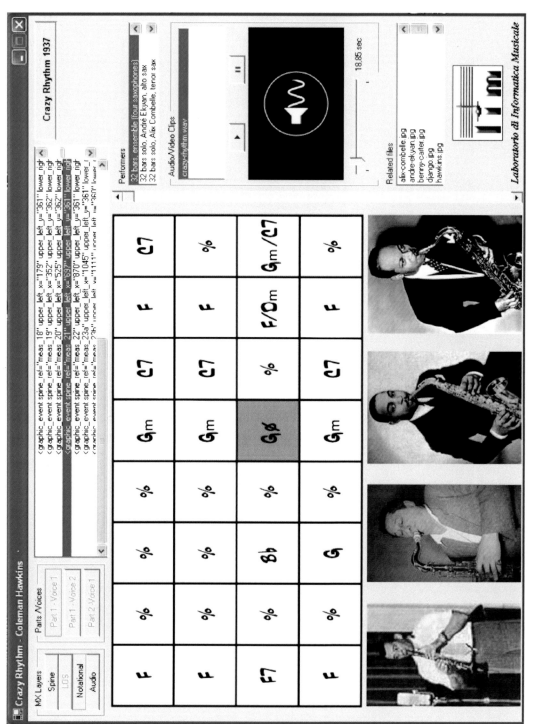

Figure 1.4. The screenshot for "Crazy Rhythm," with a harmonic grid instead of a score.

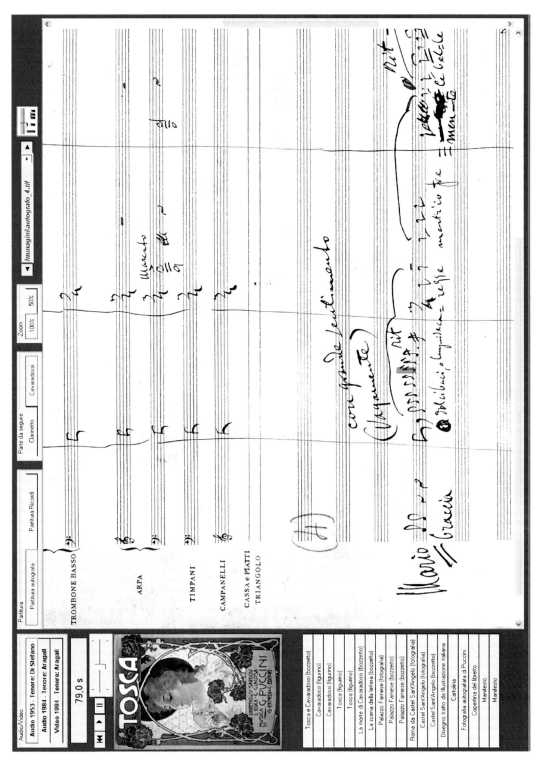

Figure 1.5. An application built on an original manuscript.

Figure 1.7. Control windows for Navigating and Interacting with Notation and Audio (NINA).

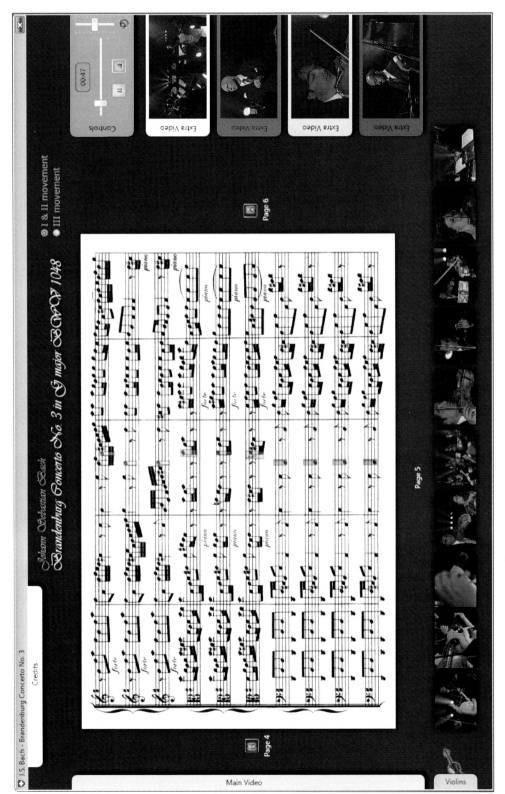

Figure 1.8. An application to control and select different videos.

Figure 1.10. The opening screen for the "La caccia" (the hunt), music by Antonio Vivaldi.

Figure 1.11. Pictures referring to themes 1, 4, 5, and 6 of "La caccia."

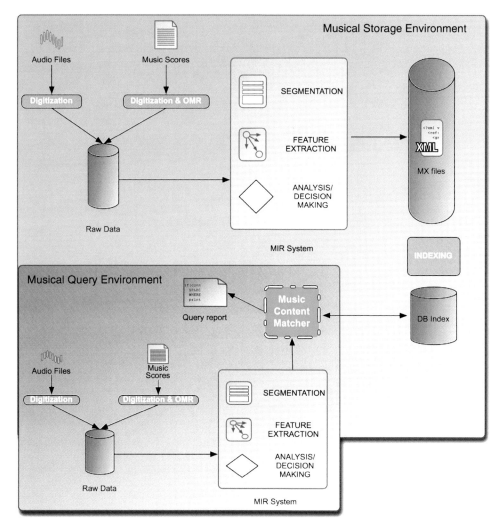

Figure 4.1. General architecture of a music search engine.

Figure 7.1. The interface of NINA.

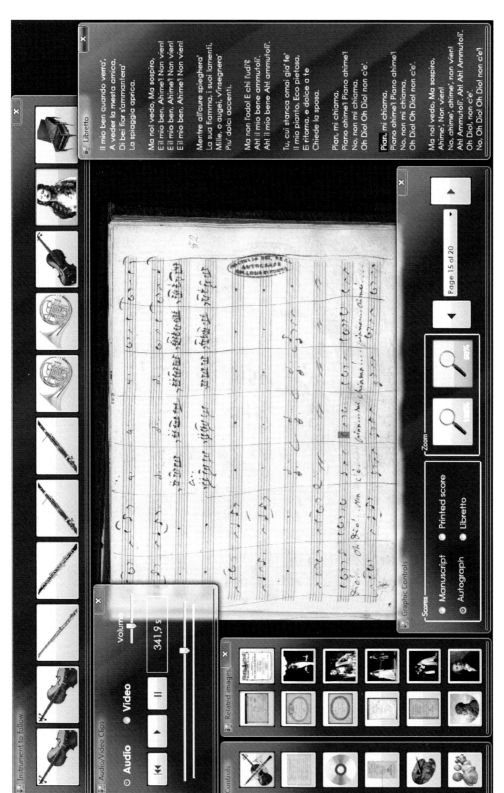

Figure 7.2. Different media objects related to the same music events.

Figure 7.2. (Continued)

Figure 7.2. (Continued)

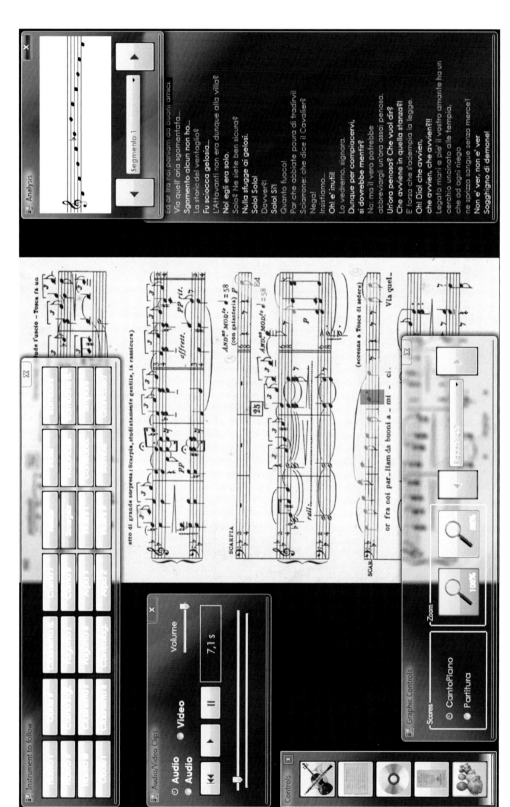

Figure 7.3. A tool to view the results of a musicological analysis.

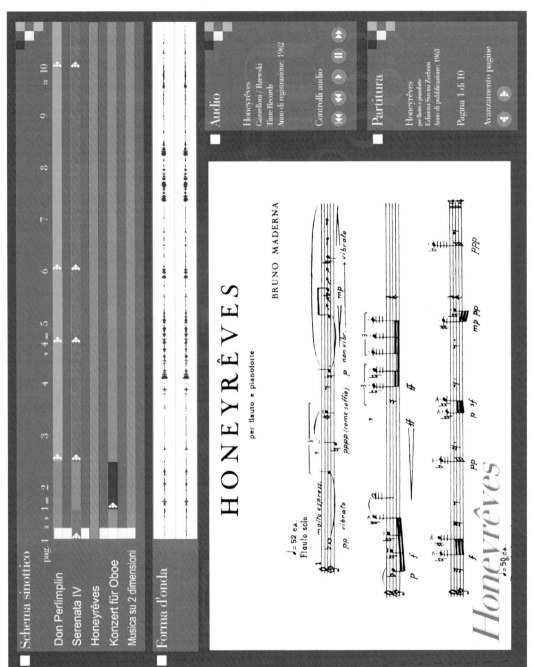

Figure 7.4. A tool to compare some works by Bruno Maderna built on the same music fragments.

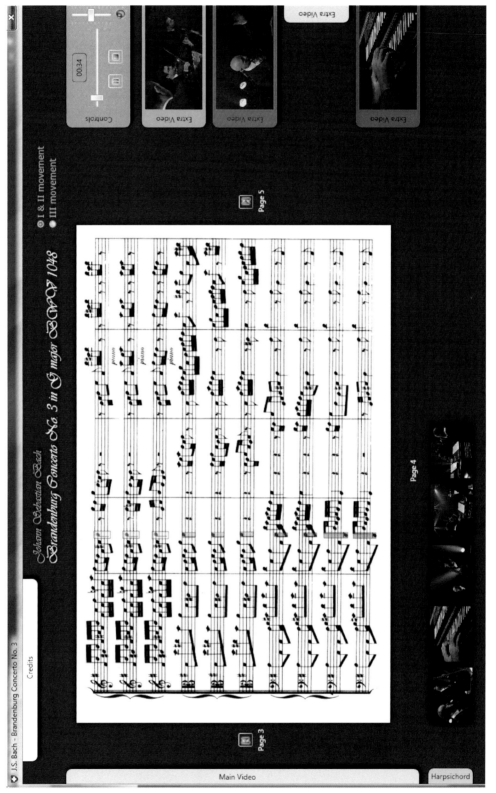

Figure 7.5. A tool oriented to music training.

Figure 7.6. The interface for multi-layer browsing applied to a pop song (a) and to city sounds (b).

Figure 7.6. (Continued)

Figure 6.10. Representation of the waveform, scaled in order to correspond to the graphical score.

automatic or a hand-made recognition of the ensemble. However, in the IEEE 1599 standard, this difficulty does not arise, since the spine is the only part to be compiled in the logic layer; hence, a list of instruments can be encoded, but this is not strictly required.

The IEEE 1599 encoding of this excerpt is the following:

```xml
<?xml version="1.0" encoding="UTF-8"?>
<!DOCTYPE ieee1599 SYSTEM "http://standards.ieee.org/
downloads/1599/1599-2008/ieee1599.dtd"[]>
<ieee1599 version="1.0" creator="StubIt">
  <general>
    <description>
      <main_title>Points contre Champs</main_title>
      <author type="composer">Bernard Parmegiani</author>
      <work_title>De Natura Sonorum</work_title>
    </description>
  </general>
  <logic>
    <spine>
      <event id="event_01" timing="0" hpos="0" />
      <event id="event_02" timing="0" hpos="0" />
      <event id="event_03" timing="0" hpos="0" />
      <event id="event_04" timing="0" hpos="0" />
      <event id="event_05" timing="0" hpos="0" />
      <event id="event_06" timing="0" hpos="0" />
      <event id="event_07" timing="0" hpos="0" />
      <event id="event_08" timing="0" hpos="0" />
      <event id="event_09" timing="0" hpos="0" />
      <event id="event_10" timing="0" hpos="0" />
      <event id="event_11" timing="0" hpos="0" />
      <event id="event_12" timing="0" hpos="0" />
      <event id="event_13" timing="0" hpos="0" />
      <event id="event_14" timing="0" hpos="0" />
      <event id="event_15" timing="0" hpos="0" />
      <event id="event_16" timing="0" hpos="0" />
      <event id="event_17" timing="0" hpos="0" />
    </spine>
  </logic>
  <notational>
    <graphic_instance_group description="Acousmographie by
Benjamin Levaux">
```

```
        <graphic_instance file_name="score\acousmographie.jpg"
file_format="image_jpeg" encoding_format="image_jpeg" position_in_
group="1" measurement_unit="pixels">
            <graphic_event event_ref="event_01" upper_left_x="403"
upper_left_y="144" lower_right_x="481" lower_right_y="275" />
            <graphic_event event_ref="event_02" upper_left_x="498"
upper_left_y="11" lower_right_x="574" lower_right_y="144" />
            <graphic_event event_ref="event_03" upper_left_x="564"
upper_left_y="143" lower_right_x="649" lower_right_y="272" />
            <graphic_event event_ref="event_04" upper_left_x="642"
upper_left_y="13" lower_right_x="721" lower_right_y="143" />
            <graphic_event event_ref="event_05" upper_left_x="718"
upper_left_y="142" lower_right_x="826" lower_right_y="270" />
            <graphic_event event_ref="event_06" upper_left_x="853"
upper_left_y="22" lower_right_x="993" lower_right_y="246" />
            <graphic_event event_ref="event_07" upper_left_x="1054"
upper_left_y="50" lower_right_x="1128" lower_right_y="252" />
            <graphic_event event_ref="event_08" upper_left_x="1197"
upper_left_y="158" lower_right_x="1243" lower_right_y="255" />
            <graphic_event event_ref="event_09" upper_left_x="1302"
upper_left_y="44" lower_right_x="1339" lower_right_y="83" />
            <graphic_event event_ref="event_10" upper_left_x="1347"
upper_left_y="137" lower_right_x="1501" lower_right_y="273" />
            <graphic_event event_ref="event_11" upper_left_x="1965"
upper_left_y="134" lower_right_x="2202" lower_right_y="278" />
            <graphic_event event_ref="event_12" upper_left_x="2230"
upper_left_y="5" lower_right_x="2356" lower_right_y="156" />
            <graphic_event event_ref="event_13" upper_left_x="2523"
upper_left_y="82" lower_right_x="2562" lower_right_y="194" />
            <graphic_event event_ref="event_14" upper_left_x="2584"
upper_left_y="137" lower_right_x="2650" lower_right_y="276" />
            <graphic_event event_ref="event_15" upper_left_x="2665"
upper_left_y="31" lower_right_x="2685" lower_right_y="136" />
            <graphic_event event_ref="event_16" upper_left_x="2746"
upper_left_y="83" lower_right_x="2787" lower_right_y="194" />
            <graphic_event event_ref="event_17" upper_left_x="2814"
upper_left_y="28" lower_right_x="2997" lower_right_y="212" />
        </graphic_instance>
      </graphic_instance_group>
    </notational>
    <audio>
      <track file_name="audio\points_contre_champs.mp3" file_format=
"audio_mp3" encoding_format="audio_mp3">
        <track_indexing timing_type="seconds">
            <track_event event_ref="event_01" start_time="4.8"
end_time="5.8"/>
            <track_event event_ref="event_02" start_time="5.9"
end_time="6.8"/>
            <track_event event_ref="event_03" start_time="6.7"
end_time="7.8"/>
            <track_event event_ref="event_04" start_time="7.7"
end_time="8.4"/>
```

```
            <track_event event_ref="event_05" start_time="8.4"
end_time="9.8"/>
            <track_event event_ref="event_06" start_time="10.1"
end_time="11.8"/>
            <track_event event_ref="event_07" start_time="12.4"
end_time="13.3"/>
            <track_event event_ref="event_08" start_time="14.1"
end_time="14.8"/>
            <track_event event_ref="event_09" start_time="15.3"
end_time="15.9"/>
            <track_event event_ref="event_10" start_time="15.9"
end_time="17.9"/>
            <track_event event_ref="event_11" start_time="23"
end_time="25.7"/>
            <track_event event_ref="event_12" start_time="26.2"
end_time="27.4"/>
            <track_event event_ref="event_13" start_time="29.8"
end_time="30.2"/>
            <track_event event_ref="event_14" start_time="30.5"
end_time="31.2"/>
            <track_event event_ref="event_15" start_time="31.4"
end_time="31.6"/>
            <track_event event_ref="event_16" start_time="32.4"
end_time="32.7"/>
            <track_event event_ref="event_17" start_time="33.2"
end_time="35.4"/>
        </track_indexing>
      </track>
    </audio>
</ieee1599>
```

6.5 CONCLUSIONS

The features of IEEE 1599 mentioned in other chapters provide substantial advantages for synthesis and manipulation of music content. To summarize, its most important characteristics are the following:

1. The possibility to represent and then extract symbolic contents from a well-defined section of the score (see Chapter 2)
2. The possibility to add performance and audio information to the original symbolic content encoded in order to provide a richer description of the original piece. The multi-layer structure and the concept of spine allow linking of the original music events to one or more corresponding representations in the performance and audio domain, while keeping them synchronized (see Chapter 5).

In conclusion, having many different performances adds considerable richness to an IEEE 1599 document, and also allows different musicological analyses within the structural layer and different graphical score versions within the notational layer.

REFERENCES

Abdallah, S.M., and Plumbley, M.D. 2004. "Polyphonic Transcription by Non-negative Sparse Coding of Power Spectra." In *Proceedings of the 5th International Conference on Music Information Retrieval (ISMIR 2004)*, pp. 10–14.

Boulanger, R. 2000. *The Csound Book*. Cambridge: MIT Press.

Cont, A., Dubnov, S., and Wessel, D. 2007. "Realtime Multiple-Pitch and Multiple-Instrument Recognition for Music Signals Using Sparse Non-negative Constraints." In *Proceedings of Digital Audio Effects Conference (DAFx)*, pp. 10–12.

Gayou, É. 2007. *GRM: Groupe de Recherches Musicales, cinquante ans d'histoire*. Paris: Fayard.

Klapuri, A., and Virtanen, T. 2008. "Automatic Music Transcription." In *Handbook of Signal Processing in Acoustics*. Springer, pp. 277–303.

Mathews, M.V., and Rosler, L. 1968. "Graphical Language for the Scores of Computer-Generated Sounds." *Perspectives of New Music*, 6(2):92–118.

Mion, P., Nattiez, J.J., and Thomas, J.C. 1982. *L'envers d'une oeuvre:* De natura sonorum *de Bernard Parmegiani*. Paris: Buchet/Chastel.

Schaeffer, P., and Chion, M. 1967. *La musique concrète*. Presses Universitaires de France.

Scheirer, E.D., and Vercoe, B.L. 1999. "SAOL: The MPEG-4 Structured Audio Orchestra Language." *Computer Music Journal*, 23(2):31–51.

Schobben, D., Torkkola, K., and Smaragdis, P. 1999. "Evaluation of Blind Signal Separation Methods." In *Proceedings of the International Workshop on ICA and BSS (ICA'99)*, pp. 261–266.

Selfridge-Field, E. 1997. *Beyond MIDI: The Handbook of Musical Codes*. MIT Press.

Smaragdis, P., and Brown, J.C. 2003. "Non-negative Matrix Factorization for Polyphonic Music Transcription." In *IEEE Workshop on Applications of Signal Processing to Audio and Acoustics*, pp. 177–180.

Virtanen, T. 2007. "Monaural Sound Source Separation by Nonnegative Matrix Factorization with Temporal Continuity and Sparseness Criteria." *IEEE Transactions on Audio, Speech, and Language Processing*, 15(3):1066–1074.

Widmer, G., and Goebl, W. 2004. "Computational Models of Expressive Music Performance: The State of the Art." *Journal of New Music Research*, 33(3):203–216.

7

IEEE 1599 APPLICATIONS FOR ENTERTAINMENT AND EDUCATION

Adriano Baratè and Luca A. Ludovico

Summary: While the previous chapter relates to past projects based on the manipulation of musical symbols and which, had the present technology been available, could have been realized with IEEE 1599, this chapter describes applications made possible by the availability of such complete and encompassing technology.

7.1 INTRODUCTION

Hardware and software interfaces for music fruition have become increasingly common in the recent past, and a large number of applications can be mentioned, ranging from portable devices to dedicated web portals. However, such applications, even those that are advanced from both a graphical and a content-related point of view, usually allow enjoyment of music in only a traditional way, and thus respond merely to a partial vision of the whole music description. On the contrary, music is made of many different and complementary aspects.

For example, music pieces are usually distributed or enjoyed as audio contents (tracks), even though they are based on symbolic content (score) and contain also text (lyrics), video (video clips), and the like. In addition, for each of the multimedia categories, a number of different cases may occur.

For example, for a pop song, related materials can include (but are not limited to):

- Score: original score, piano transcription, vocal lines with chord symbols, etc.
- Audio: radio edit, CD version, unplugged performance, etc.
- Video: official clip, recordings of live concerts, etc.

Music Navigation with Symbols and Layers: Toward Content Browsing with IEEE 1599 XML Encoding,
First Edition. Edited by Denis L. Baggi and Goffredo M. Haus.
© 2013 the IEEE Computer Society. Published 2013 by John Wiley & Sons, Inc.

To describe a music piece in all of its aspects, a suitable and comprehensive encoding for all of its symbolic and multimedia content must be provided. IEEE 1599 is such a format, since it is capable of dealing with different aspects and approaches, and of taking into account any kind of music description. It is therefore a good candidate for a comprehensive encoding of music. As will be shown, this new technology is the basis for a number of advanced applications oriented toward entertainment as well as toward music education.

7.2 IEEE 1599 FOR ENTERTAINMENT

Thanks to its particular characteristics, IEEE 1599 is a format suited for designing and developing entertainment-oriented applications.

By using ad hoc music viewers, the characteristics of which are described in Section 8.3, it is possible to enjoy music content from new perspectives: for a user, all the available materials can be presented in a unique framework that supports media heterogeneity and full synchronization. This fruition model matches the needs of both experts and untrained people. The former can appreciate the richness of media sources and digital objects related to a unique piece. It is a great experience for a music lover to compare—note by note—the performance of the same aria by Maria Callas and by Renata Tebaldi. It is also interesting for an expert to investigate the differences among great conductors, such as Arturo Toscanini, Herbert von Karajan, and Claudio Abbado, when they are performing, for instance, the same rhythmical section of a composition.

As regards the needs of the latter group, the so-called laypeople, IEEE 1599 is a container for heterogeneous materials, the richness of which can be enjoyed even by untrained people. The innovative concept is to go beyond mere audio content, such as binary files for personal audio players, by offering a complete multimedia package with audio, video, musical symbols, iconographic materials, and so on. Those digital objects are presented within a synchronized environment in which different versions are supported. For instance, a pop song can be listened to and watched in its many versions (live, radio edit, covers); a jazz standard can be compared in its many performances, with different players and ensembles; and so on. Finally, even people with no music training (e.g., no ability to read music sheets) can enjoy scores by following a cursor on the screen, and can appreciate the differences between the audio quality of a digitized vinyl disc and a new digital recording.

In addition, although only applications based on a computer viewer have been mentioned thus far, IEEE 1599 can be also applied to the creation of new media, by exploring the possibilities of support such as DVD videos and Blu-ray discs. In such a context, the format can play an additional role: instead of putting an IEEE 1599 document directly on the support, it can be used to produce the support itself. For example, consider a number of video clips related to the same song, and assume that the goal is the realization of a standard DVD video in which they constitute independent video tracks. If the source is an IEEE 1599 file containing synchronization information, an automatic system can produce a master matrix with ad hoc tagging and subdivision into chapters.

The cases mentioned do not cover all the possibilities offered by IEEE 1599; however, they provide a broad enough picture to appreciate this format and to open new possibilities in the entertainment field.

7.3 IEEE 1599 FOR MUSIC EDUCATION

Another relevant application field for IEEE 1599 is *music education*. The format supports a number of features that can be used in different ways to create ad hoc implementations, both as a guide to advanced listening and as a tool for *instrumental* and *ear training*.

In this context, the heterogeneity of descriptions and instances within each layer opens up new ways of enjoyment of a music piece. The logical score—encoded within the logic layer—can be visually represented in the notational layer not only through autographic and printed scores but also by other forms of graphical descriptions. In addition, this feature allows support for those scores that do not belong to Common Western Notation. The audio layer can provide various performances of the same piece, that is, many interpretations as well as a number of variations on the original score.

It follows that a basic application may consist of implementing a score-following software with advanced features. For instance, music students can concentrate on synchronization among audio and graphical content to learn score reading. If the granularity provided in notational and audio mappings is the single note and rest, a very accurate result can be achieved. In addition, through an ad hoc viewer, it is possible to follow full scores as well as single instrumental parts or groupings. A more advanced use of IEEE 1599 code consists of switching in real time between the current media and another in order to compare different performances of the same piece; such an application is useful for instrument players, singers, and musicologists. Similarly, other content types can be alternatively loaded, thus providing a more complete description of the piece: a trivial example is the case of different score versions, corresponding, for instance, to various editions of the same piece.

In addition to the possibility of switching both the audio and the graphical content in real time, while still preserving the overall synchronization, a high degree of interaction with the music is supported. Thanks to the mappings encoded in the audio and notational layers, graphic file areas can be made sensitive to mouse clicks and trigger a prompt re-synchronization of music content.

Moreover, two characteristics of the format can be coupled, namely:

1. The possibility to watch the score of the music and listen to it at the same time
2. The support of non-traditional scores.

A tool based on these features could be used to teach how to read and perform contemporary music.

Ear training and instrumental practice activities can be based on the IEEE 1599 technology. Thanks to audio-source separation techniques or multi-track recordings, some parts and voices can be easily removed, or mixed in differently, from the audio output by an ad hoc software. In addition, the mentioned score-following application can highlight the part the student has to perform.

Although this description concentrates mainly on the notational and audio layers, the other layers that have been left out in this discussion also contribute several other applications. In particular, the structural layer allows identification of music objects and of their relationships in a score. The meaning of the definition, as well as the possibilities of the format, is broad enough to embrace harmonic grid, segmentation, different kinds of musicological analysis, and the like. For instance, thanks to IEEE 1599, the result of an analytical process could be described by a text document that refers to a symbolic score. Hence the score could be enjoyed and understood within an integrated framework where the original score, its revised versions, its many audio descriptions, and various other items are available in a synchronized environment.

Other applications can be designed and implemented. For instance, there has been little investigation and methodological research on cultures and music genres removed from Common Western Notation, such as those studied by ethnomusicology.

In general terms, the IEEE 1599 standard shows its power when rich files can be produced, that is, when a large amount of material related to the same piece is available. All applications discussed below are based on the contemporaneous presence of heterogeneous media descriptions. While an IEEE 1599 document is valid even when only the logic layer has been compiled, most of the advanced characteristics of the applications would be lost.

However, creating a rich IEEE 1599 document could present some problems related to media linking and synchronization. Since a key concept of the format is the synchronization of all associated media, the process of adding content cannot be viewed merely as linking external files, but needs a synchronization process defined event by event. In IEEE 1599, all materials have a direct relation only with the common data structure, the spine, so that adding a new type of media has a linear cost related to the number of spine events, rather than to the synchronized media. After this process, both intra-layer and inter-layer synchronization with other objects are automatically achieved.

7.4   IEEE 1599-BASED MUSIC VIEWERS

An IEEE 1599 document typically contains a great number of heterogeneous materials. Thus, an appropriate viewer supporting different media types and their synchronization is needed, though in order to appreciate its richness a tool deeply interacting with music content can be equally well designed and implemented. It is worth noticing that, in this context, aspects such as user-friendliness, efficiency, and effectiveness are important. This subject has been addressed in Baratè and Ludovico [2008]. This section provides some guidelines for the implementation of a traditional viewer, and an advanced interactive IEEE 1599 player is discussed.

First, heterogeneity in music content should find a counterpart in the layout of controls and views. Players, panels, floating windows, or other devices should be used to present heterogeneous multimedia contents within a unique framework.

A simple way to view and navigate heterogeneous content consists of organizing different multimedia types by using different controls, and grouping a number of instances of the same type within the same control. As a matter of fact, homogeneous media types imply a similar design, both for the user and for the machine, so similar controls are required for them. For instance, the interface dedicated to audio and video content should contain the playlist of such media objects (dynamically loaded from the IEEE 1599 document) as well as the usual controls of a media player—unlike the panel dedicated to score images, which should contain the list of score versions and the list of pages of each score (once again dynamically loaded from the IEEE 1599 document) as well as navigation controls.

The simultaneous presence of all six layers, described in Chapter 2, is not strictly required for a generic music piece: for example, a jazz piece could present no score, a music work could be described as symbols without any media attached, and so on. As a consequence, the corresponding controls of the interface should be dynamically displayed or hidden according to the characteristics of the encoding.

In addition, a general approach should assign the same relevance to all forms of music description. This is a direct consequence of IEEE 1599 philosophy, where only the spine is required, whereas all other layers represent alternative ways to describe the music. As a consequence, the interface should present no "privileged" media type. Nevertheless, from a user-oriented standpoint, it is preferable to have a main window where a given medium is shown with greater emphasis and detail. A possible solution to this problem is to allow any media to be played in the main window, and resized to a secondary panel as needed. For example, in many early implementations of the IEEE 1599, viewer video files were initially loaded inside a small window, but full-screen magnification was supported.

Within a single IEEE 1599 document, synchronizable and non-synchronizable objects are present. This matter has been already discussed in Chapters 2 and 5. Audio, video, and score images usually belong to the family of synchronizable objects, while other icono-graphic materials and catalog metadata fall into the non-synchronizable family. Where a number of either homogeneous or heterogeneous synchronizable objects are available for a given music piece, IEEE 1599 implements mechanisms to provide full synchronization among them. In this way, it is possible to enjoy music in a highly integrated environment, where a cursor highlights the current note or chord in the score, while simultaneously the corresponding point in an audio track is playing. Similarly, it is possible to switch from one score version to another, or from one audio performance to another, in real time, while the music is being played. Of course, this feature is not available for non-synchronizable objects such as metadata (track title, author) or music-related material (on-stage photos, sketches, playbills).

The interface should allow the simultaneous enjoyment of all the views provided for the representation of media objects. A problem could only occur with instances belonging to the same media category: for example, listening to many performances, each with its own absolute temporization of music events, is confusing for the user and difficult to implement. Finally, non-synchronizable descriptions (such as catalogue metadata or icono-graphic content) should also be accessible, but in this case, layout requirements are less problematic.

A number of applications following these guidelines have been designed, imple-mented, and presented during international conferences, symposiums, and exhibitions in order to demonstrate the applicability of the IEEE 1599 standard to different purposes, ranging from education to cultural dissemination, from music information retrieval to entertainment, from advanced fruition of multimedia content to music-related cultural heritage.

The first experiment in this sense was the application of IEEE 1599 to jazz music. The goal was not trivial, as jazz is often based on processes of variation and improvisation whose development can be poorly encoded by a traditional score, if at all. In this case, the logic description of the score can be either based on a transcription (one of the many possible instances) or simplified to a list of generic music events (e.g., a sequence of chords or a harmonic path). This has important consequences for music education, since the user is given the possibility of comparing performances of the same jazz piece by different players from different periods, or even the solos performed during a unique session on the same harmonic path, simply jumping from one media to another.

A number of public multimedia installations based on IEEE 1599 standard have already been realized. The most relevant ones are listed below:

- *Tema con Variazioni: Musica e Innovazione Tecnologica*, Music Park Auditorium, Rome, Italy, December 2005

- *Celeste Aida: Percorso Storico e Musicale tra Passato e Futuro*, Teatro alla Scala, Milan, Italy, December 2006–January 2007
- *Napoli, nel Nobil Core della Musica*, ResidenzGalerie, Salzburg, Austria, May–June 2007
- *RAI Musical Phonology Studio, MITO Settembre Musica (seconda edizione)*, Milan, Italy, September 2008–today
- *That's Butterfly*, Castello Sforzesco, Milan, Italy, September 2009–February 2010.

The next section describes some software prototypes in detail, in order to show the flexibility of IEEE 1599.

7.5 CASE STUDIES

The case studies proposed in this section have two main goals: first, they aim at demonstrating the multimodal synchronized description of music within an IEEE 1599 document; second, they provide examples of future ways to enjoy music at different levels of comprehension and abstraction.

These two aspects have a deep impact on music education. In this context, at least three kinds of applications can be cited:

1. Tools to make available new ways to listen to music, by providing a high degree of interaction to the user together with the possibility of comparing performances
2. Tools to support musicological analysis
3. Applications oriented to music training in all its aspects.

These cases are treated in detail in the following subsections, where an example for each application will be shown.

Some characteristics are common to all applications. The user is allowed to select one among many score versions, among many audio/video tracks, and among leading instruments. A basic fruition model consists of following the evolution of the instrumental parts by listening and watching music in a synchronized fashion. A second way to enjoy music consists of switching from an aural/visual representation to another. In other words, it is possible to compare in real time different versions of the score (e.g., the handmade and the printed one) or different performances. When the user decides to switch from one representation to another, an interruption is not perceived since the process takes place in real time and all available materials are instantly re-synchronized. Finally, this model of application provides a third way to enjoy music that consists of jumping—backward or forward—from one point to another in the score, in both its visual and aural representations. The following examples should help to clarify these concepts.

7.5.1 Navigating and Interacting with Music Notation and Audio

Navigating and Interacting with Notation and Audio (NINA) was designed and implemented for the exhibition "Napoli, nel Nobil Core della Musica," held in May 2007 at ResidenzGalerie in Salzburg, Austria. One of the purposes of the exhibition was that of making music tangible and visible by bringing together all five senses, beyond just hearing. The music piece chosen for this demonstration was the operatic aria "Il mio ben quando verrà," from Giovanni Paisiello's *Nina, o sia la pazza per amore.*

The core of the application is an IEEE 1599 encoding containing synchronization among four graphic objects representing scores, two audio and video clips, and the libretto [Baggi et al. 2007].

In the context of that exhibition, a rich but simple user interface has been designed and conceived for laypeople, to let them listen to a track with various interpreted scores and to look at different score versions simultaneously.

The screenshot in Figure 7.1 illustrates the user interface of NINA. Music browsing is based on windows containing different representations of multimedia content that operate in synchronism while the music is being played. The layout is made of floating panels that can be either opened or closed depending on the user's needs. Each panel is dedicated to a specific kind of visualization. All the homogeneous objects, namely, the material belonging to the same layer, are selectable in each panel designed to manage them.

A number of selection windows are present in the interface. In the lower window there are four choices among scores that can be loaded: *autograph full score*, *historical hand-made copy*, *printed piano reduction*, and *libretto*. In the left window, the user can choose to listen to either an audio track or a video clip. The movie is launched in a dedicated player. The upper window allows selection of the instrumental part to be followed in real time on the score previously chosen.

The main part of the interface contains key graphical content, namely, the score of the aria in one of its versions. On that selection, several synchronized activities execute in real time. The music starts playing, while on the score the running cursor indicates what is being played. In addition, the interface makes it possible either to follow every instrument (as in the examples below) or to view a whole vertical line (as in common music notation software). The user can move the red cursor with the mouse and start playing from another point in the score, while the other real time windows adjust synchronously, and the audio/video player cursor changes its current position accordingly. The user is allowed to follow the evolution of any single voice. Hence, another selection window is provided in the upper part of the interface, where instruments are listed.

During the performance, the user can change the instrument to be followed, as well as the audio being played and the score. This is achieved by clicking on any point of the current graphical score (the synchronization is driven by spatial coordinates), by dragging the slider of the audio/video player (the synchronization is driven by time coordinates), and even by selecting syllables from the libretto (navigation by text content). Overall synchronization is immediately reconstructed. Figure 7.2a (autograph full score and audio), 7.2b (manuscript copy and audio), and 7.2c (printed libretto and video) show some examples.

In conclusion, NINA is a browser that represents music with readable symbols that can be accessed and manipulated even by non-musicians.

7.5.2 Musicological Analysis

Another set of tools is devoted to the visual and aural representation of the results of musicological analyses. Recall that IEEE 1599 provides a specific layer to encode structural information, that is, the structural layer, described in Chapters 3 and 4.

Figure 7.1. The interface of NINA. See color insert.

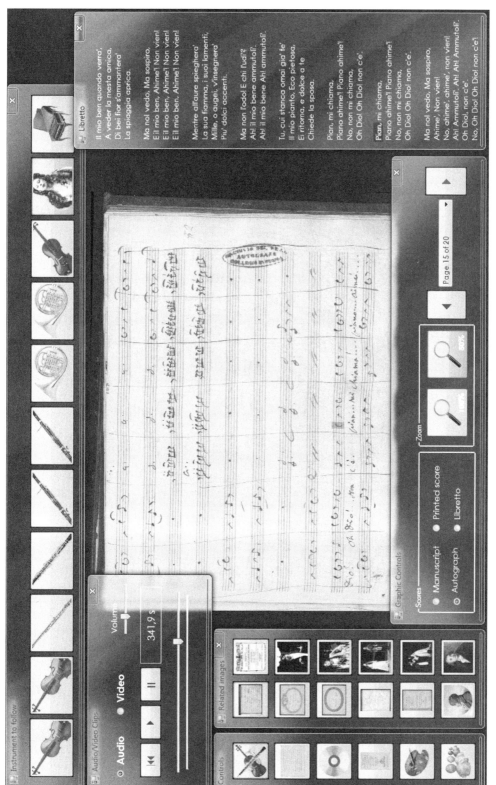

Figure 7.2. Different media objects related to the same music events. See color insert.

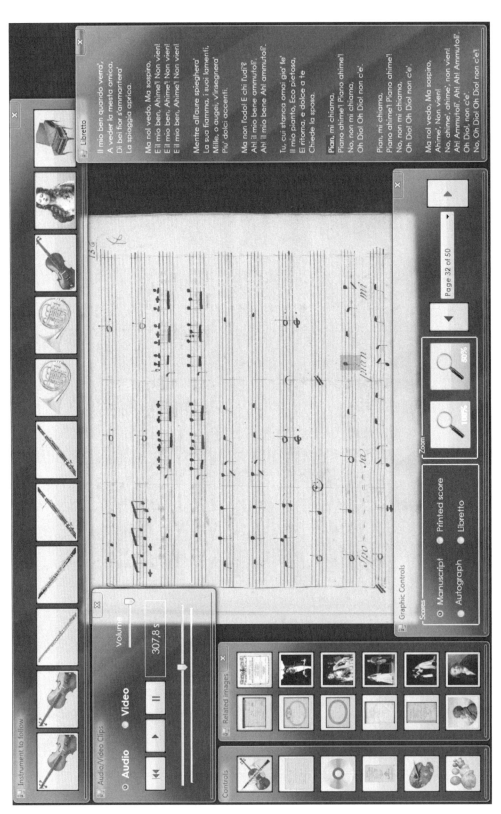

Figure 7.2. (*Continued*)

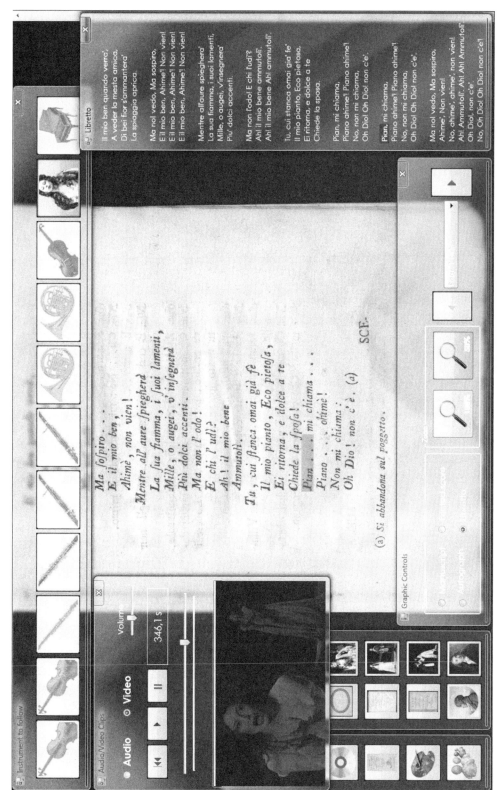

Figure 7.2. (Continued)

Once again, an interface can allow a number of different ways to enjoy music, similar to what has been stated in the previous section. However, new ad hoc navigational tools can be implemented in order to demonstrate a musicological thesis or to make it clearly tangible to the audience: for example, the navigation by music themes or a graphic panel to highlight music fragments.

Recently, two applications with musicological purposes have been designed [Baratè et al. 2009]. The first tool was developed for the conference "Il Nuovo in Musica: Estetiche, Tecnologie, Linguaggi," held in 2008 in Trento, Italy. It is similar, from a logical point of view, to the one shown in Figure 7.1, but a window with the current music phrase has been added (see Figure 7.3). As a consequence, a new navigational tool is available, aiming at the demonstration of a musicological analysis: in this case, the entire piece—a duet from Puccini's *Tosca*—is built on melodic arches of ascending/descending pitches, often split over the two characters' parts. The interface provides an effective way to listen and watch the basic idea this piece is built on.

The IEEE 1599 standard, and in particular its structural layer, can be used also to relate different pieces with common elements. This is the case of some compositions by Bruno Maderna, where the same notational and audio fragments are used, even if they are mixed and interpolated in different ways. As a result of the musicological analysis conducted by Angela Ida De Benedictis, the pieces *Don Perlimplin*, *Honeyrêves*, *Serenata IV*, *Konzert für Oboe*, and *Musica su 2 Dimensioni* end up having shared roots that can be highlighted thanks to IEEE 1599 technology. An ad hoc application has been designed and implemented for the permanent exhibition "RAI Musical Phonology Studio" in Milan, Italy. Figure 7.4 shows some screenshots. The upper part of the interface illustrates a synoptic table about the current piece and its relations with the other compositions, and it provides a navigational tool to compare shared fragments in real time.

7.5.3 Instrumental and Ear Training

Finally, it is possible to design software based on IEEE 1599 dedicated to instrument training and ear training. For this kind of application, a good integration among logic, structural, audio and video content is fundamental.

Regarding learning a musical instrument, in a multimedia interactive environment the student can watch the score in order to perform it, can listen to a pre-recorded version of the music content to reproduce it, and can even analyze the performance of an expert musician. This latter aspect becomes particularly relevant for artists such as conductors or singers, though video content in a learning contexts is interesting also for instrument performers. For example, a clip can show the positions for guitar chords or the hands of the pianist. All these aspects are supported by the IEEE 1599 standard, as shown in the previous sections. In addition, this format allows synchronized multi-track audio as well as multi-angle videos. These novel aspects contribute to create advanced interfaces for music training.

An ad hoc mixing or de-mixing of single instrument recordings allows the implementation of a software tool for both instrument and ear training. For instance, a trumpet student and a double bass student could decide to play a jazz piece together by removing the audio tracks of their parts and using the other tracks of an existing performance. With regard to ear training, a student can try to follow a given part in an orchestral recording, and then validate his or her understanding by listening to the isolated audio track. An example of application that supports part-by-part score and audio following, as well as multi-angle videos, is shown in Figure 7.5.

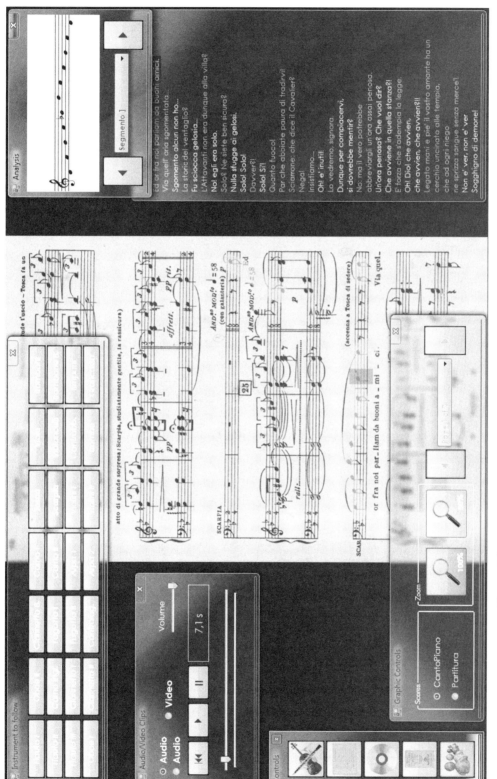

Figure 7.3. A tool to view the results of a musicological analysis. See color insert.

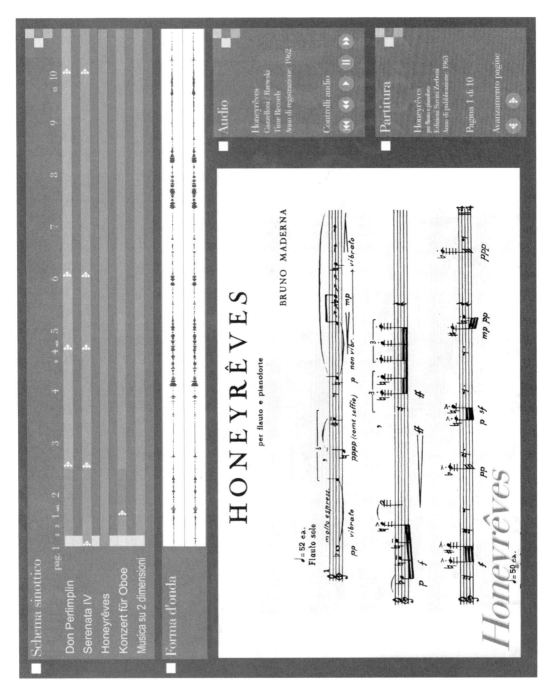

Figure 7.4. A tool to compare some works by Bruno Maderna built on the same music fragments. See color insert.

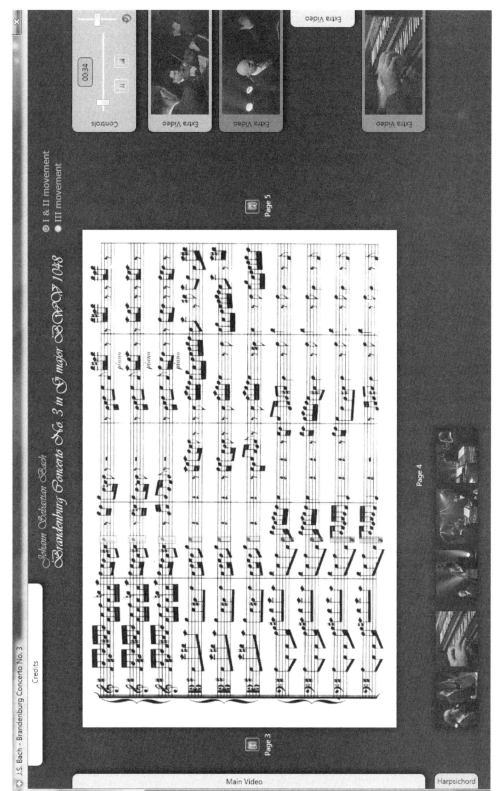

Figure 7.5. A tool oriented to music training. See color insert.

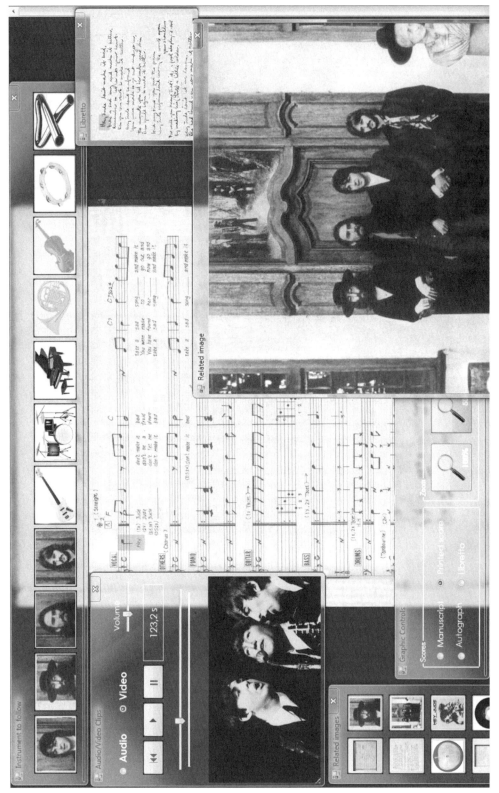

Figure 7.6. The interface for multi-layer browsing applied to a pop song (a) and to city sounds (b). See color insert.

Figure 7.6. (Continued)

7.5.4   IEEE 1599 Beyond Music

It was shown that IEEE 1599 has been applied to various aspect of the music field, and here a particular application of the standard that goes beyond its original goals will be shown. Instead of applying the format to a score, IEEE 1599 is used to represent the soundscape of a urban environment: city maps are considered versions of a score, the audio/video recordings at different hours of the day generate different performances, and finally related files are used to implement a slideshow of the route, with images and short text descriptions [Ludovico and Mauro 2009]. In the music field, a score is read from left to right, music event by music event, while in this case, the revised concept of score—namely, a map—presents a number of points of interest (such as monuments and squares) linked by a path.

Figure 7.6 shows a standard music-oriented viewer adapted to the presentation of non-musical material. Multimedia and navigation controls do not change, as the key differences between a music application and this one are due only to a different interpretation of the underlying concepts. For instance, now the media player loads an audio track of the route and the slider can go backward and forward in the audio/video material, while the main window (usually the score panel) contains one of the maps related to the path itself. The selection tools still work in real time to change the current map and audio/video track.

To demonstrate the effectiveness of the approach, three different recording sessions have been conducted in Genoa, acquiring the environmental sounds along a short pedestrian path, going from the cathedral to the harbor. This route is about 0.5 km long and takes about 7 minutes on foot. The goal of the experiment was to unveil the similarities and differences that characterize city life during the phases of a day.

This case study illustrates the potential of the format in union with a browsing tool, even in non-musical applications. In broader terms, this experience could be generalized to take into account a number of different scenarios and purposes. Other applications for art, communication, and multimedia installations could emerge.

REFERENCES

Baratè, A., and Ludovico, L.A. 2008. "Advanced Interfaces for Music Enjoyment." In *Proceedings of the Working Conference on Advanced Visual Interfaces, May 28–30, 2008, Napoli, Italy*, ed. S. Levialdi. New York: ACM Press, pp. 421–424.

Baggi, D., Baratè, A., Haus, G., and Ludovico, L.A. 2007. "NINA: Navigating and Interacting with Notation and Audio." In *SMAP 2007: Proceedings of the Second International Workshop on Semantic Media Adaptation and Personalization, London, United Kingdom, 17–18 December 2007*, ed. M.C. Angelides, P. Mylonas, and M. Wallace. Los Alamitos, CA: IEEE Computer Society, pp. 134–139.

Baratè, A., Haus, G., and Ludovico, L. A. 2009. "IEEE 1599: A New Standard for Music Education." In *Proceedings of ELPUB 2009, 13th International Conference on Electronic Publishing: Rethinking Electronic Publishing: Innovation in Communication Paradigms and Technologies*, ed. T. Hedlund and S. Mornati. Milan: Edizioni Nuova Cultura, Milan, pp. 29–45.

Ludovico, L. A., and Mauro, D. A. 2009. "Sound and the City: Multi-Layer Representation and Navigation of Audio Scenarios." In *Proceedings of the SMC 2009: 6th Sound and Music Computing Conference, 23–25 July 2009, Porto, Portugal*, ed. Á. Barbosa, F. Gouyon, and X. Serra. Porto: SMC, pp. 19–24.

8

PAST PROJECTS USING SYMBOLS FOR MUSIC

Denis L. Baggi

Summary: This chapter does not particularly refer to IEEE 1599, but describes past proj-ects that have used the technique of symbol manipulation, which has culminated in IEEE 1599. Had that technology been available at that time, it could have been used in all these projects. In this sense, it relates to Chapter 7, which describes further projects that can and will be carried out using IEEE 1599 Technology.

8.1 BRIEF HISTORY

One of the very first ideas for automatic composition mirrors the mathematical method called Monte Carlo method, namely, the generation of random numbers that are then subject to constraints, statistical or other. For example, for the computation of an otherwise intractable definite integral, a large number of virtual bullets are shot at its picture, and the ratio of the count of those below the curve and the total provides a measure of the integral.

Something similar was proposed by Mozart [Mozart] and Haydn [Haydn] (see Intro-duction): a die was used as a random number generator thanks to which musical segments were selected from tables as functions of the past segment. This way, a complete minuet could be composed.

This is also the method that has been used for the first composition by a digital elec-tronic computer, the *Illiac Suite* [Hiller and Isaacson 1959]. In the second movement, random numbers are subject to obey increasingly stringent rules of Four-Part First-Species Counterpoint, as follows:

Music Navigation with Symbols and Layers: Toward Content Browsing with IEEE 1599 XML Encoding,
First Edition. Edited by Denis L. Baggi and Goffredo M. Haus.
© 2013 the IEEE Computer Society. Published 2013 by John Wiley & Sons, Inc.

A. Random music; no rules

B. Skip-stepwise rule

C. *Cantus firmus* on C, cadence on C

D. Octave-range rule

E. Only consonant chords permitted

F. Parallel unisons, octaves, fifths, and fourths permitted

G. Parallel fourths, 6-4 chords with tenth permitted

H. Best counterpoint

And this produced the following result, a movement with 8 segments:

For the first time in the history of music it had been possible to assess the effect of rules for composing, independently of any subjective and human criteria. Every random number corresponds to a note, which is either retained if it satisfies all rules or rejected, in which case the random number generator is called again. Thus it is possible to hear, in the example of Figure 8.1, a slow convergence toward what is generally associated with 17th-century music, part H.

At the same time, the experiment shows that *randomness* does not generate a piece of music that in any way exhibits what everyone associates with music, namely, the unfolding of a narration. According to German musicologist Heinrich Schenker, composers spent centuries mastering the art of tonal music by more or less consciously adhering to an *overall structure*, that of an initial movement based on the *tonic* of the piece—the first degree of the tonality or key—a central one based on the *dominant* or fifth degree, and a final one returning to the tonic [Baggi 2010]. This is what holds a whole piece together, allowing it to avoid a perceived feeling of aimless wandering, as is often the case for pieces of pre-tonal music. And this is similar to other arts that unfold in time, such as movies, or in sequence, such as literary works, in which there is a preparation, a climax, and then a conclusion. This applies to movies, such as *Gone with the Wind*, to large literary masterpieces such as *War and Peace*, to short stories such as the ones by Edgar Allan Poe and Nathaniel Hawthorne, and also to detective stories.

Hence, at least in tonal harmony, what gives the coherence of a piece is its *harmonic structure*, namely, the progression from one assembly of voices to the next, in a "logical" way.[1] This was developed in order to provide a procedure guaranteeing a "sense" of the whole to a composer, the first step of which consists in teaching the rudiments of tonal classical harmony, from which a musician evolves.

8.2 BASS COMPUTERIZED HARMONIZATION (BA-C-H)

Tonal classical harmony is generally taught with a restricted model of music, four-part harmony [Baggi 2010], which puts the maximum emphasis on the harmonic content and much less on melodic, rhythmic, or other musical characteristics. Pieces are strictly in four voices, called from bottom to top *bass*, *tenor*, *alto*, and *soprano*—a terminology that in this context has little or nothing to do with the actual range of the voice or instrument. The tempo is 2/2 or 3/2, indicating that quarter notes have no structural importance but

---

[1] Note that jazz improvisers pay particular attention to "building a climate" and "telling a story."

are treated as passing notes. Most vertical assemblies or chords have three distinct notes, in which case one is doubled, or four distinct notes. Modulations, or changes of key, are restricted to those that are no more than one sharp or one flat away from the original one. Often the voices are in *close position*, meaning that a keyboard player would play the bass with his left hand, while the three upper parts are as close as possible to be played with the right hand.

Proficiency in this art of composing is tested by an exercise, the *realization of the unfigured bass*, in which only the bass of the whole piece is given and the student must construct the three upper parts "by ear." A first step in learning consists of learning the realization of the *figured* bass, where each bass note is accompanied by a figure specifying its harmony, allowing the student to practice *voice-leading*, or how to make the voices flow correctly according to some rules. The latter is not however an exercise to develop a sense of harmony, for which there exists an exercise dealing with *harmonizing the unfigured bass* [Rothgeb 1968], which has been studied for centuries. Clearly, the ability to realize the unfigured bass is the culmination of the learning process.

To this end, there exist booklets with examples of bass lines to be harmonized and realized [Pedron 1925], given as an exercise to students of harmony. Figure 8.2 is such an example.

Hence, the idea was to construct a computer program that passes such an exam, called Bass Computerized Harmonization (BA-C-H) [Baggi 1974], and the result is shown in Figure 8.3. In this figure, the original bass can be recognized with the addition of the upper three voices built by the program. Note that the first chord has the third on the soprano, as specified in Figure 8.2. The quarter note patterns in the bass of bars 5, 7, and 9 could have been imitated in the soprano at bars 6, 8, and 10, and the same applies for patterns of bars 13 and 15 to be copied at 14 and 16, but the program was not capable of doing that. Nevertheless, it respected the rules of voice leading, reproduced progressions as at bars 18–19, identified the modulation to G-major at bars 10–12 and to A-minor at 16, and handled the diminished chord at bar 21, ending with a suspension and the final cadence. Parallel octaves and parallel fifths do not (generally) occur.

From Figure 8.3, it can be appreciated how primitive the display technology was in 1974, as opposed to today's scores produced by any sequence (see Figure 8.7 below). It was obtained from a Calcomp plotter, with a pen used for diagrams and scientific plotting. The program itself ran in a CDC6400 with a memory of 120K 60-bit words, several orders of magnitude less of what is available today on an inexpensive PC or phone. It was written in LISP, and very few arithmetic computations took place; instead, the program had operators to compute notes, intervals, and chords, and recognize melodic patterns in the bass, thus manipulating symbols.

The program did not excel but solved problems such as the one shown above, sometimes well and sometimes with errors, such as jumps of augmented seconds. It was capable of recognizing a standard set of progressions in the bass and harmonizing them, and had some heuristics for the cases it did not know. Tempo was restricted to 2/2 and little attention was paid to the melodic line in the soprano.

8.3 HARMONY MACHINE

The idea behind the Harmony Machine is the inverse function of BA-C-H, in the sense that, if it is possible to realize any bass with a finite set of progressions and patterns, then it should be possible to build a synthesis machine that from a fixed set of options allows

Figure 8.1. Second movement of the *Illiac Suite*. The letters A, B, C, . . . , H refer to the rules in Section 8.1, at the top of p. 134.

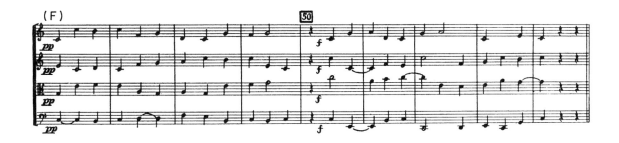

Figure 8.1. (*Continued*)

Figure 8.2. Example of bass to be realized.

Figure 8.3. Realization of the bass of Figure 8.2 by BA-C-H.

composition of the structure of (almost) any piece of music.[2] In the 1970s it became possible for computing amateurs to build simple computer systems at home around an 8-bit processor, such as the Motorola 6800, and this is how the Harmony Machine was built [Baggi 1984].

The basic hardware is shown in Figure 8.4. The processor, an eight-bit 6800 chip, is driven by the clock oscillator that also feeds the Top Octave Generator, which produces 12 notes in the highest register. The program resides in a 2K-byte EEPROM, and 256 bytes of memory serve to store intermediate results. Hence, the processor has the conventional data and address bus, in addition to a "music bus" shown below the dotted line. The Peripheral Interface Adapter connects to the keyboard that selects the progression, to the display indicating the beat and some other messages, and to a switch to select among three speeds or tempos. At the bottom there are plugs to extract each individual voice, and the same outlet allows recharging of the batteries and running from an external power supply.

---

[2] The author thanks Max Mathews for this suggestion.

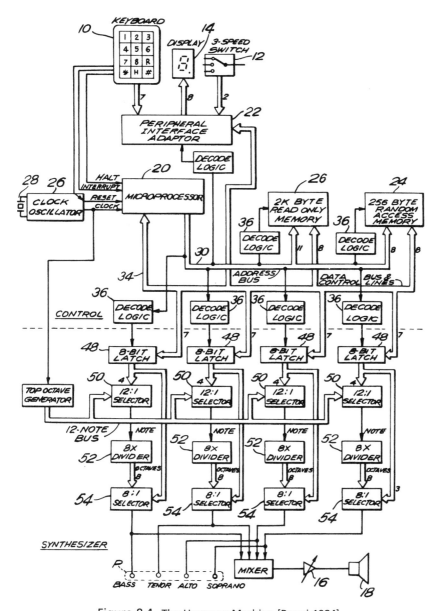

Figure 8.4. The Harmony Machine [Baggi 1984].

Generally, the music is heard through the built-in speaker. The whole is housed in a plastic box measuring $23 \times 18 \times 8$ cm, with the internal board clearly visible. Sockets for wire wrapping have been used.

The music bus is reproduced four times for all four voices. From the top octave generator, each voice is divided eight times, thus making eight octaves available. A note is defined as an eight-bit digit of which the second nibble selects the note, one out of 12, in the top octave, while the first uses three bits to select the octave. Then, four notes are sent at every beat to the data bus by the processor and are played at the speaker.

The operation occurs as follows. On turning on the machine, the display prompts with a dot to indicate readiness: key 1, 2, or 3 can be pressed to select the position of the first chord, with the octave, third, or fifth in the soprano. Then it displays a P to prompt for a progression. The user has 10 choices: the first seven are standard progressions, the eighth is the final cadence, and * and # start a modulation to other keys. The user can push a button at any time to start another progression, while the display acknowledges the command with a dot that gets turned off when the machine enters the new progression, choosing the appropriate moment for the best voice leading.

The current beat is indicated on the one-digit display, allowing some notation of the piece, and if the user does not push a button for 16 beats, or after a modulation that lasts two beats, the machine selects one at random. Likewise, if the four-part music gets too high or too low in pitch, the machine corrects the piece by selecting a progression leading to the middle register. Two extra keys allow further control: H halts the current chord, so that the user can step through a progression chord by chord, while R resets the whole.

Individual progressions have been chosen that reflect those found in harmony exercises. The tempo is strictly 2/2 and there are only whole and half notes and no quarters. The progressions are, as selected from the keyboard:

1: Circle of fifths, the bass moves up a fourth and down a fifth.
2: The bass moves up a fourth and down a third.
3: The bass moves down a third and up a second.
4: The bass is tied across the bar and moves up a second.
5: The bass is tied across the bar and moves down a second.

(Note that odd-numbered progressions make the music go down in pitch, while even-numbered ones make it go up.)

6: The bass ascends stepwise.
7: The bass descends stepwise.

   (In these cases, the music neither ascends nor descends.)

8: Final cadence, lasting three measures including the final rest.
*: Two-bar pattern modulating to the key distant one flat (e.g., from C to F, from A to D)
#: Two-bar pattern modulating to the key distant one sharp (e.g., from C to G, from E-flat to B-flat)

The novelty of this approach as compared with many of its time is that there are *no stored note patterns* in the program. Every note of every progression is computed instantly depending on the previous chord, on voice-leading rules and progressions. Hence, in theory, an infinite number of pieces can be composed and played in real time.

The program has been written in machine language for the 6800, that is, with instructions expressed with one, two, or three hexadecimal bytes. It may seem difficult to see that all these machine-language routines implement *symbol manipulation*: in other words, operators perform not arithmetic operations but computation of chords and notes, in the proper octave. Since the machine is capable of operating in any key after it has started, these operators are capable of performing in any key, which—once more—is constantly computed and not simply stored.

This was not meant to be a machine to revolutionize the state of the art. Today, programming on a much smaller notebook or smartphone would allow the realization of an algorithm far more sophisticated than the one used in the 2k PROM. However, it remains an example that it is possible, no matter the limitations of the hardware, to write systems that use symbols to represent and play music.

8.4 NEURSWING, AN AUTOMATIC JAZZ RHYTHM SECTION BUILT WITH NEURAL NETS

NeurSwing [Baggi 1992] is an automatic jazz rhythm section, molded as *neural nets*, which accepts as input the *harmonic grid* of a piece and produces as output the same piece played on piano, bass, and drums accompanying a soloist, such as a singer, or a melodic instrument player, for example, a saxophone or trumpet player. The meter is 4/4 and the tempo can be specified between 1 and 512 beats per minute—more realistically, 80–300. The output is available in real time through the speakers of a stereo set and the sound is produced by a MIDI synthesizers. Style knobs are available to the user to control the simulated rhythm section, as well as controls such as pause and stop.

Such programs have been available well before the existence of NeurSwing; however, the purpose in this case was not to create a commercial product but to simulate the way of thinking of a jazz rhythm section that, unlike existing programs, does not simply reproduce the input, but interprets and modifies it in order to push the soloist into exploring new improvisational paths.

Artificial neural nets were used not because of their learning ability, but because it was easy to express complex relations with this paradigm. Generally, in computer science, the existence of a mathematical-physical model, such as Newton's mechanics or Maxwell's electromagnetic set of equations, allows the realization of a program which is *isomorphic to the model*. For those cases in which only expert solutions based on practice are available, as for the repair of engines, knowledge engineers try to capture this practice in the form of *rule-based systems*. And for those cases for which outputs are known only to be produced by a given input, neural nets can be *trained* with an existing set of examples, with the hope that they would behave accordingly for unknown cases. However, none of that was necessary here, since the nets needed no training and the relationships were known.

Figure 8.5 shows the basic scheme of NeurSwing. The bottom neural net is a set of neurons representing nets of possible harmonic substitutions of input harmony, used to determine what will be played by piano, bass, and drums. The top net is an analogic relationship among different quantities determined by the setting of three style knobs that bias the random choice at run time.

The three knobs are meant to represent the stylistic quantities of *hot-cool, consonant/dissonant, as-is/free modifications*. From their default value at 0.5, meaning neutrality and the same probability of random choices, the knobs act as follows. The first one favors, when increased, a more present rhythm section, *hot*, to push the soloist toward a more expressionist style; while *cool* means a kind of laying back, softer tones, more transparent patterns, similar to relaxing. The second, as the name says, use definitions of tonal classical music, where dissonance implies choice of harmonic patterns with extra dissonant notes and consonance means the opposite. The third knob, which when turned high embodies what has been called *as-is-ness*, reduces alternate choices, forcing the music to adhere to the input, "as-is," reproducing the progression of the piece from the input.

As a result, no two repetitions of the piece, or *choruses*, are ever the same, since all choices are determined by a random number generator with variable seed. Extra controls

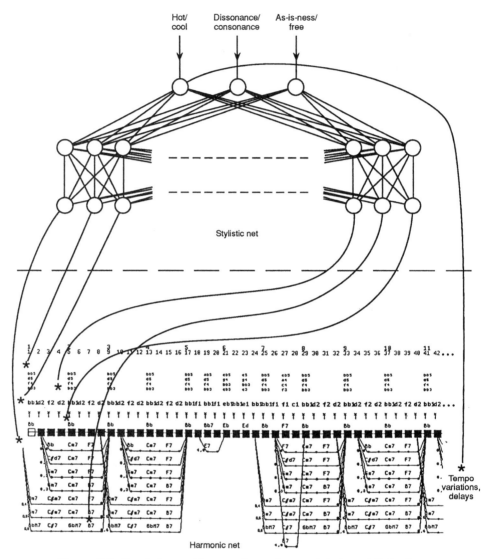

Figure 8.5. NeurSwing and its neural nets: harmonic below, stylistic above.

are pause, stop at the end of the chorus, and stop immediately. At start, the user gives the tempo and can select a debugging mode called *as-is*, which plays the input with absolutely no substitution: piano on the first beat and third if needed, bass as arpeggio of the chord, and drums simply marking the beat, which is useful to debug the input. Or the user can skip this and directly enter the chorus or improvisational mode.

The following is the hierarchical order in which the biased random choices are performed.

The first is *harmony*. All elements of the harmonic grid are matched with the known algorithm: matching pattern–matched element–substitution. Hence, for instance, a progression *dominant seventh chord–tonic chord* can be substituted with *tritone on the dominant–tonic*. Especially complex are patterns over several bars, transforming sequences of two equal chords into evolved progressions, as the example of Figure 8.6 below shows.

From harmony, most of the other choices are derived. The advantage of this rhythm section over a human one is that all three instrumentalists are aware of the basic choice and act accordingly. From harmony, the *piano notes* are obtained: these are determined such that their range lies in normal voice-leading for an accompanying jazz pianist. These notes will be played on beats determined by the *piano rhythmic patterns*, such as across two bars, 1-2- - 4l - 2 3 -, with the purpose of constantly creating a *swinging* pattern. Empty beats may receive an extra *appoggiatura*, computed from the next chord a note or a half-note above or below, hence there are four possible choices.

The notes of the bass are computed from the basic harmony, especially on strong beats, and as passing notes on weak beats to simulate a *walking bass*. An *appoggiatura* may be inserted as extra note played on the beat before the note.

The drum set consists of *kick drum*, three *toms*, the *charleston*, one *ride cymbal* one *crash cymbal*, *high hat*—closed, open, and closing—two *cowbells* used to acknowledge a command, such as changing the knob settings and signaling its execution, and *finger snaps* to mark the beginning of the piece with the usual 1-3l1-2-3-4 pattern. The patterns have been adapted from a book on drumming [Gilbert 1970], and there are two basic patterns, one used normally and another in the cool mode. Connecting patterns using the toms may be used at the junction of the eighth measure and sometimes at the fourth in a piece, and at the end to prepare the next chorus.

As mentioned, all choices are made at random. However, the knobs bias the choices as follows.

The hot-cool knob, as it gets turned high, emphasizes dense piano patterns (the piano plays on most beats of the measure), more piano appoggiaturas, a flatted fifth in dominant seventh chords somewhat more often, the piano playing louder, the walking bass tending to rise in pitch, more bass appoggiaturas, denser drums patterns and more drums fill-ins favored, and more crash cymbal. This also tends to increase the loudness of bass and drums, to let the bass play up to 3/16th ahead of the beat and the piano 1/8 ahead as if to "pull" the beat, and to accelerate the overall tempo by up to 5% per chorus. Obviously, turning it down has the reverse effect. This is just one example of the use of the system to reflect the vision of its user—in fact, in some "cool" rhythm sections of the early fifties, drummers lag behind the beat, which is the reverse of the above.

The dissonance/consonance knob favors more dissonant harmonic patterns as substitutes, a flatted fifth in the dominant seventh chord, no root position for piano chords, and half steps in piano and bass appoggiaturas. Fortunately, this criterion is easy to implement and test, thanks to the practice of tonal classical music. As should be the case in a contemporary jazz rhythm section, however, a certain quantity of dissonance is always present.

The as-is-ness/change, of no real stylistic importance, is meant as an aid to the user to learn the basic input harmony of a piece, elaborated only rhythmically and with little or no harmonic substitutions. Hence the knob emphasizes given harmony, no flatted fifths, piano root position, bass playing notes of the chord, no bass nor piano appoggiaturas, a single neutral drum pattern with no fill-ins, and no crash cymbal. Hence a user can learn the piece without the intricacies of substitutions and elaborated patterns, turning down the knob as needed.

There are therefore several options to modify the operation of the rhythm section at various levels. The most immediate is the setting of the knobs, allowing different styles to be tried; the setting of the knobs is not orthogonal. Second, the probability functions associated with each knob and choice, which are simply linear, could be easily modified to allow selected and more focused choices. Third, the patterns for harmony, piano, drum patterns, and so on are in external tables, and as long as some programming conventions are respected, they could easily be modified.

A few words about the realization are to be noted. For the software, the system has been initially implemented with the Rochester Connectionist Simulator, a collection of routines in C to simulate neurons and their connections, and all routines have been written in the C language, originally developed on a SUN Sparcstation and later ported under UNIX System V running on PCs such as SCO and Interactive UNIX. The neural nets, later implemented as C routines, operate in real time and use a specially developed UNIX driver for the MIDI interface, namely, the MPU-IPC, which is similar to the MPU 401 with added counters and real-time interrupts. The driver has been designed specifically for this project and allows use of standard UNIX system calls such as *open*, *write*, *read*, and *ioctl*, to control operation of the card. Three "tracks" of the MIDI interface have been used for piano, bass, and drums, driven in the Conductor mode. This means that the interface not only receives the MIDI data to turn a note on and off at a given loudness, but it also accepts tempo commands.

As for the hardware, it all ran on a PC with a 386 and 486 processor with an AT bus. Computation of a complete piece is made in a couple of seconds and the MIDI data are sent in real time to a Kurzweil 250RMX digital synthesizer, of which three MIDI channels have been set to play as piano, bass, and drums. Today this can be made with a standard MIDI card, provided that routines that simulate the timing of the MPU-IPC hardware are used.

Next follows an example of the operation of the system, in which a didactical example is used. Figure 8.6a is an extremely simple harmonic grid, eight bars with a single C-major chord, which is a mode similar to *as-is* and could represent the music shown in Figure 8.6b.

It is not necessary to be proficient in music reading to determine that this is an extremely boring piece. However, Figure 8.7 is what NeurSwing is capable of making from it. Even though the impression of swing, which cannot be annotated, requires this output to be heard rather than read, the variety in all instruments can be appreciated, and this contributes to making the input unrecognizable—including the two-bar snaps at the beginning; the use of a full drum set with high-hat, bass drum, snare, three toms, two ride cymbals, and two cow bells; and piano and bass *appoggiatura*s.

Thus, the system acts as benchmark to experiment with various models of swing, at several levels: first, by acting on the *controls*; then, by *biasing the choices*; then, by introducing at the code level *alternative models* for *harmonic*, *rhythmic*, and *melodic choices*; and finally, by *encoding different* and *non-linear choice functions*.

Figure 8.6a. A trivial harmonic grid.

Figure 8.6b. A musical rendition of the grid of Figure 8.6a.

Figure 8.7. One possible rendition of the pattern of Figure 8.6 by NeurSwing.

8.5 THE PAUL GLASS SYSTEM

Paul Glass is a Swiss-American composer who resides near Lugano, Southern Switzerland, especially appreciated for movie music. During his experiments in dodecaphony, he encountered the following problem: is it possible to create a sequence of 84 notes such that it is at the same time a set of 12 diatonic scales and of seven dodecaphonic series?

Figure 8.8 indicates how that works. The diatonic scales are indicated below with their tonic, and the dodecaphonic series with numbers above. Suppose starting with C-major; hence to complete the series the notes C♯, D♯, F♯, G♯, and A♯ are needed. The three keys containing such notes are B, C♯, and F♯, so let us choose B and complete the series. But then there are two notes that spill over the 12-note sequence, E and B. Therefore, the third diatonic scale that starts from the third note of the second dodecaphonic series must *not* contain them, as is the case of C♯. Hence, one has now nine notes of the series, and to complete it one needs D, G, and A. A key containing them is B♭, which therefore spills over in the next series with notes B♭, C, E♭, and F. Hence, to continue, one needs a key that does not contain these notes, and such a key is D. To complete the series, only G♯ is missing, contained, for example, in the key of A. In this way one finds the next key, and by trial and error it is possible to complete the whole, and as in the figure the following *series of keys* is obtained:

(1)   C – B – C♯ – B♭ – D – A – E♭ – A♭ – E – G – F – F♯

This particular series has the property of being *invariant under retrogression*, that is, it sounds the same if played from end to beginning, and also it *contains all intervals*, one to six semitones, from one note to the next, exactly twice because of its *symmetry*. It allows

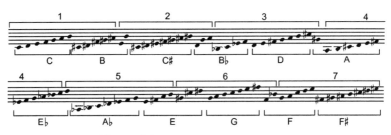

Figure 8.8. A sequence by Paul Glass.

a composition with the least possible reference to diatonic intervals and tonal centers. Notice also that its mirror-like *inversion* has the same properties:

(2)   C – C♯ – B – D – Bi♭ – D♯ – A – E – A♭ – F – G – G♭

Less obvious is that the chromatic scale also satisfies the constraints of the Glass method:

(3)   C – C♯ – D – D♯ – E – F – F♯ – G – G♯ – A – A♯ – B

but has the disadvantage of containing only one single interval from note to note, a semitone.

Even less obvious is the fact that, if at a given point a choice among different keys is possible, some of these choices prevent completion of the sequence. For instance, for the sequence of Figure 8.8, if F♯ had been chosen for the second key, the process would stop, unless one steps back and chooses B or C♯, a process that in computer jargon is called *backtracking*.

To compose, the rules of dodecaphony apply in the sense of giving freedom of choice of the note within every segment that can be found in the picture. The number of notes contained in each segment can be seen from Figure 8.8 to be

7, 5, 2, 7, 3, 4, 7, 1, 6, 6, 1, 7, 4, 3, 7, 2, 5, 7

allowing any ordering of the notes within a segment, but no repetition of the same note before all others have been exhausted.

Hence the question arises: are there other sequences of this kind, and if so, what are they and how many are there? And what are their properties, such as *symmetry* and *intervals*?

To answer such questions, in 1985 this author wrote a program in the language LISP defining operators such as compute the keys with given notes and compute the keys without given notes, from the knowledge of the chromatic key, intervals, and the like. The main algorithm is a loop that finds all 12 diatonic keys and thus the sequence that satisfies the constraints of all seven dodecaphonic series, and then all possible sequences. The unexpected result was the following:

- There are exactly 1,200 Glass sequences and their inversions, hence a total of 2,400.
- Of these, 144 are symmetric.
- Of the 2,400, some 420 contain all intervals.

Hence the results are multiples of 2, 3, 5, and 7, which may suggest a geometric interpretation of the method. The program has been tested not only with the major mode, but also with other modes, including some with a number of notes different from seven, and this has produced the following result:

- Glass sequences exist only for the Greek modes of Ionian, Dorian, Phrygian, Lydian, Mixolydian, Aeolian, and Locrian and are always the same independent of the mode.
- Altered modes such as the harmonic minor or the ascending melodic minor do not yield any solution (obtained with the descending melodic minor since it is the same at the Aeolian), and the same is true for oriental modes with seven notes, and for modes with a number of notes different from seven, as is to be expected.

Hence, Glass sequences are strictly related to the properties of the diatonic scale, namely, of scales with one group of two tones and one of three, and of the chromatic scale in the tempered system. The Paul Glass method has been used successfully in his own compositions, and the list indicates the piece and also the sequence used, according to the classification of the program:

- *Fuchs-Variationen* for cello solo, 1983, Series no. 866 (Sequence (12))
- Concerto per pianoforte estemporaneo e orchestra, 1982, Series no. 1398 (11)
- *5 Klavierstücke* (5 Piano Pieces), 1984, Series no. 1398
- "The Late Nancy Irving," for Fox Mystery Theater, 1984, Series no. 866
- *Pianto della Madonna*, words by Jacopone da Todi, 1986, Series no. 866
- *Deh, spiriti miei, quando mi vedete*, words by Guido Cavalcanti, 1987, Series no. 683
- String Quartet No. 1, 1988, Series no. 783
- *Lamento dell'acqua*, 1990, Series no. 763
- Sinfonia No. 4, 1992, Series no. 994
- *"Quan shi qu,"* 1994, Series no. 683.

The existence of Glass sequences may have important consequences for a composer of dodecaphonic music, because it favors a definition and concatenation of dodecaphonic sequences that allow a homogeneous transition and development, thus guaranteeing control over the overall structure of a piece—something akin to Schenker's finding for tonality. Glass has composed pieces that exhibit, for an unsophisticated listener, the same emotion, expectations, and development generally perceived in tonal music and not in atonal music, even though it clearly does not sound quite tonal. The disadvantage may lie in the constraints imposed on the composer, the possible absence of strong contrasts because of the homogeneity of the music—there is even something that looks like a cadence between the seventh and eight diatonic key in sequence (1). However, the project has a strong theoretical interest and demonstrates that the use of the computer and symbolic programming is not restricted to research but can give useful and enjoyable solutions to music problems.

8.6 A PROGRAM THAT FINDS NOTES AND TYPE OF A CHORD AND PLAYS IT

It is relatively easy to use the algorithm of Chord notation, as found in jazz grids, fakebooks, and guitar charts, to build a program to identify the notes of a chord from its label. The simple program included in Baggi [2010] does the following:

- It identifies the first MIDI card at address 0, which generally works, prints a description of it, and plays middle C.
- It then prompts with a ? and accepts your input: if you type the name of a chord, it will identify its notes and play it; if you type a carriage return, it replays it; if you type something syntactically incorrect, it complains and prompts again.
- If there is more than one MIDI device, the user is allowed to type S, and then all MIDI cards are identified and the user can select one.

Activation of the program will open a black DOS window running within. The following is the transcript of a typical session, from my PC with its default MIDI (the program output appears in Courier):

```
Number of MIDI devices found: 3, Device 0 taken as default.
Midi device 0 OK, note sent, everything OK.
Man id: 125, Prod Id: 70, Driver Version: 4.0
Product name: AudioPCI MIDI Synth, synthesizer.
Number of voices: 31, Number of simultaneous notes: 31, Channel
Mask: ffff
Supports separate left and right volume control.
Supports volume control.

? Cm7
c-eb-g-bb, 4 notes, minor chord.
? Ab
ab-c-eb, 3 notes, major chord
? E9
e-g#-b-d-f#, 5 notes, dominant seventh chord.
?
e-g#-b-d-f#, 5 notes, dominant seventh chord.
? B0
b-d-f-a, 4 notes, half-diminished chord.
? <control-C>
```

Symbols acceptable to the program are the following:

- Letters A to G, uppercase, to specify the root of the chord, possibly followed by the symbols # or b
- Other letters such as m, d, o, M
- Numbers such as 7, 9, 11, 13, 6, 5
- Characters such as ∧, (,), +, #, -, b, 0

with all of them in the proper sequence, as usual. Examples: D, Am7, G0, C13($\sharp$5), EM9.

If you have more than one MIDI device card in your PC, you can type S instead of a chord. Here is what I get with my three MIDI devices:

```
? S
Checking all Midi Devices

Device 0: resource already allocated,sent,OK.
Man id: 125, Prod Id: 70, Driver Version: 4.0
```

```
Product name: AudioPCI MIDI Synth
synthesizer.
# of voices: 31, # of sim. notes: 31, Channel Mask: ffff
Supports separate left and right volume control.
Supports volume control.

(next)
Device 1: OK,sent,OK.
Man id: 125, Prod Id: 68, Driver Version: 4.0
Product name: AudioPCI MIDI Out
MIDI hardware port.
# of voices: 0, # of sim. notes: 0, Channel Mask: ffff
0: Unknown dwSupport.

(next)
Device 2: OK,sent,OK.
Man id: 1, Prod Id: 10, Driver Version: 4.0
Product name: Roland MPU-401
MIDI hardware port.
# of voices: 0, # of sim. notes: 0, Channel Mask: ffff
0: Unknown dwSupport.

select device: 1
?
b-d-f-a, 4 notes, half-diminished chord.
? <control-C>
```

In this way you can hear how the same chord sounds with different devices.

Due to the volatility of MIDI devices, it is not always easy to reset them and get them to work properly. In case the program starts, but nothing or a strange instrument is heard, try to turn your computer off and then on, as this resets all MIDI synthesizers.

While the chord parser has worked for years in the program described in Section 8.4 and correctly finds notes from a harmonic grid, no guarantee is made to the accuracy of its results in a general context, and inputs are not protected.

8.7 SUMMARY OF PROJECTS

- *"Realization of the Unfigured Bass"* [Baggi 1974]: This is a problem of four-part harmony in which the bass is given and the task is to "realize" three upper voices; this program solved the exercises of a classical textbook.

- *"Common Music,"* a set of function to model some aspects of music theory to identify the key from the signature; to find the degree of a note, the interval between two notes in a given key, all permutations of a list of note, and the fundamental of a chord and its type; and to transpose a melody from one key to another [Baggi 1988].

- *Harmony Machine* [Baggi 1984], a portable music instrument built around an eight-bit processor with a 2kB program, 265 bytes of memory, built-in four-voice synthesizer, telephone-like keyboard, and switches. It allows composition and play in real time of pieces in four-part harmony, by selecting typical progressions: five periodical, two scales, two modulations, and a final cadence. Written in 6800 machine language, with the techniques of LISP.

- *NeurSwing* [Baggi 1992], a system that, given a harmonic grid like the one of Figure 8.6a, computes in real time what piano, bass, and drums play. The result is different at each repetition, and there is "analogic" control of the style and also chord substitution as jazz players do. Realized with neural nets in the language C but with LISP techniques, and played by a MIDI synthesizer.
- *Chords*, the program that given a chord label identifies its notes and type, described in Section 8.6. Written for Visual C++6.0 with the techniques of LISP included in a book on jazz structures [Baggi 2010].

8.8 CONCLUSIONS

Independently of their merit, these projects represent the effort to model some aspects of music with symbols and symbolic programming. All of them have an indirect relationship to IEEE 1599 and could actually be realized with the technology of IEEE 1599, since this represents a happy union of binary formats for, for example, audio and a symbolic language such as XML. No doubt future projects will evolve from this technology, as described in the preceding chapter.

REFERENCES

Baggi, D. 1974. "Realization of the Unfigured Bass by Digital Computer." Ph.D. thesis, University of California, Berkeley.

Baggi, D. 1984. Harmony Machine. U.S. Patent 4,468,998.

Baggi, D. 1988. "*Common Music, System of Common LISP Functions to Compute Keys, Intervals and Chords.*" Notes for CS283, Artificial Intelligence, University of California, Berkeley.

Baggi, D.L. 1992. "NeurSwing: An Intelligent Workbench for the Investigation of Swing in Jazz." In *Readings in Computer Generated Music*, ed. D. Baggi. IEEE CS Press.

Baggi, D. 2010. *An Almost Algorithmic Model of Music Theory.* ReadyNotes, IEEE CS Press. Available at http://www.computer.org/portal/web/store?product_id=RN0000014&category_id=Ready Notes, with linked sound and musical examples.

Gilbert, D. 1970. *Learn to Play the Alfred Way: Drum Set: Everything You Need to Know to Play the Drum Set.* [S.I.]: Alfred.

Haydn, J. *Giuoco Filarmonico, ossia maniera facile per comporre minuetti*, G. Ricordi & C., Milan, Italy, N. 108202.

Hiller, L.A., and Isaacson, L.M. 1959. *Experimental Music: Composition with an Electronic Computer.* New York: McGraw-Hill.

Mozart, W.A. Musikalisches Würfelspiel, *K.Anh. 294d*, Mainz, Schott's Söhne, Edition 4474.

Pedron, C. 1925. *Nuova serie di esercizi per lo studio progressivo del basso senza numeri*, n. 14847. Milan, Italy: Carish SA.

Rothgeb, J.E. 1968. "Harmonizing the Unfigured Bass: A Computational Study." Ph.D. thesis, Yale University.

APPENDIX A. BRIEF HISTORY OF IEEE 1599 STANDARD, AND ACKNOWLEDGMENTS

The initial Project Authorisation Request was accepted by the IEEE SA (http://standards.ieee.org) in 2001, and the Standards Activity Board of the Computer Society, CS SAB, became the project sponsor. It created a site describing the project (http://www.computer.org → communities → Standards Activities → SAB Sponsored Projects → Musical Applications Using XML) in 2004 (see also http://www.lim.dico.unimi.it).

An IEEE CS Conference dedicated to the project and its proposals took place in Milan in September 2002 (see the *Proceedings of the First International Conference MAX 2002: Musical Applications Using XML*, IEEE CS, Milan, Italy, September 19–20, 2002).

The abstract for a project proposal was accepted by the global fund Intelligent Manufacturing Systems (IMS) (www.ims.org) in 2002 and a preliminary project was accepted for financing by the Swiss Commission for Innovative Technology (CTI) (http://www.bbt.admin.ch/kti/index.html?lang=en) in 2004.

A first article dedicated to the standard was published in *IEEE Computer* in 2005 (see references to Chapter 1), and since then dozens of publications, lectures, and invited lectures at conferences followed.

A formal project proposal was accepted by IMS in 2005 and by the CTI in 2006 to realize the standard and applications, together with the Radiotelevisione della Svizzera Italiana (http://www.rsi.ch) and the festival Jazz Ascona: New Orleans and Classics (http://www.jazzascona.ch). The Swiss government financed the Laboratory of Musical Informatics of the University of Milan, Italy, the only specialists worldwide, its faculty, and its doctoral candidates.

The draft of the standard was approved by the New Standards Committee of the IEEE SA on June 12.

The international conference Symposium on Music, Mathematics and Multimedia took place in Lugano on October 8–10, 2008, financed by the Swiss University of Applied Sciences of Southern Switzerland, by the University of Milan, Italy, and by the City of Lugano. IEEE CS proceedings were published, which formed the basis of a special issue of the *Journal of Multimedia*, February 2009, volume 4, number 1. A special award was granted for the completion of the project at the IMS Meeting in Geneva on November 9–10, 2010.

Music Navigation with Symbols and Layers: Toward Content Browsing with IEEE 1599 XML Encoding, First Edition. Edited by Denis L. Baggi and Goffredo M. Haus.
© 2013 the IEEE Computer Society. Published 2013 by John Wiley & Sons, Inc.

APPENDIX B. IEEE DOCUMENT-TYPE DEFINITIONS (DTDs)

```
<?xml version="1.0" encoding="UTF-8"?>

<!--
 File name:          ieee1599.dtd
 Version:            1.0
 Creation date:      25/02/2007
 Last update:        08/04/2007

 Description
 IEEE 1599 format is an XML-based language aimed at a
comprehensive description of music and music-related contents.
 It has been designed in response to IEEE Recommended Practice
for Definition of a Commonly Acceptable Musical Application using
the XML Language (IEEE P1599).

-->

<!--
===================================================================
======================-->

<!-- Import of external DTDs -->

<!ENTITY % svg
 PUBLIC "-//W3C//DTD SVG 1.1//EN"
 "http://www.w3.org/Graphics/SVG/1.1/DTD/svg11.dtd">
%svg;

<!ENTITY % ChannelRequired "#REQUIRED">
<!ENTITY % mididtd
 PUBLIC          "-//MIDI Manufacturers Association//DTD MIDIEvents
1.0//EN"
 "http://www.midi.org/dtds/MIDIEvents10.dtd">
%mididtd;
```

Music Navigation with Symbols and Layers: Toward Content Browsing with IEEE 1599 XML Encoding,
First Edition. Edited by Denis L. Baggi and Goffredo M. Haus.
© 2013 the IEEE Computer Society. Published 2013 by John Wiley & Sons, Inc.

```
<!--
=====================================================================
=====================-->

<!-- Common attributes parameter entities -->

<!ENTITY % spine_ref
        "event_ref IDREF #REQUIRED">

<!ENTITY % spine_start_end_ref
        "start_event_ref IDREF #REQUIRED
    end_event_ref IDREF #REQUIRED">

<!ENTITY % accidental
        "(none | double_flat | flat_and_a_half | flat | demiflat |
natural | demisharp | sharp | sharp_and_a_half | double_sharp)">

<!ENTITY % formats
        "(application_excel | application_mac-binhex40 |
application_msword | application_octet-stream | application_pdf |
application_x-director | application_x-gzip | application_
x-javascript | application_x-macbinary | application_x-pn-
realaudio | application_x-shockwave_flash | application_x-tar |
application_zip | audio_aiff | audio_avi | audio_mp3 |
audio_mpeg | audio_mpeg3 | audio_mpg | audio_wav | audio_x_aiff |
audio_x_midi | audio_x_wav | audio_x-mp3 | audio_x-mpeg |
audio_x-mpeg3 | audio_x-mpegaudio | audio_x-mpg |
audio_x-ms-wma | image_avi | image_bmp | image_x-bmp |
image_x-bitmap | image_x-xbitmap | image_x-win-bitmap |
image_x-windows-bmp | image_ms-bmp | image_x-ms-bmp |
application_bmp | application_x-bmp | application_x-win-bitmap |
application_preview | image_gif | image_jpeg | image_pict |
image_png | application_png | application_x-png | image_tiff |
text_html | text_plain_application_postscript | video_avi |
video_mpeg | video_msvideo | video_quicktime | video_x-msvideo |
video_x-ms-wmv | video_x-qtc | video_xmpg2)">

<!-- Common Elements -->

<!ELEMENT rights EMPTY>
<!ATTLIST rights
 file_name CDATA #REQUIRED>

<!--
=====================================================================
=====================-->

<!-- Root Element -->

<!ELEMENT ieee1599 (general, logic, structural?, notational?,
performance?, audio?)>
<!ATTLIST ieee1599
```

```
                    version CDATA #REQUIRED
                    creator CDATA #IMPLIED>


<!--
================================================================
======================-->


<!-- General Layer -->

<!ELEMENT general (description, related_files?, analog_media?,
notes?)>

<!ELEMENT description (main_title, author*, other_title*,
number?, work_title?, work_number?, date*, genres?)>

<!ELEMENT main_title (#PCDATA)>

<!ELEMENT author (#PCDATA)>
<!ATTLIST author
          type CDATA #IMPLIED>


<!ELEMENT other_title (#PCDATA)>

<!ELEMENT number (#PCDATA)>

<!ELEMENT work_title (#PCDATA)>

<!ELEMENT work_number (#PCDATA)>

<!ELEMENT date (#PCDATA)>
<!ATTLIST date
          type CDATA #IMPLIED>


<!ELEMENT genres (genre+)>

<!ELEMENT genre EMPTY>
<!ATTLIST genre
          name CDATA #REQUIRED
          description CDATA #IMPLIED
          weight CDATA #IMPLIED>

<!ELEMENT related_files (related_file+)>

<!ELEMENT related_file EMPTY>
<!ATTLIST related_file
          file_name CDATA #REQUIRED
          file_format %formats; #REQUIRED
          encoding_format %formats; #REQUIRED
          start_event_ref IDREF #IMPLIED
          end_event_ref IDREF #IMPLIED
          description CDATA #IMPLIED
```

```
            copyright CDATA #IMPLIED
            notes CDATA #IMPLIED>


<!ELEMENT analog_media (analog_medium+)>


<!ELEMENT analog_medium EMPTY>
<!ATTLIST analog_medium
            description CDATA #REQUIRED
            copyright CDATA #IMPLIED
            notes CDATA #IMPLIED>


<!ELEMENT notes (#PCDATA)>


<!--
=====================================================================
=====================-->


<!-- Logic Layer -->


<!ELEMENT logic (spine, los?, layout?)>


<!-- Spine -->
<!ELEMENT spine (event)+>


<!ELEMENT event EMPTY>
<!ATTLIST event
            id ID #REQUIRED
            timing CDATA "null"
            hpos CDATA "null">


<!ELEMENT los (agogics*, text_field*, metronomic_indication*,
staff_list, part+, horizontal_symbols?, ornaments?, lyrics*)>


<!ELEMENT agogics (#PCDATA)>
<!ATTLIST agogics
            bracketed (no | yes) #IMPLIED
            %spine_ref;>


<!ELEMENT text_field (#PCDATA)>
<!ATTLIST text_field
            extension_line_to IDREF #IMPLIED
            extension_line_shape (normal | dotted | dashed) #IMPLIED
            %spine_ref;>


<!ELEMENT metronomic_indication EMPTY>
<!ATTLIST metronomic_indication
            num CDATA #REQUIRED
            den CDATA #REQUIRED
            dots CDATA #IMPLIED
            value CDATA #REQUIRED
            %spine_ref;>
```

```
<!ELEMENT staff_list (brackets | staff)+>

<!ELEMENT brackets EMPTY>
<!ATTLIST brackets
        marker (start_of_staff_group | end_of_staff_group)
#REQUIRED
        group_number CDATA #REQUIRED
        shape (square | rounded_square | brace | vertical_bar |
none) #REQUIRED>

<!ELEMENT staff (clef | ( key_signature | custom_key_signature) |
time_signature | barline | tablature_tuning)*>
<!ATTLIST staff
        id ID #REQUIRED
        line_number CDATA "5"
        ossia (yes | no) "no"
        tablature (none | french | german | italian) #IMPLIED>

<!ELEMENT clef EMPTY>
<!ATTLIST clef
        shape (G | F | C | gregorian_F | gregorian_C |
percussion | doubleG | tabguitar) #REQUIRED
        staff_step CDATA #REQUIRED
        octave_num (0 | 8 | -8 | 15 | -15) "0"
        %spine_ref;>

<!ELEMENT key_signature (sharp_num | flat_num) >
<!ATTLIST key_signature
        %spine_ref;>

<!ELEMENT sharp_num EMPTY>
<!ATTLIST sharp_num
        number (0 | 1 | 2 | 3 | 4 | 5 | 6 | 7) #REQUIRED>

<!ELEMENT flat_num EMPTY>
<!ATTLIST flat_num
        number (0 | 1 | 2 | 3 | 4 | 5 | 6 | 7) #REQUIRED>

<!ELEMENT custom_key_signature (key_accidental)+>
<!ATTLIST custom_key_signature
        %spine_ref;>

<!ELEMENT key_accidental EMPTY>
<!ATTLIST key_accidental
        step (A | B | C | D | E | F | G) #REQUIRED
        accidental %accidental; "none">

<!ELEMENT time_signature (time_indication)+>
<!ATTLIST time_signature
        visible (yes | no) "yes"
        %spine_ref;>
```

```
<!ELEMENT time_indication EMPTY>
<!ATTLIST time_indication
        num CDATA #REQUIRED
        den CDATA #IMPLIED
        abbreviation (yes | no) "no"
        vtu_amount CDATA #IMPLIED>


<!ELEMENT barline EMPTY>
<!ATTLIST barline
        style (dashed | double | final | invisible | standard |
medium | short) #REQUIRED
        extension (single_staff | staff_group | all_staves |
mensurstrich) #REQUIRED
        %spine_ref;>


<!ELEMENT tablature_tuning (string*)>
<!ATTLIST tablature_tuning
        type (D | E | G | A | baroque | flat_french | other)
#IMPLIED>


<!ELEMENT string EMPTY>
<!ATTLIST string
        string_number CDATA #REQUIRED
        string_pitch (A | B | C | D | E | F | G) #REQUIRED
        string_accidental %accidental; #IMPLIED
        string_octave CDATA #REQUIRED>


<!ELEMENT part (voice_list, measure+)>
<!ATTLIST part
        id ID #REQUIRED
        performers_number CDATA "unknown"
    transposition_pitch (A | B | C | D | E | F | G) #IMPLIED
    transposition_accidental %accidental; #IMPLIED
        octave_offset CDATA #IMPLIED>


<!ELEMENT voice_list (voice_item+)>


<!ELEMENT voice_item EMPTY>
<!ATTLIST voice_item
        id ID #REQUIRED
        staff_ref IDREF #REQUIRED
        notation_style (normal | rhythmic | slash | blank)
#IMPLIED>


<!ELEMENT measure (voice+ | multiple_rest | measure_repeat?)>
<!ATTLIST measure
        number CDATA #REQUIRED
        id ID #IMPLIED
        show_number (yes | no) #IMPLIED
        numbering_style (arabic_numbers | roman_numbers | small_
letters | capital_letters) #IMPLIED>
```

```
<!ELEMENT multiple_rest EMPTY>
<!ATTLIST multiple_rest
        number_of_measures CDATA #REQUIRED
event_ref IDREF #IMPLIED>


<!ELEMENT measure_repeat EMPTY>
<!ATTLIST measure_repeat
        number_of_measures CDATA #REQUIRED
event_ref IDREF #IMPLIED>


<!ELEMENT voice (chord | rest | tablature_symbol | gregorian_
symbol)+>
<!ATTLIST voice
        voice_item_ref IDREF #REQUIRED
        ossia (yes | no) "no">


<!ELEMENT chord (duration, augmentation_dots?, (notehead+ |
repetition), articulation?)>
<!ATTLIST chord
        id ID #IMPLIED
        %spine_ref;
        stem_direction (up | down | none) #IMPLIED
        beam_before (yes | no) "no"
        beam_after (yes | no) "no"
        cue (yes | no) "no"
        tremolo_lines (no | 1 | 2 | 3 | 4 | 5 | 6) #IMPLIED>


<!ELEMENT repetition EMPTY>

<!ELEMENT duration (tuplet_ratio?)>
<!ATTLIST duration
        num CDATA #REQUIRED
        den CDATA #REQUIRED>


<!ELEMENT tuplet_ratio (tuplet_ratio*)>
<!ATTLIST tuplet_ratio
        enter_num CDATA #REQUIRED
        enter_den CDATA #REQUIRED
        enter_dots CDATA #IMPLIED
        in_num CDATA #REQUIRED
        in_den CDATA #REQUIRED
        in_dots CDATA #IMPLIED>


<!ELEMENT rest (duration, augmentation_dots?)>
<!ATTLIST rest
        id CDATA #IMPLIED
        %spine_ref;
        staff_ref IDREF #IMPLIED
        hidden (no | yes) #IMPLIED>


<!ELEMENT tablature_symbol (duration, augmentation_dots?, key+)>
<!ATTLIST tablature_symbol
```

```
                   id ID #IMPLIED
                   %spine_ref;
                   stem_direction (up | down | none) #IMPLIED
                   beam_before (yes | no) "no"
                   beam_after (yes | no) "no">

<!ELEMENT key (tablature_pitch, tablature_articulation?, tie?,
tablature_fingering?)>
<!ATTLIST key
                   id ID #IMPLIED
                   staff_ref IDREF #IMPLIED>

<!ELEMENT tablature_pitch EMPTY>
<!ATTLIST tablature_pitch
                   string_number CDATA #IMPLIED
                   key_number CDATA #REQUIRED>

<!ELEMENT tablature_articulation EMPTY>
<!ATTLIST tablature_articulation
                   shape (cross | tie | other) #REQUIRED>

<!ELEMENT tablature_fingering (#PCDATA)>
<!ATTLIST tablature_fingering
                   shape (number | dot | other) #REQUIRED>

<!ELEMENT gregorian_symbol (notehead+)>
<!ATTLIST gregorian_symbol
                   id ID #IMPLIED
                   neume (punctum | virga | punctum_inclinatum | quilisma |
apostrofa | oriscus | podatus | pes | clivis | flexa | epiphonus
| cephalicus | bistropha | bivirga | trigon | torculus |
porrectus | scandicus | salicus | climacus | tristropha |
trivirga | strophicus | pressus | custos) #REQUIRED
                   inflexion (no | resupinus | flexus) "no"
                   subpunctis (no | praepunctis | subpunctis | subbipunctis
| subtripunctis | subquadripunctis | subquinquipunctis) "no"
                   interpretative_mark (no | vertical_episema | horizontal_
episema | liquescens) "no"
                   mora (yes | no) "no"
                   %spine_ref;>

<!-- Articulation signs -->

<!ELEMENT articulation (normal_accent | staccatissimo | staccato
| strong_accent | tenuto | stopped_note | snap_pizzicato |
natural_harmonic | up_bow | down_bow | open_mute | close_mute |
custom_articulation)*>

<!ELEMENT normal_accent EMPTY>

<!ELEMENT staccatissimo EMPTY>

<!ELEMENT staccato EMPTY>
```

```
<!ELEMENT strong_accent EMPTY>

<!ELEMENT tenuto EMPTY>

<!ELEMENT stopped_note EMPTY>

<!ELEMENT snap_pizzicato EMPTY>

<!ELEMENT natural_harmonic EMPTY>

<!ELEMENT up_bow EMPTY>

<!ELEMENT down_bow EMPTY>

<!ELEMENT open_mute EMPTY>

<!ELEMENT close_mute EMPTY>

<!ELEMENT custom_articulation (svg)>

<!ELEMENT notehead_ref EMPTY>
<!ATTLIST notehead_ref
        %spine_ref;>

<!ELEMENT notehead (pitch, printed_accidentals?, tie?, fingering?)>
<!ATTLIST notehead
 id ID #IMPLIED
 staff_ref IDREF #IMPLIED
 style (normal | harmonic | unpitched | cymbal | parenthesis |
circled | squared) #IMPLIED>

<!ELEMENT pitch EMPTY>
<!ATTLIST pitch
        step (A | B | C | D | E | F | G | none) #REQUIRED
        octave CDATA #REQUIRED
        actual_accidental %accidental; #IMPLIED>

<!ELEMENT printed_accidentals (double_flat | flat_and_a_half | flat
| demiflat | natural | demisharp | sharp | sharp_and_a_half |
double_sharp)+>
<!ATTLIST printed_accidentals
        shape (normal | small | bracketed) "normal">

<!ELEMENT tie EMPTY>

<!ELEMENT fingering EMPTY>
<!ATTLIST fingering
        number (1 | 2 | 3 | 4 | 5) #REQUIRED>

<!ELEMENT double_flat EMPTY>
<!ATTLIST double_flat
        parenthesis (yes | no) "no">
```

```
<!ELEMENT flat_and_a_half EMPTY>
<!ATTLIST flat_and_a_half
        parenthesis (yes | no) "no">


<!ELEMENT flat EMPTY>
<!ATTLIST flat
        parenthesis (yes | no) "no">


<!ELEMENT demiflat EMPTY>
<!ATTLIST demiflat
        parenthesis (yes | no) "no">


<!ELEMENT natural EMPTY>
<!ATTLIST natural
        parenthesis (yes | no) "no">


<!ELEMENT demisharp EMPTY>
<!ATTLIST demisharp
        parenthesis (yes | no) "no">


<!ELEMENT sharp EMPTY>
<!ATTLIST sharp
        parenthesis (yes | no) "no">


<!ELEMENT sharp_and_a_half EMPTY>
<!ATTLIST sharp_and_a_half
        parenthesis (yes | no) "no">


<!ELEMENT double_sharp EMPTY>
<!ATTLIST double_sharp
        parenthesis (yes | no) "no">


<!ELEMENT augmentation_dots EMPTY>
<!ATTLIST augmentation_dots
        number CDATA "1">


<!ELEMENT lyrics (syllable+)>
<!ATTLIST lyrics
        part_ref IDREF #REQUIRED
        voice_ref IDREF #REQUIRED>


<!ELEMENT syllable (#PCDATA)>
<!ATTLIST syllable
        start_event_ref IDREF #REQUIRED
        end_event_ref IDREF #IMPLIED
        hyphen (yes | no) "no">


<!ELEMENT horizontal_symbols (arpeggio | bend | breath_mark |
chord_symbol | dynamic | fermata | glissando | hairpin | octave_
bracket | pedal_start | pedal_end | percussion_beater |
percussion_special | slur | special_beam | tablature_hsymbol |
repeat | coda | segno | fine | multiple_ending | custom_hsymbol)*>
```

```
<!ELEMENT arpeggio (notehead_ref+)>
<!ATTLIST arpeggio
          shape (wavy | line | no_arpeggio) #REQUIRED
          direction (up | down) "down">

<!ELEMENT bend EMPTY>
<!ATTLIST bend
  id ID #IMPLIED
          %spine_ref;
  type (single | double) "single"
          to_pitch (A | B | C | D | E | F | G | up | down)
#REQUIRED
          to_accidental %accidental; #IMPLIED
  to_octave CDATA #IMPLIED>

<!ELEMENT breath_mark EMPTY>
<!ATTLIST breath_mark
          id CDATA #IMPLIED
          type (comma | caesura) #REQUIRED
          staff_ref IDREF #IMPLIED
          %spine_start_end_ref;>

<!ELEMENT chord_symbol (#PCDATA)>
<!ATTLIST chord_symbol
          id CDATA #IMPLIED
          %spine_ref;>

<!ELEMENT dynamic (#PCDATA)>
<!ATTLIST dynamic
          id CDATA #IMPLIED
  extension_line_to IDREF #IMPLIED
  extension_line_shape (normal | dotted | dashed) #IMPLIED
          staff_ref IDREF #IMPLIED
          %spine_ref;>

<!ELEMENT fermata (#PCDATA)>
<!ATTLIST fermata
          id ID #IMPLIED
          %spine_ref;>

<!ELEMENT glissando EMPTY>
<!ATTLIST glissando
  id ID #IMPLIED
          start_event_ref IDREF #REQUIRED
          end_event_ref IDREF #IMPLIED>

<!ELEMENT hairpin EMPTY>
<!ATTLIST hairpin
          id CDATA #IMPLIED
          type (crescendo | diminuendo) #REQUIRED
          staff_ref IDREF #IMPLIED
          %spine_start_end_ref;>
```

```
<!ELEMENT octave_bracket EMPTY>
<!ATTLIST octave_bracket
        id CDATA #IMPLIED
        type (8va | 8vb | 15ma | 15mb) #REQUIRED
        staff_ref IDREF #REQUIRED
        %spine_start_end_ref;>


<!ELEMENT pedal_start EMPTY>
<!ATTLIST pedal_start
        id ID #IMPLIED
        %spine_ref;>


<!ELEMENT pedal_end EMPTY>
<!ATTLIST pedal_end
        id ID #IMPLIED
        %spine_ref;>


<!ELEMENT percussion_beater (#PCDATA)>
<!ATTLIST percussion_beater
 id CDATA #IMPLIED
 type (bow | snare_stick | snare_stick_plastic | spoon_shaped |
guiro | triangle | knitting_needle | hand | hammer | metal_
hammer | wooden_timpani_mallet | light_timpani_mallet | medium_
timpani_mallet | heavy_timpani_mallet | light_vibraphone_mallet |
medium_vibraphone_mallet | heavy_vibraphone_mallet | light_
bassdrum_mallet | medium_bassdrum_mallet | heavy_bassdrum_mallet
 | steel_core_bassdrum_mallet | coin | brush | nails) #REQUIRED
   start_event_ref IDREF #REQUIRED
   end_event_ref IDREF #IMPLIED>


<!ELEMENT percussion_special (#PCDATA)>
<!ATTLIST percussion_special
 id CDATA #IMPLIED
 type (play_on_border | stop_drumhead | muffle_with_harmonics |
muffle | rub | shake) #REQUIRED
   %spine_ref;>


<!ELEMENT slur (svg?)>
<!ATTLIST slur
 id ID #IMPLIED
        %spine_start_end_ref;
        shape (normal | dashed | dotted) "normal"
        bracketed (no | yes) "no">


<!ELEMENT special_beam (notehead_ref+)>
<!ATTLIST special_beam
        id CDATA #IMPLIED
        fanned_from CDATA #IMPLIED
  fanned_to CDATA #IMPLIED>


<!ELEMENT tablature_hsymbol (tablature_element | barre)+>
<!ATTLIST tablature_hsymbol
```

```
            id CDATA #IMPLIED
            %spine_ref;
    string_number CDATA #REQUIRED
    start_fret CDATA #REQUIRED
    fret_number CDATA #REQUIRED>


<!ELEMENT tablature_element EMPTY>
<!ATTLIST tablature_element
            shape (empty_circle | full_circle | cross | rhombus | 1
| 2 | 3 | 4 | T) #REQUIRED
    string_position CDATA #REQUIRED
    fret_position CDATA #REQUIRED>


<!ELEMENT barre EMPTY>
<!ATTLIST barre
            start_string_position CDATA #REQUIRED
  end_string_position CDATA #REQUIRED
  fret_position CDATA #REQUIRED>


<!ELEMENT repeat (repeat_text?, (jump_to, end?)+)>
<!ATTLIST repeat
            id ID #IMPLIED
            %spine_ref;>


<!ELEMENT repeat_text (#PCDATA)>


<!ELEMENT jump_to EMPTY>
<!ATTLIST jump_to
            id ID #IMPLIED
            %spine_ref;>


<!ELEMENT end EMPTY>
<!ATTLIST end
            id CDATA #IMPLIED
            %spine_ref;>


<!ELEMENT segno (#PCDATA)>
<!ATTLIST segno
            id ID #IMPLIED
            %spine_ref;>


<!ELEMENT coda (#PCDATA)>
<!ATTLIST coda
            id ID #IMPLIED
            %spine_ref;>


<!ELEMENT fine (#PCDATA)>
<!ATTLIST fine
            id ID #IMPLIED
            %spine_ref;>
```

```
<!ELEMENT multiple_endings (multiple_ending+)>
<!ATTLIST multiple_ending
        id ID #IMPLIED>
<!ELEMENT multiple_ending EMPTY>
<!ATTLIST multiple_ending
        id ID #IMPLIED
 number CDATA #REQUIRED
 %spine_start_end_ref;
 return_to IDREF #IMPLIED>

<!ELEMENT custom_hsymbol (svg)>
<!ATTLIST custom_hsymbol
 id ID #IMPLIED
        start_event_ref IDREF #REQUIRED
        end_event_ref IDREF #IMPLIED>

<!ELEMENT ornaments (acciaccatura | baroque_acciaccatura |
appoggiatura | baroque_appoggiatura | mordent | tremolo | trill
| turn)*>

<!ELEMENT acciaccatura (chord+)>
<!ATTLIST acciaccatura
 id ID #IMPLIED
        %spine_ref;
        slur (yes | no) "no">

<!ELEMENT baroque_acciaccatura EMPTY>
<!ATTLIST baroque_acciaccatura
 id ID #IMPLIED
        %spine_ref;
        style (vertical_turn | mordent | flatte | tierce_coulee |
slash | backslash) #REQUIRED>

<!ELEMENT appoggiatura (chord+)>
<!ATTLIST appoggiatura
 id ID #IMPLIED
        %spine_ref;
        slur (yes | no) "no">

<!ELEMENT baroque_appoggiatura EMPTY>
<!ATTLIST baroque_appoggiatura
 id ID #IMPLIED
        %spine_ref;
        style (hairpin | plus | slash | backslash | pipe |
double_slur | up_hook | down_hook) #REQUIRED>

<!ELEMENT mordent EMPTY>
<!ATTLIST mordent
 id ID #IMPLIED
        %spine_ref;
        type (upper | lower) "upper"
        length (normal | double) "normal"
```

```
                    accidental %accidental; "none"
                    style (normal | up_hook | down_hook) "normal">

<!ELEMENT tremolo EMPTY>
<!ATTLIST tremolo
 id ID #IMPLIED
 %spine_start_end_ref;
                    tremolo_lines (1 | 2 | 3 | 4 | 5 | 6) #REQUIRED>

<!ELEMENT trill EMPTY>
<!ATTLIST trill
 id ID #IMPLIED
          %spine_ref;
          accidental %accidental; "none"
          style (t | tr | tr- | plus | double_slash | caesura_
double_slash | slur_double_slash | mordent | double_mordent)
#IMPLIED
          start_hook (none | up | down) "none"
          end_hook (none | up | down) "none">

<!ELEMENT turn EMPTY>
<!ATTLIST turn
 id ID #IMPLIED
          %spine_ref;
          type (over | after) #REQUIRED
          style (normal | inverted | cut | vertical) #REQUIRED
          upper_accidental %accidental; "none"
          lower_accidental %accidental; "none">


<!-- Layout -->

<!ELEMENT layout (page+, text_font?, music_font?)>
<!ATTLIST layout
          hpos_per_unit CDATA #REQUIRED
          measurement_unit (centimeters | millimeters | inches |
decimal_inches | points | picas | pixels | twips) #REQUIRED>

<!ELEMENT page ((standard_page_format | custom_page_format),
layout_system*, layout_images*, layout_shapes*)>
<!ATTLIST page
          id CDATA #REQUIRED
          number CDATA #IMPLIED>

<!ELEMENT standard_page_format EMPTY>
<!ATTLIST standard_page_format
 format (a0 | a1 | a2 | a3 | a4 | a5 | a6 | a7 | a8 | b0 | b1 |
b2 | b3 | b4 | b5 | b6 | b7 | b8 | c0 | c1 | c2 | c3 | c4 |
c5 | c6 | c7 | c8 | ansi_a | ansi_b | ansi_c | ansi_d | ansi_e |
arch_a | arch_b | arch_c | arch_e | arch_e1 | quarto | foolscap |
executive | monarch | government_letter | letter | legal |
ledger | tabloid | post | crown | large_post | demy | medium |
royal | elephant | double_demy | quad_demy | statement)
#REQUIRED>
```

```
<!ELEMENT custom_page_format EMPTY>
<!ATTLIST custom_page_format
        width CDATA #REQUIRED
        height CDATA #REQUIRED>


<!ELEMENT layout_system (layout_staff+)>
<!ATTLIST layout_system
        id CDATA #IMPLIED
        upper_left_x CDATA #REQUIRED
        upper_left_y CDATA #REQUIRED
        lower_right_x CDATA #REQUIRED
        lower_right_y CDATA #REQUIRED>


<!ELEMENT layout_staff EMPTY>
<!ATTLIST layout_staff
        id ID #IMPLIED
        staff_ref CDATA #REQUIRED
        vertical_offset CDATA #REQUIRED
 height CDATA #REQUIRED
        show_key_signature (yes | no) "yes"
        show_clef (yes | no) "yes"
        show_time_signature (yes | no) "no"
        ossia (yes | no) "no">


<!ELEMENT layout_images EMPTY>
<!ATTLIST layout_images
 file_name CDATA #REQUIRED
 file_format %formats; #REQUIRED
 encoding_format %formats; #REQUIRED
 horizontal_offset CDATA #REQUIRED
 vertical_offset CDATA #REQUIRED
 description CDATA #IMPLIED
 copyright CDATA #IMPLIED
 notes CDATA #IMPLIED>


<!ELEMENT layout_shapes (svg)>
<!ATTLIST layout_shapes
   horizontal_offset CDATA #REQUIRED
   vertical_offset CDATA #REQUIRED>


<!ELEMENT text_font (font)>


<!ELEMENT music_font (font)>


<!--
=================================================================
====================-->


<!-- Structural Layer -->


<!ELEMENT structural (chord_grid*, analysis*, petri_nets*, mir*)>
```

```
<!-- Chord Grid -->

<!ELEMENT chord_grid (chord_name+)>
<!ATTLIST chord_grid
 id ID #IMPLIED
 author CDATA #IMPLIED
        description CDATA #IMPLIED>

<!ELEMENT chord_name (#PCDATA)>
<!ATTLIST chord_name
        root_id IDREF #REQUIRED>

<!-- Analysis -->

<!ELEMENT analysis (segmentation, relationships?, feature_
object_relationships?)>
<!ATTLIST analysis
 id ID #IMPLIED
 author CDATA #IMPLIED
 description CDATA #IMPLIED>

<!ELEMENT segmentation (segment+)>
<!ATTLIST segmentation
 id ID #IMPLIED
 description CDATA #IMPLIED
 method CDATA #IMPLIED>

<!ELEMENT segment (segment_event+, feature_object*)>
<!ATTLIST segment
 id ID #REQUIRED>

<!ELEMENT segment_event EMPTY>
<!ATTLIST segment_event
 %spine_ref;>

<!ENTITY % added_feature_object_classes "">

<!ELEMENT feature_object (simple_description
 %added_feature_object_classes;)>
<!ATTLIST feature_object
 id ID #IMPLIED
 name CDATA #REQUIRED>

<!ELEMENT simple_description (#PCDATA)>

<!ELEMENT relationships (relationship+)>

<!ELEMENT relationship EMPTY>
<!ATTLIST relationship
 id ID #REQUIRED
 description CDATA #IMPLIED
 segment_a_ref IDREF #REQUIRED
```

```
 segment_b_ref IDREF #REQUIRED
 feature_object_a_ref IDREF #IMPLIED
 feature_object_b_ref IDREF #IMPLIED
 feature_object_relationship_ref IDREF #IMPLIED>


<!ELEMENT feature_object_relationships (feature_object_
relationship+)>


<!ELEMENT feature_object_relationship (ver_rule)>
<!ATTLIST feature_object_relationship
  id ID #REQUIRED>


<!ELEMENT ver_rule (#PCDATA)>


<!-- Petri Nets -->


<!ELEMENT petri_nets (petri_net+)>


<!ELEMENT petri_net (place | transition)+>
<!ATTLIST petri_net
        id ID #IMPLIED
 author CDATA #IMPLIED
        description CDATA #IMPLIED
 file_name CDATA #REQUIRED>


<!ELEMENT place EMPTY>
<!ATTLIST place
        place_ref CDATA #REQUIRED
        segment_ref IDREF #REQUIRED>


<!ELEMENT transition EMPTY>
<!ATTLIST transition
        transition_ref CDATA #REQUIRED
        feature_object_relationship_ref IDREF #REQUIRED>


<!-- Music Information Retrieval -->


<!ELEMENT mir (mir_model+)>


<!ELEMENT mir_model (mir_object+, mir_morphism*)>
<!ATTLIST mir_model
 id ID #IMPLIED
 description CDATA #IMPLIED
 file_name CDATA #IMPLIED>


<!ELEMENT mir_object (mir_subobject+, mir_feature*)>
<!ATTLIST mir_object
 id ID #IMPLIED
 description CDATA #IMPLIED
 displacement_ref CDATA #IMPLIED>
```

```
<!ELEMENT mir_subobject (mir_feature*)>
<!ATTLIST mir_subobject
 id ID #IMPLIED
 description CDATA #IMPLIED
 displacement_ref CDATA #IMPLIED
 segment_ref IDREF #IMPLIED>

<!ELEMENT mir_feature EMPTY>
<!ATTLIST mir_feature
 id ID #IMPLIED
 description CDATA #IMPLIED
 displacement_ref CDATA #IMPLIED>

<!ELEMENT mir_morphism (mir_feature*)>
<!ATTLIST mir_morphism
 id ID #IMPLIED
 description CDATA #IMPLIED
 domain_ref IDREF #REQUIRED
 codomain_ref IDREF #REQUIRED
 displacement_ref CDATA #IMPLIED>

<!--
========================================================================
======================-->

<!-- Notational Layer -->

<!ELEMENT notational (graphic_instance_group | notation_instance_
group)+>

<!ELEMENT graphic_instance_group (graphic_instance+)>
<!ATTLIST graphic_instance_group
        description CDATA #REQUIRED>

<!ELEMENT graphic_instance (graphic_event+, rights?)>
<!ATTLIST graphic_instance
 description CDATA #IMPLIED
        position_in_group CDATA #REQUIRED
        file_name CDATA #REQUIRED
        file_format %formats; #REQUIRED
        encoding_format %formats; #REQUIRED
        measurement_unit (centimeters | millimeters | inches |
decimal_inches | points | picas | pixels | twips) #REQUIRED>

<!ELEMENT graphic_event EMPTY>
<!ATTLIST graphic_event
        %spine_ref;
        upper_left_x CDATA #REQUIRED
        upper_left_y CDATA #REQUIRED
        lower_right_x CDATA #REQUIRED
        lower_right_y CDATA #REQUIRED
        highlight_color CDATA #IMPLIED
 description CDATA #IMPLIED>
```

```
<!ELEMENT notation_instance_group (notation_instance+)>
<!ATTLIST notation_instance_group
          description CDATA #REQUIRED>

<!ELEMENT notation_instance (notation_event+, rights?)>
<!ATTLIST notation_instance
 description CDATA #IMPLIED
          position_in_group CDATA #REQUIRED
          file_name CDATA #REQUIRED
          format CDATA #REQUIRED
 measurement_unit CDATA #REQUIRED>

<!ELEMENT notation_event EMPTY>
<!ATTLIST notation_event
 %spine_ref;
 start_position CDATA #REQUIRED
 end_position CDATA #REQUIRED
 description CDATA #IMPLIED>

<!--
==================================================================
=====================-->

<!-- Performance Layer -->

<!ELEMENT performance (midi_instance | csound_instance | mpeg4_
instance)+>

<!ELEMENT midi_instance (midi_mapping+, rights?)>
<!ATTLIST midi_instance
 file_name CDATA #REQUIRED
          format (0 | 1 | 2) #REQUIRED>

<!ELEMENT midi_mapping (midi_event_sequence+)>
<!ATTLIST midi_mapping
          part_ref IDREF #REQUIRED
          voice_ref IDREF #IMPLIED
          track CDATA #REQUIRED
          channel CDATA #REQUIRED>

<!ELEMENT midi_event_sequence (midi_event | sys_ex)+ >
<!ATTLIST midi_event_sequence
          division_type        (metrical | timecode) #REQUIRED
          division_value NMTOKEN #REQUIRED
 measurement_unit (ticks | sec) #REQUIRED>

<!ELEMENT midi_event (%MIDIChannelMessage;)*>
<!ATTLIST midi_event
          timing CDATA #REQUIRED
 %spine_ref;>

<!ELEMENT sys_ex (SysEx)>
<!ATTLIST sys_ex
          %spine_ref;>
```

```
<!ELEMENT csound_instance (csound_score | csound_orchestra)+>

<!ELEMENT csound_score (csound_spine_event+, rights?)>
<!ATTLIST csound_score
        file_name CDATA #REQUIRED>


<!ELEMENT csound_spine_event EMPTY>
<!ATTLIST csound_spine_event
        line_number CDATA #REQUIRED
        %spine_ref;>


<!ELEMENT csound_orchestra (csound_instrument_mapping*, rights?)>
<!ATTLIST csound_orchestra
        file_name CDATA #REQUIRED>


<!ELEMENT csound_instrument_mapping (csound_part_ref | csound_
spine_ref)+>
<!ATTLIST csound_instrument_mapping
        instrument_number CDATA #REQUIRED
        start_line CDATA #IMPLIED
        end_line CDATA #IMPLIED
        pnml_file CDATA #IMPLIED>


<!ELEMENT csound_part_ref EMPTY>
<!ATTLIST csound_part_ref
        part_ref IDREF #REQUIRED>


<!ELEMENT csound_spine_ref EMPTY>
<!ATTLIST csound_spine_ref
        %spine_ref;>


<!ELEMENT mpeg4_instance (mpeg4_score | mpeg4_orchestra)+>
<!ELEMENT mpeg4_score (mpeg4_spine_event+, rights?)>
<!ATTLIST mpeg4_score
        file_name CDATA #REQUIRED>


<!ELEMENT mpeg4_spine_event EMPTY>
<!ATTLIST mpeg4_spine_event
        line_number CDATA #REQUIRED
        %spine_ref;>


<!ELEMENT mpeg4_orchestra (mpeg4_instrument_mapping*, rights?)>
<!ATTLIST mpeg4_orchestra
        file_name CDATA #REQUIRED>


<!ELEMENT mpeg4_instrument_mapping (mpeg4_part_ref | mpeg4_spine_
ref)+>
<!ATTLIST mpeg4_instrument_mapping
        instrument_name CDATA #REQUIRED
        start_line CDATA #IMPLIED
        end_line CDATA #IMPLIED
        pnml_file CDATA #IMPLIED>
```

```
<!ELEMENT mpeg4_part_ref EMPTY>
<!ATTLIST mpeg4_part_ref
        part_ref IDREF #REQUIRED>

<!ELEMENT mpeg4_spine_ref EMPTY>
<!ATTLIST mpeg4_spine_ref
        %spine_ref;>

<!--
=================================================================
======================-->

<!-- Audio Layer -->

<!ELEMENT audio (track+)>

<!ELEMENT track (track_general?, track_indexing?, rights?)>
<!ATTLIST track
 file_name CDATA #REQUIRED
 file_format %formats; #REQUIRED
 encoding_format %formats; #REQUIRED
 md5 CDATA #IMPLIED>

<!-- General Sub-Layer -->

<!ELEMENT track_general (recordings?, genres?, albums?,
performers?, notes?)>
<!ATTLIST track_general
        geographical_region CDATA #IMPLIED
        lyrics_language CDATA #IMPLIED>

<!ELEMENT recordings (recording+)>
<!ELEMENT recording EMPTY>
<!ATTLIST recording
        date CDATA #REQUIRED
        recorded_part CDATA #IMPLIED
        studio_name CDATA #IMPLIED
        studio_address CDATA #IMPLIED>

<!ELEMENT albums (album+)>

<!ELEMENT album EMPTY>
<!ATTLIST album
        title CDATA #REQUIRED
   track_number CDATA #IMPLIED
        carrier_type CDATA #IMPLIED
        catalogue_number CDATA #IMPLIED
        number_of_tracks CDATA #IMPLIED
        publication_date CDATA #IMPLIED
        label CDATA #IMPLIED>

<!ELEMENT performers (performer+)>
```

```
<!ELEMENT performer EMPTY>
<!ATTLIST performer
        name CDATA #REQUIRED
        type CDATA #REQUIRED>


<!-- Indexing Sub-Layer -->

<!ELEMENT track_indexing (track_region*, track_event+)>
<!ATTLIST track_indexing
        timing_type (samples | time | seconds | time_frames |
frames | measures | smpte_24 | smpte_25 | smpte_2997 | smpte_30)
#REQUIRED>

<!ELEMENT track_region EMPTY>
<!ATTLIST track_region
 name CDATA #REQUIRED
 description CDATA #IMPLIED
 %spine_start_end_ref;>

<!ELEMENT track_event EMPTY>
<!ATTLIST track_event
 start_time CDATA #REQUIRED
 end_time CDATA #IMPLIED
 %spine_ref;
 description CDATA #IMPLIED>
```

APPENDIX C. IEEE 1599 DEMONSTRATION VIDEOS

These are videos taken of a user navigating IEEE 1599 applications:

"Il mio ben quando verrà," from Giovanni Paisiello's *Nina, o sia la pazza per amore*, which allows choice of instrument, voice, and different versions of the score and the libretto: http://www.mx.lim.dico.unimi.it/videos/ieee1599_movie_short.wmv

Brandenburg Concerto No. 3, by J.S. Bach, allowing selection of viewing different sections of the orchestra, from several different vantage points, running simultaneously: http://www.mx.dico.unimi.it/videos/rtsi_movie.wmv

Music Navigation with Symbols and Layers: Toward Content Browsing with IEEE 1599 XML Encoding, First Edition. Edited by Denis L. Baggi and Goffredo M. Haus.
© 2013 the IEEE Computer Society. Published 2013 by John Wiley & Sons, Inc.

INDEX

Music Navigation with Symbols and Layers: Toward Content Browsing with IEEE 1599 XML Encoding,
First Edition. Edited by Denis L. Baggi and Goffredo M. Haus.
© 2013 the IEEE Computer Society. Published 2013 by John Wiley & Sons, Inc.